Stereotyping
The Politics of Representation

MICHAEL PICKERING

D1579327

palgrave

First published 2001 by
PALGRAVE
Houndmills, Basingstoke, Hampshire RG21 6XS and
175 Fifth Avenue, New York, N.Y. 10010
Companies and representatives throughout the world

PALGRAVE is the new global academic imprint of
St. Martin's Press LLC Scholarly and Reference Division and
Palgrave Publishers Ltd (formerly Macmillan Press Ltd).

ISBN 0–333–77209–1 hardback
ISBN 0–333–77210–5 paperback

This book is printed on paper suitable for recycling and
made from fully managed and sustained forest sources.

A catalogue record for this book is available
from the British Library.

Library of Congress Cataloging-in-Publication Data

Pickering, Michael
  Stereotyping : the politics of representation / Michael
Pickering.
    p. cm.
  Includes bibliographical references and index.
  ISBN 0–333–77209–1 (cloth) — ISBN 0–333–77210–5 (pbk.)
    1. Stereotype (Psychology) 2. Group identity. 3. Prejudices.
    I. Title.

  HM1096 .P53 2001
  303.3'85—dc21   2001021436

Editing and origination by
Aardvark Editorial, Mendham, Suffolk

10 9 8 7 6 5 4 3 2 1
10 09 08 07 06 05 04 03 02 01

Printed in China

In memory of
Doreen Barker (1931–1996)
and Lilian France (1914–2000)

Contents

List of Figures

Preface

Stereotyping is a problem that refuses to go away. It recurs, across various contexts and discourses, as a divisive and troubling issue, and remains a central source of contention in the politics of representation. Yet what it involves as a symbolic process, and how it may be considered as a critical concept, are themselves part of the problem. These questions are not as straightforward as they may seem, and the general purpose of this book is to examine them in their fuller complexities and difficulties. The major proposition it operates with is that stereotyping has to tell a bigger story. It has to be made part of a bigger story. The story to which I attempt to relate it unfolds in each of the succeeding chapters. Separately, they provide new episodes in the telling of this story, for they all cover different areas of enquiry. Together, as the task of the book as a whole, they bring these different areas into critical synthesis in the hope of regenerating the stereotype as a key concept of cultural analysis. I want to begin by outlining how they each contribute to the book's overall concerns and main lines of argument.

The critical analysis of stereotyping is usually devoid of any sense of its career as a concept. In the early chapters I try to redress this situation by examining the main elements in the development of its use, the problems these involve and some of the contradictions between them. Tracing these back to the initial formulation of the concept in the early 1920s by Walter Lippmann brings us again into confrontation with the founding quality of dilemma which underlies it. One of the most significant problems associated with stereotyping is the subsequent avoidance of this quality in those areas of study which have made central use of it. Its uses in psychology and communications research have proceeded with little reference to each other, as both have pursued one half of the dilemma to the detriment of the other. In these early chapters, I attempt to work through both the psychological and the cultural analysis of stereotyping in order that they may be made to interrogate each other. The intention is to bring the two dimensions of the dilemma of stereotyping back together again. This is the first part of building up a bigger story.

The next involves a realignment of stereotyping with its twin concept of the Other. This concept is often deployed without reference to that of the stereotype, which for some has apparently become outmoded, even annulled by its more fashionable successor. For me they are necessarily twinned, for the simple reason that they address the same cultural and psychological processes involved in self/other relations. In the face of these relations, both stereotyping and constructions of the Other operate as strategies of symbolic containment and risk, for that which they seek to resolve into steadfast fixity is, by that move, potentially reanimated as the threat which such strategies wish to keep constantly at bay. They both involve attempts to combine and contain contrary themes, but in so doing keep those contrary themes in active view. Stereotyping and constructions of the Other share these paradoxical features.

The concept of the Other does progress beyond that of the stereotype in three major ways. First, it keeps both the stereotypical target and those who are involved in processes of 'othering' in view of each other. This is important because, in this particular form of symbolic exchange, the ways in which they are related are central to the politics of representation. The concept of the Other does not just involve exposing the misrepresentation involved. It also grounds this in the structures and relations of power which give it its binding force. Second, in its more productive uses it has directed attention to the ambivalences and contradictions attendant on strategies of 'othering', and so not lost sight of the dilemma underlying the process of stereotyping, which is the problem that has beset many applications of the stereotype concept in the past. Third, it involves a fuller and more fruitful theorising of that with which it deals, even though this has often become wilfully carried away with itself and resulted in sometimes difficult, if not obscure and rebarbative, styles of writing. The various uses of the concept of the Other are not equally helpful, and my preference is for its early treatment in the work of Simone de Beauvoir and Franz Fanon. Tracing the concept back to their pioneering uses of it provides a sound base for considering its more recent adoption by such writers as Homi Bhabha and Gayatri Chakravorty Spivak, as well as bringing the critical analysis of both the gendered and racialised Other into an earlier conjunction than that flagged up by postcolonial theory. Going beyond theoretical uses of the concept in contemporary fashion is central to the historical trajectory of this book.

Trying to tell the story of stereotyping in historical terms, to relocate it within various histories in which it has been a central component, is the more general aim of the book. This historical perspective on stereotyping has been missing from many treatments of it. What it means is working towards a better understanding of how, throughout modernity, it has developed as a process and been deployed as a practice. It involves showing how, as process and practice, stereotyping is endemic to modernity. Apart from looking into the development of its conceptual postulates and applications, I attempt to do this in various ways. The middle chapters of the book relate the concepts both of stereotyping and the Other to questions of belonging in the modern world – to the nation and a national cultural past, and to differential stages of civilisational progress measured in terms of social evolution and racial hierarchisation – as well as to questions of power and authority in the contexts of nation-building, colonialism and imperialism. This is important because many stereotypical constructions of the Other, as representations of other cultures and other countries, are rooted in nineteenth-century nationalisms and in the pseudoscientific rationalisations of racial difference developed at that time, in European societies conceiving themselves as modern. They derived also from the racialised images of other people, such as the Chinese and the Irish as well as those diverse ethnic groupings of the sub-Saharan African continent, utilised in the popular fiction of empire. Chapter 5 considers these constructions of both 'high' and 'low' culture alongside each other.

Among other reasons, the long-term temporal perspective adopted in this book is important in trying to unravel the tangle between the idea of nationality and that of 'race'. As Paul Gilroy (1999) has noted, this 'goes back to the formation of nationalism as a way of managing historical time according to a logic that uses race to solve wider problems of belonging and fate'. I frame my historical analysis of these constructions with sections which develop a more theoretically oriented discussion. First, in Chapter 3, I relate them to the idea of primitivism, which was centrally involved in the management of historical time and the rhetoric of belonging and fate. Second, in Chapter 6, I outline and critically assess Orientalism, colonial discourse analysis and postcolonial theory.

The critique of static, chronocentric treatments of the stereotype and their lack of an adequate historical grounding is advanced further in the last two chapters of the book. These are concerned first, with deviancy theory and the analytical model of the moral panic, and second, with the figure of the stranger in the modern city and in modern cultural life. The dual emphasis given in Chapter 6 to power and resistance in relation to the politics of representation is continued in Chapter 7, which deals with the social construction of deviant Otherness and the reinscription of deviance as an expression of resistance. In dealing with deviancy theory, I trace its historical development through its relations with the idea of normality within modernity, for this is the unexamined basis from which deviancy is alleged to depart. I also argue for a more historically informed approach to questions concerning the relations between social infractions and practices of judgement and censure. In dealing with the stranger and with the quality of strangerhood, I trace the ways in which they have been conceived within the sociological tradition, from Simmel through to Bauman. I use the conception of the stranger resulting from this tradition as a way of returning to the dilemma of stereotyping, the emphasis with which the book begins. I also use it to return to the key issue of ambivalence, the thematic significance of which is sounded at various points throughout the book as a whole, but is given greatest salience in the concluding chapter because of its direct relevance to the sociology of strangerhood.

These are then the final elements which I bring to the task of making stereotyping part of a bigger story than that which is apparent in off-the-peg complaints of biased images in contemporary media representations, and in superficial conceptions of 'distortions' of an otherwise readily apprehended social reality.

Representations consist of words and images which stand in for various social groups and categories. They provide ways of describing and at the same time of regarding and thinking about these groups and categories. They may also affect how their members view themselves and experience the social world around them. Public representations have the power to select, arrange, and prioritise certain assumptions and ideas about different kinds of people, bringing some to the fore, dramatising and idealising or demonising them, while casting others into the social margins, so that they have little active public presence or only a narrow and negative public image. These practices are central to the politics of representation. Representation involves processes of 'speaking for' and 'speaking of' those who are represented. The politics of representation cover both the power to speak of and for others, whether in news narratives, social documentaries, feature films or advertising, all of which follow their own formal rules and conventions. The consequences of providing accounts and images of others for structures and relations of social power are central to the analysis of any study of symbolic representations, where questions of under-representation, over-representation and misrepresentation are necessarily high on the critical agenda.

The ways in which cultural forms relate to the social world in which they circulate are rarely straightforward, however, at least in their broader implications. It is high time we moved firmly away from simplistic assumptions about the transparency of, say, the media/social reality relationship, where media discourse simply reflects an objectively given social reality and misrepresentation is understood as an obvious distortion of that objective reality. Such assumptions have at times characterised criticism of stereotyping in the past. What remains crucial to the critique of stereotyping is not only the question of who speaks for whom and with what consequences, but also the question of how stereotypes relate to conceptions of what is held to be 'natural' or 'normal', how they create and sustain a common sense of the proper limits of what is accepted as legitimate and right. The complexities of this will be dealt with at various points in the book, but here I want simply to note that if we approach these conceptions and limits as animated at those various points of reference beyond itself of a cultural text, then this depends not only on how a text is discursively constructed, but also on how it is sociologically understood. In attending to media accounts and narratives, viewers, listeners and readers interpret them in different ways, depending on who they are, where they are, and when, in and across historical time they engage with texts and images. We need to remember that what is taken as normal or legitimate, in the production and consumption of such texts and images, is never absolute, never fixed for all time, and always the site of different and conflicting ways of knowing it. Keeping this point in mind is always a helpful starting point in thinking about any form of representation.

An account or image which provides a portrayal of others is historically contingent. It is dependent on particular conceptions of their social and psychological make-up, and particular codes and conventions for representing these in discourse. These change over time. What is regarded as a satisfactory account in one period will be seen in a succeeding period as artificial, misconceived, skewed in a particular direction, or simply dated, as will the means for providing the account which were codified and conventional in that period. Forms of social representation are never static partly because discourse about the 'social' changes to accommodate historical change and movement, and partly because such discourse involves struggles over the meanings and definitions of social representations which are being fought between different interest groups and value systems in society, in and over time. It is as a result of these accommodations and struggles as well that the form and content of cultural representations change. Certainly, how questions of representation and referentiality should be approached in social and historical analysis involves far more than this. I have explored some of the hermeneutic issues which they raise in a previous book (1997a). Such issues will be followed through in this book, but the point to insist on here is that, in the critical study of stereotypes, a historical dimension is vital for understanding how they have acquired their symbolic cargo of meanings and values, and how this cargo has been carried through time, in a complex relation of continuity and change. The most significant way in which stereotyping must be made part of a bigger story is by rehistoricising it, and that in the end is my most abiding intention in this book.

In writing it, I have incurred various debts. I would like to thank Michael Billig and Graham Murdock, with whom I discussed the project on which this book is based in its early stages. Graham has continued to provide important moral support as the book has progressed. The place where I teach, in the Department of Social Sciences at Loughborough University, has provided a stimulating and congenial atmosphere in which to work on this book. I would particularly like to thank friends and colleagues in the communication and media studies section of the department – David Deacon, John Downey, Natalie Fenton, Peter Golding, Sharon Lockyer and Dominic Wring, as well as Graham – for their encouragement and efforts to create the necessary space for research and writing. I would also like to thank Roy Shuker, who edited an edition of *Delta*, a journal of the Education Department at Massey University, New Zealand, where I first broached some of the ideas in this book, and John Corner, who invited me to take them forward in a review essay for *Media, Culture and Society* (see *Delta*, 45, March 1991: 91–7; and *Media, Culture and Society*, 17, 1995: 691–700). I am grateful to the editorial board of both journals for their permission to draw on these publications here. Catherine Gray at Palgrave has been a constructive critic and discerning editor. The book benefits considerably from her involvement. In preparing the book for publication, my greatest critical debt is to Keith Negus of Goldsmith's College who highlighted certain inadequate aspects of the first complete draft of the book, and urged me to clarify some of its general lines of argument. My subsequent revisions have perhaps not gone far enough in matching up to his sceptical appraisal and constructive advice, but I am sure that the book has considerably benefited from them, and I would like to offer my sincere gratitude for the time taken to read through my first manuscript.

Three friends, now dead, were in my mind throughout the writing of this book. In tribute to their memory, thanks to Barry Troyna, who first generated my interest in stereotyping and whose work has stimulated my own thinking; to Allon White, who first directed me to media studies and whose work has been a continuing inspiration; and to Peter Laver, whose comradeship and turn of mind remain a source of solace and influence. Sadly as well, two close family relations passed away during the time this book was taking shape, either in my mind or on paper. The book is dedicated to them both. Finally, I want to acknow-ledge my immediate family. Thank you to Karen for her intolerance of bigotry and social discrimination, as well as sharing her life with me, to Lucy for her good humour and love of music, to Joseph for his wonderful pictures and love of football – and to all of them together for their love and forbearance as I have taken up too much valuable time in writing this study of the dynamics of stereotyping.

Acknowledgements

The author and publisher wish to thank the John Johnson Collection, Bodleian Library, for their help in obtaining Figures 3.1 and 5.1 and their permission to use these; also Malika Slaoui for permission to use Figure 6.2 from *The Orientalist Poster: A Century of Advertising Through the Slaoui Foundation Collection* published by Malika Editions.

Every effort has been made to trace all the copyright holders but if any have been inadvertently overlooked the publishers will be pleased to make the necessary arrangements at the first opportunity.

Chapter 1

The Concept of the Stereotype

Truth does less good in the world than its appearances do harm.

LA ROCHEFOUCAULD, 1931: 136

Stereotyping as Gain and Loss

The stereotype remains an important concept in contemporary cultural analysis. In the study of what is still sometimes called 'mass communications', the process and effects of stereotyping have long been of concern. Stereotyping has become a focal issue in other areas of study as well. Its causes and consequences have been taken up in cultural history, human geography and social anthropology, and in various social movements such as feminism, anti-racism and gay rights activism. Yet as soon as one begins to explore these uses and applications of the concept, a rather peculiar situation presents itself. Although its application in uncovering prejudiced views in various representations of social identity is always a welcome move, too often there is an imbalance between the deployment of it as a critical tool and any conceptual elaboration of what it involves. If stereotyping is a major discursive device in the ideological construction of social groups and categories, we cannot assume that its significance and force as a concept is transparent and so able to be applied uninspected in analytical work on the politics of representation.

In the first two chapters I want to ask what a stereotype is, what it consists of and in what ways it can be said, conceptually, to hang together in any coherent and consistent manner. This will involve outlining the main ways in which the stereotype and stereotyping processes have been conceived, and highlighting the main problems and shortcomings involved in these conceptions. I shall do this not only by dealing with the salient features of stereotyping, but also by tracing the history of the concept during the course of the twentieth century. The story of its developing uses is often ignored in work on stereotyping. It is important because, among other reasons, such uses are not always

1

consistent with each other, and in some cases are clearly contradictory. In order to understand how such inconsistencies have arisen, we need to consider how the concept was initially formulated, and then adopted and applied in different fields. We need to return stereotyping to the bigger story it has always belonged to, but which has too often been neglected. This is the project of the book as a whole. I want to begin by singling out for special comment three major aspects of the argument I shall develop.

First, we need to distinguish more clearly between categories and stereotypes. This is important if we are to avoid using these two terms interchangeably in a way which renders one or the other of them potentially redundant. They have separate meanings. Insisting on these provides a way of countering the claim that we cannot live without stereotyping. As we shall see, such a claim is central to the approach to stereotyping taken in cognitive psychology, but it is commonly made in a variety of other fields of study, such as media and literary studies, sociology and political science (see for example, Gilman, 1985, discussed below; also Holquist, 1989; Potter, 1998: 53–4; Gillespie, 1999; Glynn et al., 1999: 147–58; Kolakowski, 1999: 139–43). Thinking in relation to categories is a necessary way of organising the world in our minds, creating mental maps for working out how we view the world and negotiating our ways through it in our everyday social relations and interactions. It would be difficult to imagine how the world would seem without using categories in general speech and writing as basic tools for organising our understanding.

But in addressing the claim that we cannot *not* engage in processes of stereotyping, I want to argue that categories as cognitive devices are not the same as stereotypes. They are not synonyms for each other, even if the two do overlap at times. To see them as equivalent obscures the distinctive properties of stereotyping. Without an adequate identification of these properties we will not be able to get a critical purchase on the ways in which evaluations of stereotyping and categorisation have been deployed as a rhetorical strategy, as for instance when distinctions are made between them in terms of an apparently clear-cut, rational/irrational split. This serves to distance those who (rationally) study stereotyping from those who (irrationally) engage in it, with the result that those wielding racist or xenophobic stereotypes become conveniently isolated as the problem to be studied, while those who study stereotypes are exonerated from any charge of prejudice or unthinking bias. Examples of this spurious application of the distinction between categories and stereotypes will be discussed later on.

Despite the fact that it can be rhetorically turned to one's own advantage, the distinction is not thereby drained of all value. It remains important. While we need to understand stereotypes as elements of broad cultural practices and processes, carrying with them quite definite ideological views and values, they are not necessarily integral to our perceptual and cognitive organisation of the social worlds we live in.

A further point follows from any sensible distinction between categories and stereotypes. If we need categories as a way of organising our sense of the world, we should not exaggerate their significance or elevate them to a supreme position as a unit of thought. Categories are not fixed for all time. They can be used flexibly and their designations can be disputed. In our social understanding, in the stories we tell each other and ourselves about the world we live in, we make all sorts of mental moves over and beneath the categories we operate with. Categories should not be regarded as *the* elemental structure of thought.

Second, we need to bring back into the frame the central dilemma at the heart of stereotyping. This was prominent enough in the ways in which it was first thought about, early in the twentieth century, but too often this dilemma has been lost sight of in much subsequent work. It is, at base, to do with questions of order and power. Stereotyping may operate as a way of imposing a sense of order on the social world in the same way as categories, but with the crucial difference that stereotyping attempts to deny any flexible thinking with categories. It denies this in the interests of the structures of power which it upholds. It attempts to maintain these structures as they are, or to realign them in the face of a perceived threat. The comfort of inflexibility which stereotypes provide reinforces the conviction that existing relations of power are necessary and fixed.

In a world that is constantly changing, we are confronted all the time with certain social events, circumstances and developments which show that this is not the case. When we remember this, when we recognise that what appears to be fixed in place can be modified or altered, as the world changes, we are confronted by the dilemma underlying the impulse to resort to the imprecise referencing of a stereotypical attribution. We can then move either way. We either reproduce a given stereotype in our occasioned uses of it, as a short cut in representing a sense of order to ourselves, or we refuse the stunted abbreviation of a social group or subculture which a stereotype entails by opting for a more particularised, less one-sided description. This is the dilemma which stereotyping faces: to resort to one-sided representations in the interests of order, security and dominance, or to allow for a more complex vision, a more open attitude, a more flexible way of thinking. Stereotyping functions precisely in order to forget this dilemma. It attempts to annul the dilemma that lies within it and has brought it into existence, to hide from what is at the heart of the situation it initially responds to.

Any dilemma implies choice, the decision to move between one or other among two or more opposed alternatives. Dilemmas involve contrary notions or conflicting options, but with stereotyping, movement between them is not necessarily a matter of straightforward choice. There is no absolute yardstick for weighing up what is at stake in stereotyping. This does not mean that the different possibilities involved should simply be ignored. Stereotyping attempts to dissipate the tension between these possibilities, but it's the possibilities themselves which enable us to argue against stereotyping. We can begin to address how the process of stereotyping operates by bringing out again the different options it has already foreclosed. Emphasising its paradoxical features provides a means of getting a critical purchase on stereotyping. For example, despite the imprecise referencing it involves, which we may come to recognise, stereotyping creates the illusion of precision in defining and evaluating other people. Exposing these contrary elements points to the dilemma annulled by stereotyping, even as it acts as the originating spring which brings the process into operation. The paradoxical features of stereotyping are the visible traces of the condition of dilemma it has attempted to make invisible, and this condition always connects back to the ways in which order and power interact.

Stereotypes are usually considered inaccurate because of the way they portray a social group or category as homogeneous. Certain forms of behaviour, disposition or propensity are isolated, taken out of context and attributed to everyone associated with a particular group or category. Stereotypes render uniform everyone associated with a particular feature, such as being a woman who is blonde-haired or a man who is black-skinned; they are reduced to the characteristic isolated by the stereotype in its designation of what being blonde or black means. For those who use a particular stereotype, this may create an element of order by seeming to lock a category irrevocably into its place, in an apparently settled hierarchy of relations. The feeling of security or superiority resulting from this may help to explain why such imprecise referencing of other people or other cultures spreads rapidly and is taken up uncritically on a widespread basis. The imprecise representations involved in this process of social dissemination create the illusion of precision, of order, of the ways things should be. This is convenient for existing relations of power because it lends to them a sense of certainty, regularity and continuity.

The dilemma remains. For if we move from the perspective of order to that of power, we can see that what has been a gain for some, entails a loss for others. The evaluative ordering which stereotyping produces always occurs at a cost to those who are stereotyped, for they are then fixed into a marginal position or subordinate status and judged accordingly, regardless of the inaccuracies that are involved in the stereotypical description given of them.

Stereotyping imparts a sense of fixedness to the homogenised images it disseminates. It attempts to establish an attributed characteristic as natural and given in ways inseparable from the relations of power and domination through which it operates. If a social group or category is stereotyped as inherently lazy, stupid, childish or dishonest, the ascription acts not only as a marker of deviancy, making it marginal to the moral order, but also as a revalidation of that which it is measured against and found wanting. This twofold movement is integral to the ways in which stereotypes function as a form of social control. The assessment that is offered in a stereotype is based on the leading precepts and preoccupations of those who reproduce them, and it is this assessment that underlies the perception and positioning of the 'difference' it regards.

Foregrounding the dilemma underlying stereotyping is also important because it touches on some of the major difficulties of living in modernity. I shall discuss various manifestations of these difficulties in what follows, as for instance in relation to social constructions of deviancy in the modern world (Chapter 7) and encounters with strangers in the modern metropolitan city (Chapter 8). The initial definition of stereotyping that I want to offer is made directly in connection with these difficulties. In approaching stereotyping as a process for maintaining and reproducing the norms and conventions of behaviour, identity and value, the intention is to extend and refine this definition in relation to the various areas and themes discussed in the rest of the book. For now it is important to note that emphasising normative values and established conventions via stereotyping always entails some form of judgement about differences, about what departs from the putative sameness endorsed by the process of stereotyping in the interests of configurations of order. Such judgements are an expression of power, even among the relatively powerless, since the norms which are reinforced by stereotyping emanate from established structures of social dominance. For example, stereotypes of women in the Victorian period were divided between two polar opposites: the fragrant angel in the house and the fallen woman in the street. This is sometimes represented in historical analysis as the madonna/whore dichotomy, but it is the

Figure 1.1   The dichotomous stereotypes of the fragrant angel in the house (top) (Shoberl, 1838) and the fallen woman in the street (bottom) (*34th Annual Report of the Female Mission to the Fallen*, London, 1892)

same impossibly split model for female behaviour and identity. In its impossibilities for actually lived social experiences, it spoke only to masculine values and patriarchal knowledge. In both cases, as well as in their mutually defining combination, the stereotype was used to evaluate, control and subordinate women to male power over them. Both stereotypes were based on the assumption of comprehensive, naturalised and fixed gender patterns operating as a compelling guide for norms of behaviour, identity and value appropriate to male and female spheres.

At the same time, in a crucial pivotal movement, the rigid separation of these spheres generated an inveterate misinterpretation of the difference they were designed to keep apart. Once any form of difference becomes diametrically set apart from the self-identity of those who define it, any encounter with the difference so constructed is likely to lead to suspicion, confusion and wrongful attribution. Again, this is often interwoven with the identification of disorder from a self-arrogated perspective of order, where the sources of disorder are always over on the other side from those defining it. Stereotypes thrive on such mismatches between sharply distinct categories or category systems, and from them they derive the diverse imagery of surfeit and danger associated with those on the other side of order. Such images make the practitioners of one set of cultural practices different to the structures of another 'seem volatile, unpredictable, irrational, inconsistent, capricious, or even dangerous' (McDonald, 1993: 225). Yet it is precisely by making them seem so that stereotyping betrays itself. The imagery of surfeit and disorder produced by category mismatches renders the norms which stereotyping protects seem less stable and less centred than the process itself attempts and hopes to ensure. The dilemma it tries to annul springs back into view. Stereotyping constructs difference as deviant for the sake of normative gain, but in doing so it raises the spectre of that which it lacks and has lost in the gain. In trying to counter something dreaded, or compensate for something deficient, stereotyping characteristically oversteps the mark. It is through this overstepping of the mark that stereotyping betrays itself.

This is another of its paradoxical features. In what follows we shall explore the complexities that are involved and how they can be analysed, but the point to stress at the outset is the distinctiveness of category mismatches as a characteristic of modernity. Such mismatches are by no means unique to modernity, but they have in themselves and in their likelihood increased enormously over the course of the last two centuries or so, as encounters with other cultural practices have proliferated, whether through processes of industrialisation, urbanisation and massive population movement, or through overseas European expansion and the development of colonialism and imperialism. These are the changed conditions in which stereotyping has arisen and intensified, as a specific ideological aspect of the experience of modernity. It has, accordingly, to be understood in the context of those conditions.

The third aspect of my argument which I want to emphasise at the start follows directly from this point. We need to overcome the obsessively present-centred orientation of much of the work on stereotyping, both within media and cultural analysis and within social psychology, these being the two most important areas of research in which stereotyping has been subject to serious critical treatment. Such critical treatment seems at times to be imprisoned within a view of the world bounded by its attention to the present, permitting no view from its narrow cell of the sweeping panorama of the past. Against this we need not only to understand the concept of the stereotype historically, but also to understand the *content* of stereotypes historically – to bring the repressed historical dimension of stereotyping back into the light of its analysis in the present. To some extent this has begun to happen already. In some of the historical work on colonialism and imperialism, for instance, there is a sensitivity to the need to bring cultural analysis to bear on the historical events and processes associated with empire and its nationalist corollaries.

Yet despite some important exceptions, a historical dimension remains a significant lack in both cultural studies and social psychology, speaking of these in fairly general terms. I shall try to redress this imbalance by giving due emphasis to the ways in which many stereotypes owe their resilience to the historical accretions and sedimentations of meaning and value they carry as elements within the cultural repertory available to people in their multiple relations with others. It is this aspect of stereotypes which may help us explain why they can lie dormant for considerable stretches of time, apparently overcome and forgotten, yet suddenly, without any immediately identifiable reference backwards, can also re-emerge with little of their former strength diminished, and be powerfully applied in new social situations and contexts. It is because certain stereotypes may seem to rise without a trace that we need to excavate their obscured routes of development, and historical cultural analysis is best suited to this task. This is even more urgently the case when, in historical work itself, stereotyping is claimed as a cultural universal, as will be seen in Chapter 2 when we come to examine Sander Gilman's conceptualisation of the stereotype in his important historical work on representations of race, sexuality and madness.

In dealing with stereotypes in this book, I shall try to show the importance of taking a historical view of the processes they have been involved in on a broader scale. These include processes associated with building a national identity and nationalist sense of belonging, with the rhetorical deployment of primitivist stereotypes, with stereotypical responses to other ethnicities and cultures in the colonial encounter and the imperial relation, with representations of gender, sexuality and 'race', with Orientalism and its symbolic uses of a mysterious and exotic Orient, with constructions of social deviancy, and with the specific perturbations generated by the ambivalent figure of the stranger. All of these are discussed at length in the book as a whole. I shall also seek to consolidate the relationship of the stereotype to the concept of the Other, which is more fully elaborated in its particular operations at least partly because it became intellectually more fashionable over the last quarter or so of the twentieth century. There is a further need to align the stereotype more explicitly with the concept of the stigma, and I shall do this where it is relevant to any aspect of the discussion. Initially however, it is important that the concept of the stereotype is examined in its own right, and it to this task that we shall now turn in order to assess the extent to which its conceptual weight matches up to its rhetorical force.

The Classical View of Stereotyping

As with the cliché, the term 'stereotype' was in the first place taken metaphorically from the trade vocabulary of printing and typography, where it referred to text cast into rigid form for the purposes of repetitive use. In this respect the analogy still applies, but the conceptual meaning of the term as it has developed from the late-nineteenth century is neither straightforward nor unproblematic. It has been used in different ways, with different meanings and associations of value, in various fields and disciplines, and it has a range of connections with other forms of representation. As it has been most significantly deployed in psychological studies and in media and cultural analysis, it is on these that I shall concentrate in these opening chapters. In the general field of psychology, the concept has been subject to extensive experimental research that goes back to the 1930s. There have been numerous attempts to refine its definition and application since that time, and more recently it has been considerably overhauled, particularly in relation to social identity theory and its close kin, self-categorisation theory. In media and cultural studies, by contrast, the term has had widespread application, across a broad analytical range, but the small amount of conceptual treatment it has received has been very mixed in its results. There has also been little effort to engage substantively with the broad psychological literature on stereotyping. In this and the following chapter, I shall seek to make good this omission and engage with work on the psychology of stereotyping from the perspective of cultural analysis.

In his study of prejudice, the renowned psychologist Gordon Allport defined the stereotype as: 'an exaggerated belief associated with a category. Its function is to justify (rationalise) our conduct in relation to that category' (1954: 191). This often-quoted definition heralds many of the conventionally identified features of the stereotype, and it will be useful to start with a summary of them before discussing some of the difficulties they entail.

One aspect of the classical view of stereotypes has already been mentioned. This is the idea that social stereotypes exaggerate and homogenise traits held to be characteristic of particular categories and serve as blanket generalisations for all individuals assigned to such categories. The images and notions connected with them are then consensually shared in the interests of the social group among whom they are widely utilised and diffused. Such images and notions are usually held to be simplistic, rigid and erroneous, based on discriminatory values and damaging to people's actual social and personal identities. In the classical view, stereotypes have been regarded as necessarily deficient. They distort the ways in which social groups or individuals are perceived, and they obscure the more complex and finite particularities and subjectivities tangled up in the everyday lives of groups and individuals. They are seen as deficient either because they encourage an indiscriminate lumping together of people under overarching group-signifiers, often of a derogatory character, or because they reduce specific groups and categories to a limited set of conceptions which in themselves often contradict each other. Stereotypes are also discriminatory because the stunted features or attributes of others which characterise them are considered to form the basis for negative or hostile judgements, the rationale for exploitative, unjust treatment, or the justification for aggressive behaviour. In a word, stereotypes are bad. Politically, they stand in the way of more tolerant, even-handed and differentiated responses to people who belong to social or ethnic categories beyond those which are structurally dominant. Intellectually, they are poor devices for engaging in any form of social cartography, and for this reason should be eradicated from the map of good knowledge.

There are obvious progressive aspects to this general conception of stereotyping, which have been widely influential in relation to either some or all of the range of features identified. For example, where it has been recognised as an important educational topic, schoolchildren have been alerted to the psychological harm stereotyping may cause or the cultural disrespect it may convey to, say, ethnic groups other than their own. In the study of media and cultural representations, university and college students have become critically aware of the use of stereotypical images or allusions, across a range of forms and genres. This has provided them with a means of establishing their analytical bearings in identifying the workings of media texts and images. Within the professions, those responsible for personnel and policy management are considerably more sensitive to the transmission of xenophobic, racist and sexist values through stereotypical references, or the implementation of stereotypical notions, than they were fifty or more years ago. Government ministries and interstate institutions have developed greater sensitivity to the ways in which stereotypes affect people's jobs and career prospects, constrict their freedom of movement and hamper their ability to settle in particular regions or districts. There is at least less inclination, compared with earlier periods within modernity, to lump people together under a stereotypical group-signifier. Overall, the classical conception of stereotyping, as I have outlined it, has helped to heighten people's consciousness of stereotyping as an everyday cultural process, spread a broader acceptance of the ways in which stereotypes act as vehicles for the conveyance of social prejudice and discrimination and promoted greater mutual tolerance and understanding. Just as these seem obvious steps forward, so also does it seem obvious that at least some of the features of stereotyping identified in the classical view are empirically valid. When their general properties are spelt out, it seems clear to many people that this is how stereotypes operate and these are the effects they can have.

Nonetheless, the classical view of stereotyping raises certain perhaps less obvious problems. To begin with, taking stereotypicality as indicative of a misinformed attitude, irrational value or inaccurate representation implies that there are always firm grounds for rectifying it. It is by no means certain that this will necessarily follow, once the critique has been conducted. Instead of assuming that it will, we need to ask if we are faced with the rhetoric of realism, facticity, authenticity and rationality operating imperially to guarantee the truth of arguments against bigotry and intolerance. For some, the remedy lies in the provision of more ample information and more representative images. Such provision is obviously to the good, as for instance is shown by a recent study of the stereotype of the negligent, irresponsible, and often 'single' pregnant drug user (Murphy and Rosenbaum, 1999). The reasoning behind its advocacy is that if stereotyping's error of description and judgement is based on a lack of information, of detailed empirical evidence, then surely the error will evaporate once such information and evidence are supplied. Maybe, but unless there is a ready predisposition to stand corrected, this remedy amounts to little more than wishful liberal thinking. If its logical premises were generally valid, then misogyny or homophobia would soon become as psychologically outmoded as the four cardinal humours. As examples offered in counterpoint to this, we may grant that during the long Victorian period, which extended into much of the twentieth century, stereotypes of women and homosexuals to a great degree stood in lieu of concrete or undistorted evidence. For many people, poverty of information may well have been the breeding ground for fears and fancies, from whatever source these were sown. But the equation of lack of information and the perpetuation of stereotypes is too easy. The provision of complex information does not necessarily mean that certain stereotypes will then be abandoned, for their 'rigidity and resistance to information which contradicts them is undoubtedly one of their most salient features' (Tajfel, 1981: 133).

While the empirical demonstration of falsification does not guarantee any necessary diminution of stereotyping, particular instances of it may of course prove vulnerable to modification or erosion. If this was not the case the political purpose of this book would be instantly cut from under its feet. One reason they are so vulnerable is that they always operate within a given ideological field, not for all time but in relation to definite social needs and conditions which may change. The degree to which stereotypes of black people or any other people have proved resistant or responsive to change has depended on the social and historical circumstances in which they have operated, their rhetorical status in cultural processes of meaning-construction, and the extent of the self-rewarding emotional, moral, political or other investments which their perpetrators have had in their long-term preservation. Stereotypes remain fairly stable for quite considerable periods of time, and tend to become more pronounced and hostile when social tensions between different ethnic or other groupings arise. 'They do not present much of a problem when little hostility is involved, but are extremely difficult to modify in a social climate of tension and conflict' (Tajfel and Fraser, 1978: 427). The case for their modification is then more urgent and imperative, but this can never be advanced very far if their lineage is not clearly identified. Times when they are apparently dormant may lull us into forgetting this lineage, yet it is this which partly gives force to their recrudescence in a climate of tension and conflict. One of the arguments of this book is that stereotypical critique is always inadequate when it is not informed by a historical understanding of its despised object. Such an understanding is, indeed, all the more vital when hostility is involved.

A further problem with the classical view of the stereotype is that of simplicity. In one of the most important critical appraisals of it within media and cultural studies, Teresa Perkins suggests that this feature of the stereotype is true in so far 'as all typifications are simplifications since they select common features and exclude differences'; to this extent 'all typifications are undifferentiated (and in that sense they are also erroneous)'. She goes on to say that while this seems to be the case with the stereotype of the happy-go-lucky Negro, simplicity may be better described as abstractness in that it operates 'on a higher level of generalisation than other typifications' (1979: 139). This is useful, for what is implied in such stereotypes is more than simply the mental state of being, in Carlyle's description, 'a merry-hearted, grinning, dancing, singing, affectionate kind of creature, with a great deal of melody and amenability in his composition' (Carlyle, 1897: 8). Surrounding this Sambo image, for the civilised English, lay assumptions of an inherent inability to be serious, rational, responsible, busy, industrious; properly to exploit and develop the material resources of the earth; adequately to attain self-government and an individual or collective *amour-propre*. The case of Haiti provides an instructive illustration of these self-justifying assumptions (see Rigby, 1996: 15–18; also James, 1994 and Farmer, 1994). The British envoy, Sir Spencer St John, wrote in his memoir, *Hayti or the Black Republic* (1884):

> I know what the black man is, and I have no hesitation in declaring that he is incapable of the art of government, and that to entrust him with framing and working the laws for our islands is to condemn them to inevitable ruin. What the negro may become after centuries of civilised education I cannot tell, but what I know is that he is not fit to govern now. (cited in Rigby, 1996: 17)

Throughout the period of British slave-trading and slavery, colonialism and empire-building, the economically convenient idea that blacks in Africa or in the African diaspora were not fit to govern themselves was the firm conclusion following from the insulting claim that they were not capable of being responsible: 'The moral inferiority of colonised people, of which subjugation was a prime consequence and penalty, was most clearly demonstrated in their unwillingness to assume roles of responsibility' (Achebe, 1989: 79). The claim itself, in other words, was a direct consequence of the happy-go-lucky stereotype, which was always chief among the most desired plantocratic, explorer and settler representations of blacks because of its convenient function in justifying (rationalising) conduct in relation to them. So, as soon as we start to explore the semantic hinterlands of this particular black stereotype, we find ourselves in the midst of the expansive terrain of colonialist and imperialist discourse.

The point of this example at this stage is twofold. First, it demonstrates that it is 'misleading to say stereotypes are simple rather than complex. They are simple and complex' (Perkins, 1979: 139). Stereotypes generally exhibit contrary features. Ideologically, it is their purpose to bind such features together. Second, the example shows how deeply rooted the notion of the 'irresponsible' black person has been, how historically extensive it has been in justifying (rationalising) black people's subordination to whites, particularly in times of intense white–black conflict, or alternately in memory of such times. It is for both these reasons that I shall devote a good deal of this book to an excavation of 'black' stereotypes in colonialist and imperialist discourse.

Clearly, there are ways in which stereotypes can be shown to be inadequate as representations when they stand in for the many aspects of social life, experience and identity which are ignored, marginalised or distorted in mainstream culture and mainstream channels of communication. The importance of this kind of critique is indisputable, as for instance is exemplified by the contribution of feminist scholarship to media studies. Before this contribution was made, stereotypes of women and the media's role in their development, reinforcement and maintenance went largely unquestioned. But while female stereotypes are now contested, it remains the case that detailed comparison does not provide a straight road either to the opposite of error or to its dissolution. Resting one's case on the empirical establishment of stereotypical error considerably underestimates the play of ideological forces set in motion by processes of stereotyping. It is not as if there is any direct, unilinear connection between stereotypical images, social roles and relations, and patterns of enculturation. In the past, the comparative study of stereotypes and social experience has tended to assume a pre-existent 'reality-out-there' against which images and representations can be transparently measured and found wanting.

Underpinning the classical view, this assumption has been responsible for the empiricism inherent in much of the thinking on stereotyping.

Yet huge difficulties are involved in defining the 'reality' evoked in calls for more 'realistic' images of women in the media, and not only for reasons of subjective interpretation. There is, for instance, considerable confusion as to whether stereotyping should be condemned for *not* being realistic (in falsely representing women, for example, as innately promiscuous and wanting sex with men at any time) or being too realistic (in accurately representing women's many domestic services to men). These different examples of stereotypical complaint are taken from Martin Barker's excellent study of comics like *Jackie, Bunty* and *Beano*. As he makes clear, such complaints are 'sharply at odds with each other'. The first may block our perceiving the world as it is, while the second may 'stop us seeing anything but the world as it is' (1989: 207). Stereotypes may thus be condemned because they are untrue and because they are true. We may well ask – how could this be?

In beginning to move toward some resolution of these kinds of difficulty, I have so far outlined some of the characteristic features of the stereotype in its classical conception, and examined the claim that their alleged simplicities of representation and deficiencies of knowledge can be overcome through the addition of sufficient information about the targeted categories. I have tried to show that this remedy is itself simplistic and deficient when it is assumed that counterbalancing information will, on its own, be adequate for the eradication of any given stereotype. It may or may not. The provision of additional information is not in itself a wrong move, but it cannot be offered as a guarantee of the reality of what has otherwise been falsely represented. While the definition of that reality is always part of what is at stake in any construction of it, the necessary struggle over the meanings of cultural representations cannot depend on straightforward appeals to empirical truth outside the circuits of interpretation in which they are mediated and negotiated.

The implications of this will be explored in detail throughout the book. For now it is important to recognise that this struggle over meaning is precisely where the critique of stereotyping needs to be located. One of the strategies which such a critique can then employ is to highlight the ways in which the apparent gains of stereotyping over its targeted categories coexist uneasily with anxieties over what might have been lost in normative comparisons with those categories. Here it is important to distinguish between contradictions in the conceptual model of stereotyping and the contradictions underlying the stereotype of any particular social category. While in the end they must be taken as inseparable, it is, I think, useful to distinguish between them because it is only by doing so that we will be able to shed light on the problem of negotiating the fine line that divides warranted generalisation about differences and unwarranted depictions of the differences of other people or other cultures. This problem, I suggest, always has the quality of a dilemma attached to it. In the final section of this chapter I want to explore this quality of dilemma further, for it is one which lies at the very heart of the concept of stereotyping. It has been there right from the beginning.

Stereotyping and Modernity

The fundamental dilemma at the heart of the stereotyping concept ultimately derives from the way in which it was initially formulated by the political columnist and writer Walter Lippmann in the early 1920s. At that time, Lippmann (1889–1974) worked on the editorial staff of the *New York World*, to which he had moved after helping to found the liberal *New Republic*. He was already well known for his earlier books, such as *A Preface to Politics* (1962) and *Drift and Mastery* (1961), although he only came to earn an international reputation later through his syndicated newspaper column 'Today and Tomorrow'. Lippmann was not the first to refer to stereotyping in the modern sense. For example, the term was used in something approaching this sense by a late nineteenth-century periodical writer when he defined a nation as 'a certain section of mankind having certain characteristics which have become stereotyped in the passage of generations' (Wyatt, 1897: 523), and although he did not use the term, the American sociologist W.I. Thomas identified one of the major components of the classical view of stereotyping when he wrote, in the opening years of the twentieth century:

> Following the method of the artist and caricaturist, the experts of the yellow press produce an essential untruth by isolating and over-emphasising certain features of the original without getting clean away from the copy. By this principle an individual or institution is isolated for intensive and unremitting attention. (Thomas, 1908: 492–3)

Lippmann was, nevertheless, the first to give critical definition to the stereotype in its modern sense in his book *Public Opinion* (1965). The importance of this text, initially published in 1922, is summed up by James Carey's description of it as 'the founding book of American media studies' (Carey, 1989: 75). Its pioneering treatment of the stereotype has had an enduring influence, and not only in media studies. Lippmann is widely credited with introducing the term 'stereotype' into the terminology of the social sciences more generally (see for example, Harding, 1968: 259; Condor, 1988: 70), although it has been in social psychology that its influence has been most strongly felt.

This achievement has to be seen in the context of Lippmann's legacy as a whole, which is not that easy to assess, and only partly because of the inconsistencies in his thinking. He deserves credit for his serious re-evaluation of the liberal model of citizenship and his considered appraisal of some of the obstacles standing in the way of effective political democracy, particularly in relation to the role of the media in the political process. Media stereotyping was one of the specifically modern political problems which he dealt with in connection with this process. Against this, his political judgements and suggested remedies for social and political problems were sometimes damaging and dangerous. In Alexander Cockburn's view: 'most of the time he was wrong about everything, consistently receptive to blunder [and] on the rare occasions when he was right no one paid the slightest attention' (1987: 194).

Among the most significant blunders made by Lippmann, two in particular are worth noting. In a notorious case of the 1920s, two Italian-born anarchists, Nicola Sacco and Bartolomeo Vanzetti, were tried and executed for robbery and murder. The trial took place amid a storm of anti-Red hysteria, with the two men, one a shoemaker and the other a poor fishmonger, made to symbolise 'everything that seemed terrifying and alien to many Americans' (Steel, 1980: 228). In the face of international lobbying against the miscarriage of justice involved in their conviction, a commission headed by the President of Harvard University, A. Lawrence Lowell, confirmed the guilty verdict and rejected the case for a retrial. Lippmann both endorsed Lowell's report and refused to condemn the execution of the two men. His public commentary on the Sacco and Vanzetti affair displayed three characteristic weaknesses: an ill-judged even-handedness, an overzealous respect for authority, and an anti-popular preoccupation with social stability. The second example also involved stereotypical prejudice against perceived aliens. In 1942, following the attack on Pearl Harbor, an anti-Japanese moral panic swept the west coast of North America. Lippmann's commentary on this wave of racist hysteria added a powerful impetus to calls for the relocation of Japanese-Americans. After being forced to forfeit their homes and businesses, they were herded into trucks and resettled in concentration camps in remote areas of the west.

These two examples from Lippmann's record obviously lend considerable support to Cockburn's verdict, despite its rather harsh and ungenerous tone. Yet Lippmann's identification of stereotyping as a serious problem in opinion formation and reproduction presents us with one of those rare occasions when he was right, or at least half right, and where people did subsequently pay attention, albeit selectively.

In discussing stereotyping, what Lippmann identified was one of the abiding problems of modernity. This involves the various ways in which the need for sound, reliable knowledge of the complexities of the modern world is compromised by the reliance of public knowledge on inadequate and manipulated media representations. In Lippmann's view, these are inadequate and manipulated not necessarily because of 'any malevolent plan', but because, for sound, commercial reasons, they follow 'the line of least resistance' in relation to existing prejudices, as for instance in the journalistic amplification of the stereotypes of foreigners (1915: 57). In the light of this problem, he conceived of the stereotype in two opposed ways. On the one hand, he viewed stereotypes as inadequate and biased, as endorsing the interests of those who use them, as obstacles to rational assessment, and as resistant to social change. In this first, political sense, he contrasted stereotyping with 'individualised understanding' (Lippmann, 1965: 59). On the other hand, he regarded stereotyping as a necessary mode of processing information, especially in highly differentiated societies, an inescapable way of creating order out of 'the great blooming, buzzing confusion of reality' (ibid: 63). In this second, psychological sense, he equated stereotyping with broader patterns of typifying and representing, and indeed with our general means of thinking and making sense of the world and the peoples within it.

Stereotyping in the first sense advanced by Lippmann clearly involves a loss, the loss of an individualised understanding of other people, whether these are foreigners or those in other social classes and communities outside our own situated experience. In the second sense, it would seem, equally clearly, to involve a gain in helping us to make sense out of the diversely blooming and buzzing forms of life that swirl around us in the modern social world. Lippmann was not unaware of the contradiction between these two perspectives on stereotyping. He actually saw it as an endemic problem in modern societies and sought to devise a solution to the dilemma it poses. It was not a happy one. What he proposed would be a nightmare of centralised, technocratic mediation and social planning. In the scenario he presented, regiments of specially trained experts, whose minds are 'unclouded by prejudice and stereotypes', would 'objectively' settle disputes for us and 'rationally' manage society on our behalf.

Despite this nightmare scenario, Lippmann's sturdy critique of theories of citizenship based on the omnicompetent, sovereign individual subject certainly remains valid, as does his radical scepticism towards utilitarian conceptions of freedom (Lippmann, 1925: 39; see also Carey, 1989: 75–8). He starkly revealed the discrepancies between liberal democratic ideals and the tendency in 'mass society' to control information flow, co-ordinate public opinion and engage in organised surveillance. It is in the light of these discrepancies that we can identify Lippmann's central problematic. This was the epistemological nature of the *relation* within modernity between complexity-reducing processes in the assimilation of experience and the media's reinforcement of social stereotypes – the 'pictures in our heads' of 'the world outside'.

This can be taken in two ways. On the one hand, it leads to the view that stereotyping is inevitable, since it follows from the effort to make sense, to create order, out of an otherwise confusing social reality. On the other, it leads to the view that stereotypes can be criticised, and thus subverted, on the grounds that they rationalise prejudice towards particular categories because the pictures of them formed in our heads are reductive – they are pictures with much of the experiential complexity of 'individualised understanding' stripped away. It is the combination of these two senses of stereotyping in modern social life which constitutes the epistemological dilemma that for Lippmann bedevils modern social and political life. This dilemma is a challenge to classical political theory because of the increasingly mediated forms of modern social relations, and the scale and scope of modern social organisation. While the democratic process demands that we make rational judgements about a range of important issues affecting social and political life, our knowledge of the external world is closely related to our stereotypical mental pictures of it which media representations tend to enhance rather than erode.

Lippmann's interest in stereotypes was thus directed to the common-sense social and political uses to which they are put. What counted most of all was 'the character of stereotypes, and the gullibility with which we employ them' (Lippmann, 1965: 60, 63–4). For him, this gullibility was particularly encouraged in the news discourse of modern communications media. Such discourse does not foster understanding of social and historical processes but only registers, in any particular news story, 'an aspect that has obtruded itself' (ibid: 216). In so doing, it recycles existing stereotypes in inflated form, or implants new ones in the receptive ground to whose preparation it has contributed. The participation of news discourse in the growth of public knowledge is then 'about as useful as that of an astrologer or an alchemist' (Steel, 1980: 173). The critical focus here was very much on the sociological dimension of the dilemma. Lippmann clearly recognised the ideological importance of stereotypes and social propaganda in democratic as well as other political systems. It could be said that he did not fully explore the dark, tangled area 'where propaganda and stereotype meet deep-seated myths and draw their strength from them' (Stafford, 1984), but he certainly did understand the ideological strength that is involved, the powerful illusion of necessity imparted to the status quo. In his definition, stereotypes are: 'the projection upon the world of our own sense of our own value, our own position and our own rights' (Lippmann, 1965: 64).

It is when we come to the question of how to move beyond the stereotypes that support opposed views and values that Lippmann seems to lose sight of the dilemma which he had put on the political agenda. The flaws that follow from this are twofold. First, the need for a sceptical appraisal of forms of collective representation in 'mass' culture is undermined by the unexamined assumption that stereotyping is indispensable for public knowledge in highly differentiated modern societies. It is even rendered redundant by the claim that it is central to all moral codes and derives from an essential human propensity (Lippmann, 1965: 81, 145; Steel, 1980: 181). The two-sided politics of representation become fatally subsumed by a one-sided psychology of perception and cognition. The second flaw follows from this, for if such indispensability leads to inadequate cultural representations which undermine democratic principles and exacerbate social conflicts, then the path towards informing public opinion correctly lies in the provision of scientific (objective and value-neutral) truth. Here his ideas about scientific explanation, information-processing and stereotypicality were wrong-headed on a number of counts, some of them downright alarming in their anti-democratic implications, as Martin Barker among others has demonstrated (Barker, 1989). What Lippmann opted for – a bureaucracy of experts organised in specially designated intelligence bureaux – would ostensibly depoliticise the public sphere. Despite these flaws, he did retain some sense of the ways in which stereotypes are part of the apparatus of social control: 'he who captures the symbols by which public feeling is for the moment contained, controls by that much the approaches of public policy' (Lippmann, 1965: 133). The crucial issue is whether the contribution which stereotypes make to institutional forms of social control should be endorsed in the interests of order, or critiqued as strategies of power. The importance of this is that it is the critical nature of the dilemma raised by stereotyping which stereotypes themselves function to conceal or forget.

The emphasis in Lippmann's writing tends to be on a hit-or-miss pragmatic approach to the interests of order rather than to a more consistent critical examination of consensual support for 'particular definitions of reality, with concomitant evaluations, which in turn relate to the disposition of power within society' (Dyer, 1979: 17). With this emphasis, he scuttled the dilemma he had posed in relation to stereotyping by siding with the need for order, for elitism and for mastery. In view of this, the problem with Lippmann's epistemological problematic is that it tends towards a fixity of the relation between complexity-reducing processes and prejudiced forms of representation, and does so because the conception of understanding upon which it relies was insufficiently social, as if 'individualised understanding' could be developed by the individual as an isolated atom in the social body as a whole. The sociological dimension of the dilemma of stereotyping, which involves the generation of collectively animated discussion and debate, becomes lost from view. What remains instructive in Lippmann's early writings is that, in his attempt to think through the issues it raises, he himself embodied the dilemma posed by the problem of stereotyping. Hence his vacillation between belief in the need to secure the mastery of order and authority, and belief in the need for a critical examination of the partiality and contingency of representation in the service of public knowledge. Beyond this, it is the underlying dilemma involved in processes of stereotyping which is of enduring interest, and in the next chapter we shall see how different responses to it were subsequently developed.

Chapter 2

The Dilemma of Stereotyping

> *The ultimate aim does not consist of attempting to prevent the*
> *categorisation of human beings into distinct groups – this would*
> *be impossible and not even desirable – but of helping to create*
> *'neutral' categories, within which each human being is evaluated*
> *in terms of specific information about him, and not in terms of*
> *a powerful evaluative frame of reference applying to the category*
> *of which he happens to be a member.*
>
> HENRI TAJFEL, 1963: 14

Pathologising Prejudice

The two most significant areas of academic work in which the concept
of the stereotype was taken up after Lippmann were communications
research and social psychology. During the inter-war years, both were
strongly influenced by the behaviourist stimulus–response paradigm.
This was based on the assumption of direct effects following, without
modification, from a given impulse or signal. In media research it was
manifest in the widely influential conception of communication as a
linear process occurring between an active sender providing a powerful
message and a passive receiver reacting dumbly to what was transmitted.
In this model of direct causal impact in the communication process, the
media were seen as manipulating and seducing an inert and tractable
audience, easily swayed by propaganda, stereotyping and social myth.
Behaviourism chimed in here with the theory of a 'mass society' of
isolated individuals cut adrift from any settled patterns of belonging and
order, and thus vulnerable to immense media influence over attitudes
and beliefs. The 'direct effects' model not only made stereotyping seem
irresistible. It also overshadowed theoretical approaches to the study of
propaganda, grounded in political theory and the political economy of
communications, that were concerned with questions of public opinion,

democratic participation, social administration, legitimation and control in the modern nation-state (see Robins et al., 1987). While these questions were tackled in the mid-twentieth century mainly within a functionalist sociological framework, this did at least keep in partial view the other side of Lippmann's dilemma, with its focus on stereotyping in strategies of power, in what he referred to as the manufacture of consent (Steel, 1980: 172).

Echoes of this phrase reverberated through post-1960s' media research, in which the critical sense of the stereotype was again taken up in relation to a range of different cultural forms and genres. For example, numerous content studies have identified descriptively and evaluatively stereotypical images of minorities and outgroups as sources of public misapprehension and vehicles of ideological views and beliefs, of manufactured consent. Yet against this general advance, there was little attempt to interrogate the conceptual model of stereotyping. This contrasts with the commonplace emphasis in social psychology on the second of Lippmann's two senses, that of information-processing. Over the last twenty years or so, this emphasis in psychological research has led to a conceptual preoccupation with cognitive strategies and their shortcomings rather than, as in media studies, with the politics of representation. These two different areas of work on stereotyping have in each case concentrated on one of its key dimensions to the detriment of the other. The dilemma which they pose when brought into conjunction has consequently been played down.

While this needs to be recognised, such divergence of approach to stereotyping has not in fact been quite so stark. A concern with prejudice did make for a common link between media research and social psychology. It is for this reason that Gordon Allport's famous definition of the stereotype has been commonly cited in media and cultural analysis. The common link was with stereotypical content viewed more or less intrinsically as negative and erroneous, and it connected back to the work of Katz and Braly in the early 1930s (Katz and Braly, 1933, 1935). In psychological research, their checklist methodology and theoretical concern with prejudicial values staked out the general terrain of preoccupation and approach for work on stereotyping for the next forty years or so, despite a few dissident voices from within the discipline. Initially, this marked a shift from 'race-psychology', which had endorsed the case for racist social policy, to the study of individual attitudes and values held towards racially stereotyped groups. In one sense the move was obviously commendable. In another, it proved all too convenient in switching the blame for prejudice from psychologists themselves, who had previously lent support to racist values, to their newly identified 'irrational' subjects. Switching the blame in this way served to recuperate a sense of their professional integrity and to re-establish the basis of their superior rationality (Samelson, 1978). The study of stereotypes then became confined to a search for the intra-psychic causes of prejudice and bigotry. This consolidated the classical view of the stereotype as a deficient unit of knowledge, but with the deficiency now utterly divorced from the politics of representation. The result of this is that the bulk of psychological research on racism has been anodyne and palliative, with psychologists themselves, for methodological and theoretical reasons, effectively encouraged 'not to see themselves as part of the problem' (Howitt and Owusu-Bempah, 1994: 85, also 86–97).

In some ways the work of Theodor Adorno in social psychology diverged from this approach, but in others it was not that dissimilar. Adorno was concerned with the capacity for authoritarian behaviour which some people possess and others do not. He wanted to see how the development of this capacity was connected to family and social structure. The book which he helped to write on the authoritarian personality (Adorno et al., 1995) is justly celebrated for its ambitious attempt to fuse neo-Marxism with neo-Freudian psychoanalysis in examining the socio-psychological make-up of the potential fascist. In this project, stereotypes were seen through the prism of rigid prejudice and dogmatic conventionalism. They were the irrational cognitive product of certain people whose intolerance was deeply rooted in a typical personality structure formed in the hierarchical and conformist societies associated particularly, but by no means exclusively, with the rise of Nazism and Fascism in the 1920s and 30s. Although he attended closely to the social conditions of anti-Semitism in the book he co-wrote with Max Horkheimer, *Dialectic of Enlightenment* (Adorno and Horkheimer, 1979), the work on authoritarianism tended to 'take the irrationality out of the social order' by imputing it to individual respondents: 'by means of this substitution it is decided that prejudiced respondents derive their judgements in an irrational way' (Hyman and Sheatsley, 1954: 109). It is through this substitution that Adorno's work converged with the psychological approach of pathologising prejudice in 'irrational' individuals. The attraction of this procedure belies the difficulty of explaining how virulent prejudices are able to spread across a social formation. If, for instance, we take the case of white South Africans during the era of apartheid, understanding the widespread social distribution of their racist values and beliefs is obstructed by the tendency to assign rigidly intolerant judgements to a single personality type. The individualist focus is in this sense misplaced, primarily because 'racist, sexist or xenophobic prejudices are frequently not held for deep-seated motivational reasons, but because they form part of the "common sense" which is generally accepted in racist, patriarchal or nationalist societies' (Billig, 1995a: 664; cf. Tajfel, 1981: 16).

The theoretical preoccupation with prejudice in social psychology was extrapolated out almost entirely from one side of the dual conception of stereotyping in Lippmann's initial formulation. As a result, the inherent negative/positive contradiction at the heart of the concept was largely buried in mid-century scholarship. The epistemological dilemma which has been its most interesting characteristic from the start was virtually lost from sight.

The 'kernel of truth' hypothesis, once widely accepted in the social sciences, did in a peculiar way attempt to address the contradiction between a necessary economy of attention and reductive views of others by advancing the notion that although stereotypes deindividualise, they nevertheless validly depict certain basic characteristics of social or ethnic groups (see for example, Klineberg, 1950). This may at first seem reasonable in allowing a certain feasibility to stereotypes, and so explaining how, through the comfort of their imprecision, they come to be widely accepted. But if we push at the logic of this hypothesis we soon arrive at an absurd consequence: the endorsement of white racism on the grounds that African-Americans, say, are in the kernel of their 'black souls' actually how they are alleged to be in racist stereotypes. This particular explanation of stereotyping was also inadequate for failing to discuss the problem of conformity to stereotypical behaviour by subordinated groups as a result of the structures of power between groups in society, not to mention acts of playing, strategically, at such conformity, or parodying stereotypicality through stylistic excess. Such covert acts were among the few forms of resistance available to African-Americans, as a socially powerless sector of the United States' population, in the period prior to the civil rights movement of the 1960s. Further, in attempting to question the degree to which stereotypical attributes are wholly negative, the 'kernel of truth' idea assumed that hard-and-fast measures of accuracy are actually possible. Recurrently, this has been an easy step to take and, unsurprisingly, such measures have proved elusive. Against the persistent notion of a germ of accuracy in stereotypes, it is important to insist on seeing them as 'common-sense' rhetorical figures. It is pointless trying to gauge whether or not they are accurate. What counts is how they circulate, and with what consequences, as base coins in the economy of discourse and representation; how they attain their symbolic currency among those involved in their exchange.

Gordon Allport also attempted to take up the uneasy ambiguity of sense associated with Lippmann's writing, but he did so on the basis of a distinction between rational categorisation and irrational stereotyping. For Allport, all categorisation entails over-generalisation and simplification, but this only turns into damaging prejudice when new knowledge does not lead to revision and change. Again, and all too conveniently, it is only in those with defective character structures that this problem becomes serious. This differentiation has been widely influential. Richard Bolton, for example, in his edited collection dealing with the history of photography, describes 'healthy stereotypes' as 'temporary coping mechanisms' which are modified or discarded 'when confronted by the specifics of experience', unlike 'unhealthy' stereotypes which are rigidly closed and used as mechanisms of assimilation and control (1989: 266). Pathologising prejudice in this manner lays stress on individual failings or weaknesses. By this move it displaces attention from the ways in which it is rooted in relations of power, patterns of privilege and vested interest, inequalities of income and broad disparities in the distribution of resources and opportunities. Thus Allport argues that 'it is only within the nexus of personality that we find the effective operation of historical, cultural and economic factors' (Allport, 1954: xviii). This encapsulates the distinctive weakness of mid-century psychological approaches to stereotyping, prejudice and conflict.

Pathologising prejudice was a serious wrong move. But there remain serious difficulties in characterising the distinctive features of stereotyping itself. The difficulties begin with knowing how to specify the difference between an accurate image and an inadequate stereotype, or between necessary categorisation and defective stereotyping. Again, this is part of the legacy of Lippmann's ideas. What is 'accurate' or 'necessary' so often turns out to be a particular and preferred version, the grounds of which either go unspecified or rely on the grand legitimations of science or political ideology. Even in empirical terms, these differences are sometimes devilishly hard to pin down, but the empirical disqualification of stereotypes is not the difficulty in question. It is rather to do with the rhetorical force generated by these differences, in which the prejudiced are always 'them', never 'us'. This move creates a means of dissociation and disavowal, for who in the first place wants to be judged as prejudiced, bigoted, intolerant? Even fascists deny that they are prejudiced and seek to deracialise their racist attitudes by reference to traditional values, to a sense of fairness or the idea of a given community (Billig, 1991: 122–41, and see Billig, 1978).

Speak of prejudice and you will rapidly encounter devices in argument and discourse for turning it into the appearance of something else, such as rational justification or only partially applicable bias. Yet these devices are not just found in everyday social interactions. They have long functioned as exteriorising strategies in social science academic discourse. They work by finding the evidence of irrational or deformed feelings, of rigidly dogmatic ideas or emotionally sustained values, in deficient individual 'others', not in 'ourselves'. It is not 'we' who are prejudiced, for 'our' response is based on a strict appraisal of 'the known facts'. This is then the real difficulty, for if we say that those who employ stereotypes are prejudiced, have we not fallen into the trap of employing a prejudiced judgement ourselves? Barry Glassner describes the difficulty in this way: 'By lumping a group of people together and calling them 'prejudiced' or 'abnormal' or 'subjects', social scientists have been able to do comparisons of 'them' and 'us'; and the irony of this is that it constitutes a prejudicing strategy itself' (1980: 120).

This second-order prejudicing strategy has the rhetorical effect of removing the tarnish of prejudice from 'our' values and underwriting their validity and authority. More or less the same move has been made in media studies. The analytical identification of stereotypical attribution in media texts and representations easily serves to distance 'us' from the ignominy of prejudice, with the stain of such ignominy in those texts and representations providing an alibi for our own freedom from contamination. This helps to stabilise the professional identities of researchers or teachers. It can lead to a sense of complacency or sanctimony which is glibly passed on to students. In Ellen Seiter's view: 'Too often communications students leave the university with a heightened sense of moral outrage over the grievous practices of television networks, while they remain smugly (and erroneously) confirmed in their own freedom from racism, or sexism or elitism' (1986: 24). The stereotype used as a tool of ideological analysis can easily switch to its use as a foil for its ideological practice. Once again, the dilemma underlying it conveniently slides away and becomes lost from critical view.

Naturalising Stereotyping

So what are the alternatives to these self-serving distinctions between popular-consumer sheep and cultural-critical goats? To tackle this question we need to examine a little further the relation between categorisation and stereotyping as this was initially deployed. Between the 1920s and 60s, the prevalent response to the dilemma at the heart of the stereotype concept was to dissociate the two aspects of the relation. Again, Allport's conception was representative of this step: 'A stereotype is not identical with a category; it is rather a fixed idea that accompanies the category' (1954: 191), and it is this fixed idea which obstructs rational thinking and tolerance towards others. Categorisation by contrast was posited as necessary and normal. Only in certain individuals does this process harden into the vindictive negativity of stereotypical attribution. Within psychology this evasive handling of the conceptual dilemma of the stereotype did not change significantly until the advent of social cognition research. This represented an interesting shift.

While recognising certain negative conceptual features of the stereotype, the social cognition perspective avoided the individualised psychopathology of prejudice, and admitted the presence of discrimination in all of us, again usually for reasons of cognitive parsimony. This initiated a move away from the analysis of stereotypical content to the study of stereotyping as a process. The result was a view of stereotyping as a requisite component of ordinary cognitive functioning, rather than as a symptom of a specific character structure. What was most distinctive about this shift to a cognitive perspective during the 1970s was the view of stereotypes and stereotyping alike as 'nothing special', 'as not essentially different from other cognitive structures and processes' (Ashmore and Del Boca, 1979: 28). The fundamental contradiction in thinking about the stereotype was renegotiated by focusing on the more positive, 'screening', 'short cut' and 'coping' strategies of stereotyping, even though bias and distortion continued to be acknowledged at times as a consequence of the kind of perceptual schema which the stereotype represents.

In switching from the pathologisation of prejudice to the naturalisation of stereotyping, the social cognition approach to stereotyping replaced one set of problems with another. Among these was an excessive and mechanistic emphasis on the ordering and classifying function of the intellect, with an accompanying failure, despite its label, to place sufficient emphasis on the social. Let us take each of these in turn.

Through the use of specific criteria of selection, categories are formed in order to classify and arrange phenomena into units containing similar attributes or characteristics. But they are only one feature of the way we think. Intellectually, we do not just think and talk in relation to categories. We also have regard for distinctions within categories, for deviations from the generically familiar, for instances as well as universals, for idiosyncrasies as well as collective attributes. Three other points need to be briefly noted. First, categories themselves can be elastic in form. They are not necessarily rigid or clearly separate from others, with hard or fixed boundaries between them, although that is precisely the illusion created when categories do harden into stereotypes. Second, categories can be used in conjunction with 'individualised understanding'. There is no deep divide lying inevitably between social categories and the description of particular, individualised people within those categories. Third, as Michael Billig has cogently argued, categorisation is dependent on particularisation, since a category is always distinguished from what is specific or singular. In cognitive psychological theory, the process of particularisation is usually ignored, resulting in a 'one-sided picture' (Billig, 1985: 82, and see 1996b, Chapter 6). Cognitive approaches make thinking appear *too* ordered, for we think flexibly and ambivalently as well as in relatively hard-and-fast ways. We discursively manoeuvre and position ourselves around a range of self/other relations, in situated contexts of thinking and talking. Because of this undue bias towards 'deep structure' category-thinking, social cognition approaches blur the boundary-crossings of categories into stereotypes. This problem is not helped by the assumption that social categories themselves provide the valid empirical base in relation to which, somehow or other, a stereotype constitutes a perception gone awry. The question of how such 'mistakes' or 'fixed ideas' are determined remains elusive. Stereotyping becomes simply 'the outgrowth of normal cognitive processes' (Taylor, 1981: 83). From here there lies an open road to political fatalism, for why should racist stereotyping be of interest except as an illustration of general cognition? (Hamilton, 1981 provides examples of this position.)

A more important break followed the development of social identity theory by Henri Tajfel and others in that it attempted to re-centre the 'social' in social psychology. Following Sherif (1967), discriminatory values were located in inter-group behaviour rather than in individual attitudes, while social identities were seen as based comparatively on ingroup/outgroup differentiations. In this way, an ingroup's positive distinctiveness accrues from the comparison for reasons of self-esteem. The evaluative distinctions which result from this process were then considered as the key functional component of stereotypes. If this is so, how can it be applied in cultural analysis?

The question of stereotyping in imperialist discourse, which will be discussed more fully later in the book, provides an example of such application. In such discourse, social categories of identity have historically been focalised through national identity, although always from a particular perspective, which is determined by diverse relations of social power, such as those of social class and gender as well as race. Where this corresponds to self/group/national esteem (and the linkages between these are obviously problematic) there exists an act or process of evaluation. Nationalism in this sense is at once an ideology of the first person plural and the third person plural: 'we' are who 'we' are because 'we' are not 'them', not 'foreign' – which is always a specific category of otherness (Billig, 1995b: 78–9). The positive value attached to 'our' social/national identity in imperialist discourse implies not only categorisation but also diverse forms of comparative assessment. The power-relations to which such discourse historically spoke in the European context required reaffirmation as a prerequisite of their cultural if not social reproduction, so that those included within any ingroup category were favourably constituted and given positive identity.

While, as I shall go on to argue, the specificities of stereotypical representation tend to be occluded in social identity theory, one of the most important lessons to be taken from it is that the need for such a positive ingroup characterisation entails negative contrast with other social categories. This provides a rich soil for the growth of discriminative thinking and practice. A note of caution is in order, however. The negatively charged representations of colonised 'natives' should not be viewed simply as the provision of opprobrious images that could be used in the justification of empire. This would be to invert the historical cause-and-effect relations of racism. Racist ideology did not arise and develop during the nineteenth century as a means of laying down a foundation of values and beliefs that could then be used as a basis for constructing the imperialist edifice. Rather, such ideology in Europe and the Americas developed out of the economic exploitation of colonial resources, including 'native' labour power: 'Europeans abroad found it necessary to rationalise that exploitation in racist terms' (Rodney, 1982: 89).

Shortcomings in Stereotyping Research

Social identity and self-categorisation theory have been helpful in shifting the focus from individualistic conceptions of group membership to group-oriented self-perception, and in attempting to explain the socio-psychological processes that generate conflict between social groups. The self-categorisation approach, however, adds little if any refinement of the significantly greater achievements of social identity theory, although ironically, considering its title as a theory, it does place more stress on the 'depersonalisation' of self-perception and action in shared social identity. What this basically means is that the more individuals identify with particular groups, so their individual identities will become less salient. To this extent, self-conception becomes integrally bound up with the positive ratifications of the social and national categories to which individuals believe they belong. This is taken to be an almost ubiquitous process by which interpersonal relations are restructured into inter-group conflict. In its elaborated forms the proposition seems reasonable, but in explanatory terms it renders resistance to group-articulation, and refusals of stereotypical values in inter-group relations, as anomalous or dysfunctional, and begs the big and important question of how social identities change.

What is worse is that inter-group relations are rendered as a sort of abstract social algebra remotely distanced from the everyday world of discrimination against social difference in its oppressive stereotypical forms, whether this is in the motor car manufacturing industry or the school playground. Hogg and Abrams do at least express this conception of the relationship between ingroup self-categorisation and stereotyping relatively clearly in saying that as people's 'behaviour becomes more normative their category membership becomes more salient' (1988: 172). Hardly a big surprise, as any stereotyped victim is likely to tell them. This is, nevertheless, the way in which self-categorisation theory attempts to map the psychological integration of self into group and the psychological processes that operate through the 'social' in order to sustain the distinctions and divisions between groups. It results in the 'social' being admitted back into social psychology in an extremely limited way.

One reason for this is that, despite the sophisticated treatment of particular concepts, in theoretical terms the approach is decidedly old-fashioned. Individuals are reduced to the isolated, autonomous, perceptual atoms reminiscent of 'mass society' theory, whereas the 'social' is conceived statically in terms of sets of interlocking, hierarchical functional units reminiscent of structural-functionalism (Hogg and Abrams, 1988: 18). In addition, as Wetherell and Potter have argued, social identity and self-categorisation theories do not move much beyond social cognition research. On the one hand, they continue to operate more within a perceptualist than a sociological framework, where the cognitive acts involved in group membership are viewed as universal and inevitable, while on the other, they take social categories and groups as a priori, preformed, 'historically and culturally given in advance'

(Wetherell and Potter, 1992: 47–8). The assumption of transhistorical psychological functions leads inevitably to an ahistorical understanding of the constitution of social groups.

This relates to another inadequacy. What is equally dispiriting to the limited theoretical reach of social identity and self-categorisation approaches is their lack of reference to the symbolic dimension of social encounters. What they fail to tackle are the cultural forms of relations between discrimination and group *amour-propre*, taken either as representations with specific discursive properties or as these are mediated by experientially lived relations and practices within specific space–time locations. For both approaches, the social group is an empty category, a category without cultural meaning or specificity. A further aspect of this inadequacy is any concerted attempt to engage with the ways in which contemporary media contribute to the production and reproduction of stereotypes. This contribution is obviously significant in that, in the West at least, the media constitute the most significant forms and channels of cultural representation and exchange. If we then look at one of the more recent social psychological texts on stereotyping we find little more than a slight nod in the direction of media representations, as for example in citing a stereotypical racist joke from the best-selling British tabloid newspaper, the *Sun*, but these representations are not taken up in their own right. While the authors acknowledge the importance of the media transmission of stereotypes, they simply refer to Ashmore and Del Boca – social psychologists both – in support of the claim that media research says little of the mechanisms by which stereotyping operates (Leyens et al., 1994: 37, 40–1; and see Ashmore and Del Boca, 1981: 25).

This all depends on what is meant by 'mechanisms'. I acknowledged earlier in this chapter that the neglect of the cognitive 'mechanisms' of stereotyping has been a weakness in media research, with Teun van Dijk's impressive work on language, racist ideology and the media forming a significant exception. Conversely, however, the attention given in media and cultural studies to the structural features of text and talk – their communicative 'mechanisms' – has been lacking in much social psychology, with ethogenic and discursive psychology being the only significant exceptions on the other side. Even if we just stick with the example of the racist joke as a cultural form, the considerable amount of work in cultural analysis that has been concerned with the ideological representation of stereotypes within the dynamics of the joke-frame and the joking relationship could have been fruitfully drawn on by Leyens and his co-authors if they had wanted to do more than merely cite an example. But this is of course only one specific form. Stereotypes have been researched across a range of media representations and genres. There are even various compendia which summarise and review this extensive body of research (for example, Friedman, 1977; Signorielli, 1985; Gunter, 1986). As Martin Barker has somewhat disparagingly put it, the 'search for "stereotypes" in the media has become a small industry in its own right' (Barker, 1989: 206). Yet it is not just the inattention to particular modern cultural forms which is disturbing. What is also out of the reckoning are the consequences of our media experience in itself.

For example, through modern communications media we are drawn ever closer to events that are distant in space, and yet as images of what is faraway become increasingly familiar, we struggle to find an appropriate scale for assessing this wider scope of experience in relation to our lives as we live them, still largely in particular places, however rapidly these may change. And as images of what is spatially distant now reach us with minimal temporal delay, we experience a sense of separation from what is more locally past, in the time of previous generations, as if their experience was that of some once faraway people. There is little point in simply lamenting these contrary turns in our experience, yet every point in critically recognising them and understanding how they are negotiated and assimilated, in our ongoing social life. Unlike Lippmann's writing in its own time, contemporary theories of group formation and group divisions in the discipline of social psychology appear curiously removed from contemporary social and cultural life.

Leyens and his associates do acknowledge and take account of what they call the cultural level, although this parsimonious acknowledgement fails to recognise that culture, like language, operates at every level. In doing so they attempt to overcome the empiricism of social cognition research by emphasising other criteria of adequate judgement beyond claims to a common or objective reality. By means of these criteria people attempt to match and maintain personal and social integrity, adhere to social norms and values, and express judgements in correspondence with the theoretical knowledge they have of the world. In combination these should act together to 'constitute an enlightening *gestalt* that gives meaning to the world and allows communication' (Leyens et al., 1994: 6). This is the basis of what Leyens and his co-authors call social judgeability theory. Its intention is to move epistemic validity from centre-stage in stereotyping and related research, and give greater recognition to the pragmatic criteria of social validity. What they stress is that social judgement is based not only on claims of correspondence to 'objective' reality, but also on cultural rules and resources that provide a ground for deeming particular 'targets' judgeable, and for establishing the entitlement to form a judgement. This is fine so far as it goes, but the more telling difficulties go deeper, and I want to mention three of these in particular.

First, in revisionist social psychology stereotyping is generally investigated in scientistic terms, with an excessive reliance on experimental data at the expense of, say, any exploration of intellectual and cultural history, or relevant work done in media studies. Feminist media scholarship, whose analysis of stereotyping Liesbet van Zoonen characterises as one of the significant 'new' themes it has taken up and revitalised, is one example of this. The perspective of gender involved in such scholarship points to its relative neglect in social identity theory (van Zoonen, 1994; Williams, 1984). While media studies and cultural history in themselves need to acknowledge and engage critically with social psychology's rethinking of the stereotype concept, the problems associated with social identity theory and its descendants could at least be ameliorated by attending to work on the slippery relations between categorisation and prejudice in other disciplines and fields of study. While these relations do need to be approached in psychological terms, they cannot be adequately understood in ways divorced from their particular social, cultural and historical contexts, all of which (as Tajfel himself recognised) inform the thinking of the experimental subject (Tajfel, 1981, Chapters 1 and 2; and see Billig, 1994).

The second point of frustration is reached after recognising the rich corpus of research and theorisation which has emerged from work on stereotyping from Tajfel onwards, and after taking into account the move onward in the revisionist denial of stereotyping as necessarily erroneous, misconceived, over-generalised or negative. The frustration here derives from the realisation that dealing with the contradictory senses of the stereotype concept by sharply differentiating between stereotypes and stereotyping is to use the psychology of stereotyping to justify the politics of stereotypes. Such a move is clearly illustrated by the statement that the 'major function of attaching labels to different racial and ethnic groups is to impose order on a chaotic environment' (Stephan and Rosenfield, 1982: 95). This is an insidious step. It makes the imposition of order a rationale for racism. It concentrates exclusively on the cognitive processes associated with stereotyping at the expense of its cultural and political dimensions; and it ties up 'race' with 'notions of chaos and impending social disorder' (Condor, 1988: 79). The effect of this is a drastic loss of the critical edge kept sharp in media and cultural studies. It takes us away, yet again, from the task of bringing together in a new synthesis the two halves of the contradiction in the stereotype concept, of renegotiating the opposed senses of the term that were sprung in Lippmann's initial formulation. The aim must be to develop alternative forms of analysis that overcome the ideological separation of the politics and psychology of the stereotyping process itself.

The third source of frustration with the 'new' revisionism in theorising stereotyping is one already touched on. This is that it is ahistorical in its approach and implications, neglecting the specificities of cultural identity and representation, and assuming universal psychological similarities in group identification. The demarcation between stereotypes and stereotyping presupposes the contingency and changeability of the former and the transhistorical functioning of the latter. This vitiates any attempt to explain how stereotypical images and representations are eroded, become dormant for a considerable period, and then either regain their previous force or finally lose their persuasive capacity altogether. In this way, within social psychology, the difficulties of dealing with stereotypes as sites of cognitive and affective ambivalence are handled by creating a false dichotomy between the strategic use of stereotypes as superficial, as for example in making certain normative accommodations, and stereotyping as generated by a deeper and more genuine grammar of motivations. In Billig's judgement, social identity theory, particularly in its self-categorisation version, tends to 'flatten out different ways of representing the world', ways which are cultural and historical in character and not functionally equivalent because imagined differently. So, for instance, national identity loses its specific meanings if conceived as 'just another form of "group identity"' and understood in terms of a psychologically constant 'inner response to a motivational need' (Billig, 1995b: 67–8).

Ironically, there is a parallel flattening-out tendency in some uses of the concept of the Other in contemporary forms of cultural theory, with postcolonial literary theory providing a prominent example (see McClintock, 1995: 9–17). This concept, along with postcolonial theory, will be taken up in subsequent chapters. Here we may note that prejudiced thinking about other social or ethnic categories may indeed operate with a monolithic construction, but this is perhaps more characteristic of the special case of a siege mentality. Stereotypes are more usually used in ways which are not uniform but part of 'a culturally shared scale of valuations': 'If the imagining of foreignness is an integral part of the theoretical consciousness of nationalism, then foreignness is not an undifferentiated sense of "Otherness"' (Billig, 1995b: 80;

cf. Myrdal, 1944 and Devine, 1989). Stereotypes may contradict each other, but they are also used as ways of making distinctions between forms and modes of 'otherness', whether this is applied to 'foreign' countries or within one's own. Obviously, the Other *as* Other remains an analytically useful concept in that outgroups are more generally described and perceived in terms of stereotypical attributions than ingroups: '"we" often assume "ourselves" as the standard, or the unmarked normality, against which "their" deviations appear notable' (Billig, 1995b: 83). During the modern period, however, a prejudice against prejudice has grown increasingly pervasive. As a result, the association of stereotypes with prejudice means that the prejudice they entail has self-defensively to be denied, as most obviously with a proleptic 'I am not prejudiced but ...' disclaimer prior to their use. This cognitive and affective tension has been central to the development of racist ideology in Britain where the conflict behind 'I am not prejudiced but ...' expresses a conflict within individuals between contrasting ideological themes (Billig, 1991: 127). This is not so much a case of having your ideological cake and psychologically eating it, as of conducting an argument with(in) yourself for the sake of self-justification. Putting it another way, modern prejudice expresses itself effectively when evacuated from the category of 'prejudice': 'The contradictory demands of justifying and criticising national prejudice can be seen in the everyday discourse of racism' (ibid: 134).

The relative neglect of stereotypical content in favour of allegedly underlying cognitive structures tends to lead to the conceptual isolation of 'permanances' in social relationships and interaction, such as simplification or prejudgement (the literal meaning of prejudice). The problems of this apparent simplification have already been touched on. It is clearly too simple to see prejudice and reason in polarised negative/positive terms, or 'to decide everything before the judgement seat of reason' alone (Gadamer, 1975: 241). If we move beyond this, we may then recognise that prejudgement directs our ongoing experience and our ability to experience (ibid: 9). This is quite different to claiming prejudgement of others as an instrumental permanence, as does Glassner (1980: 70–4), who espouses a Husserlian notion of 'essences' consisting of immutable elements without which phenomena cannot be imagined. The folly of this lies in trying to move beyond a history that cannot be moved beyond. This is a definite weakness in Glassner's approach to social prejudice. His resort to 'a kind of meta-empiricism', predicated on a sense of that which 'make[s] the phenemenon what it is', relies on the unassailable certainty of a 'principle of the phenemenon beneath its everyday properties' (1980: 27, 35). The implication is that this principle is absolute and historically invariant, and this is then realised in Glassner's definition of stereotyping as 'a form of everyday induction' where individuals are attributed to 'an alleged characteristic of their group' (all A are B) as a process enabling people 'to reduce cognitive uncertainties about targets and to permit predictable reactions to these targets' (ibid: 85, 88). We are back again with one half of Lippmann's problematic shorn asunder from the other, with the historically contingent politics of stereotypical representation buried out of sight beneath a universalised process of stereotype inductions. The statement that 'the line between prejudicing and "normal" social-mental phenomena is either very thin or non-existent' (Glassner, 1980: 85) not only begs the question of what is 'normal' and how a sense of this is consensually maintained, which I shall address in Chapter 7. It is also remarkably deficient in explanatory power. If there is little chance of distinguishing between stereotypical prejudice and categories as forms of mental organisation, why do we have the concept of the stereotype in the first place?

The problems raised by revisionist social psychology in its approach to stereotyping stem from the splitting apart of the two opposed dimensions in the stereotype concept, so that the psychological process of stereotyping becomes conceived as decontaminated from the politics of stereotypical representation. I have suggested that media studies has privileged the ideological dimension of stereotypical content at the expense of the cognitive features of stereotyping as a process, and that the reverse has tended to apply in important areas of recent psychological theory. It is important now to note that the latter tendency is in fact contrary to the approach which Tajfel advocated.

While Tajfel agreed that an 'understanding of the cognitive "mechanics" of stereotypes is essential for their full and adequate analysis', he criticised social psychological research which did not take the 'social' as 'the fulcrum' of analytical work on stereotypes. The study of the social functions of stereotypes was for him 'an indispensable part of the social psychologist's job' (1981: 4, 9, 143). Cognition was important for Tajfel in that stereotypes are derived from the mental process of categorising, but this too often leads to a tunnel focus on intra-psychic mechanisms. What is much more significant is their process of being or becoming social, as when they are 'shared' by 'large numbers of people within social groups or entities – the sharing implying a process of effective diffusion'. For Tajfel, this was the missing dimension in social psychological research: 'the large-scale diffusion of hostile or derogatory social "images" of outsiders has not been, to my know-ledge, the subject of explicit applications of cognitive theories in social psychology'. And again: 'social psychological theories of stereotypes have not been much concerned in the past with establishing the links between [their] collective and individual functions' (ibid: 145, 155, 158). Tajfel attempted to remedy this by proposing 'a sequence of analysis which would *start* from the social functions' rather than the other way round (ibid: 161, emphasis in original). It is only through such a re-sequencing of steps in the analysis that we shall begin to unravel the

> spiral effect in which the existence of prejudice at large not only provides additional support and rewards for hostile judgements, [but] also removes the possibility of a 'reality check' for these judgements which then feed upon each other and become more and more strongly entrenched in the form of powerful social myths. (ibid: 134)

Stereotyping as Social Exorcism

Tajfel's important reformulation of analytical procedure has become seriously attenuated in much recent psychological work on stereo-typing. His message has not been heeded. As we have seen, however, this is true not only of Tajfel's own field. The problems arising from the tendency to separate the opposed dimensions of the stereotype concept are evident not only in social psychology, but also in cultural history. This is one of the fields in which my own work is conducted, and I shall draw on it in later chapters. In view of this, I want to finish this chapter by looking briefly at the conceptualisation of the stereo-type in the work of a historian. This is Sander Gilman's important study of the social history of stereotypes. In his treatment of the question of difference, which is necessarily central to such history, Gilman has, in the specific cases he has dealt with, produced fruitful contributions to historical cultural studies, but his conceptual approach to stereotyping is, at the very least, troublesome. In what follows, I shall try to outline its main lines of weakness.

As with social identity theory, although he only draws on it indi-rectly, Gilman rejects the liberal-humanist assumption that stereotyping is the chief perpetrator of the ill-doings of misprision, exclusion and injustice. His approach runs counter to this moral piety in contending that stereotypes are integral to 'the myth-making made necessary by our need to control the world'. This clearly echoes Lippmann's less directive conception, borrowing from his mentor, William James, of the need to create order out of 'the blooming, buzzing confusion of reality'. Gilman sees myth-making as an aspect of symbolisation, understood in Cassirer's sense as 'an essential aspect of mental processes' providing 'the matrix for structures of order' (Gilman, 1985: 16–18, 1991: 3; see also Hamburg, 1956). Although Gilman explains stereotypes in terms of 'underlying cognitive structures', he draws not on 'new' social psychology but on psychoanalysis, and in particular on object-relations theory (see for example, Gilman, 1976: 126–38, 1991: 11–12). This is in itself an interesting move, but as he does this it is disappointing to find him transmuting the historical into his own version of 'essences' or 'permanances' by stating that stereotyping is an indispensable feature of our functioning in the world. It answers an 'innate and ungovernable human need'. This unsurpassable 'need' of order is said to be rooted in the childhood development of self-identity whereby the child's 'sense of self itself splits into a "good" self, which, as the self mirroring the earlier stage of the complete control of the world, is free from anxiety, and the "bad" self, which is unable to control the environment and is thus exposed to anxieties' (1985: 17, 1991: 11–12). What follows from this is the projection of the 'bad' self onto the 'bad' object, with a subsequent division of the world into 'us' and 'them'. Stereotypes, in adult usage, are then figured as the 'palimpsests on which the initial bipolar representations are still vaguely legible' (1985: 18).

There is an enormous leap here. Gilman jumps dizzily from a conception of the emergence of a sense of differentiation of self and world in infancy, to the varied deployment of vocabularies of stereotypical terms in the cultural interaction of adult social groups. This is a form of infantile determinism. It reifies the splitting defence mechanism of the earliest stages of childhood life, and is without any power to explain how, in later life, we can come to be tolerant, caring or compassionate. It has little to say about the ways in which, as adults, we engage critically with a world we have culturally inherited. In his attempt to map out a developmental approach to stereotyping, Gilman over-psychologises the process. He sees stereotyping, at root, in terms of a generalised psychic function, as if all forms of symbolic expression and practice can be traced back to certain fundamental attributes of the human mind. It is difficult to see how his explanatory stress on psychic traumas in the emergence of subjectivity during childhood can be satisfactorily reconciled with his acknowledgement of the specific cultural and historical imprints of stereotyping, and of the relations between stereotyping and inequalities and hierarchies of social structure. Apart from only making gestures in their direction, the single means by which Gilman attempts this reconciliation is by reference to the 'deep structure' that links childhood self-differentiation and adult stereotyping in particular social contexts.

This is decidedly vague. We are told that the two are 'parallel, but not identical', that the former 'reappears in the adult as a response to anxiety', that the 'sense of order the adult maintains is much like the structure of order which precedes the earliest stage of individuation' (1985: 19). But what is meant by 'parallel', by 'reappearance', by 'much like' in these assertions? ('Echoes' is another effortlessly applied epithet.) The linkages are almost spectral in quality, while the concept of 'deep structure' evacuates historical contingency, social processes and the intricacies of cultural dynamics quite out of the analytical terrain. At the very least, it relegates them to a level of merely describable superficiality, as if all cultural practice was a matter of docile habituation. This is, indeed, what results in Gilman's outline: 'Since all of the images of the Other derive from the same deep structure, various signs of difference can be linked without any recognition of inappropriateness, contradictoriness, or even impossibility' (1985: 21). This statement is condescending and simplistic. It throws a blind across any specific uses of such recognition, never mind the pleasures it might unfold. In the light of what has been said about the complexity and variability of attitudes, meanings and practices surrounding prejudice, Gilman's Manichean conception of human thinking and interaction renders the process of stereotypical 'othering' intractable. As he openly acknowledges, we cannot function without stereotypes. They are necessary parts of our lives, and so are ungovernable.

Gilman's approach to stereotyping contains important insights – as, for instance, in his recognition not only of 'good' and 'bad' stereotypes, but of the indeterminate line between them, so that the 'most negative stereotype always has an overtly positive counterweight' (ibid: 20). 'Good' and 'bad' stereotypes are intertwined. It is because of this that people can move between stereotypes which idealise other social groups and those which, in the interests of order and control, demonise them, making them figures of fear and derision. Conceptualising stereotypes in this way can be effectively applied in historical cultural analysis, as I hope to show later in the book. But again, Gilman reveals some of the pitfalls that are involved. It is worth mentioning just a couple of them. First, he has recourse to the distinction between a common-or-garden stereotyping which 'all of us need to do to preserve our illusion of control over the self and the world', and pathological stereotyping which cannot differentiate between particular individuals and stereotypical categories, and which consequently become rigidified as lines of demarcation between self and Other (1985: 18). This is little more than a reworking of the spurious distinction between categorisation and stereotyping, the inadequacies of which have already been discussed. Gilman's second application is rather more sound. Here he sees stereotypes developing and gaining force when self-integration is threatened, when anxiety undermines our sense of order and control: 'we project that anxiety onto the Other, externalising our loss of control' (ibid: 20). Although there is considerable evidence in favour of locating stereotyping processes in such instabilities and insecurities and the emotions they arouse, this is a rather one-sided explanation. It has little to offer in accounting for, say, the adult fascination with stereotypes as a fantasised expression of desire for the Other, whether explicitly forbidden or not, or the less covert and less private manifestation of carnivalesque delight in the theatrical or ritualistic display of grotesque Otherness, which children have delighted in across many generations.

If Gilman's approach to stereotyping is something of a conceptual mish-mash, this perhaps only illustrates, once again, the abiding difficulties attached to it as a process of cultural representation and as a matrix of perception and action. It is because of the real tangle of these difficulties that I have dwelt on them at such length. Gilman's version of the tendency to pathologise prejudice is, at least in cultural history, an analytical wrong-step, not because prejudice is never pathological, but because it leads to the absurdity of seeing all 'bad' stereotypical representations in terms of desperate anxieties and absolute demarcations of 'difference', and all transmission and acceptance of them, at whatever level, as psychologically disturbed or diseased. Again, in looking ahead to the discussion of colonialism and empire in Chapter 5, this would mean identifying imperialist discourse without exception as a form of mental illness, rather than a historically based ideology which became part of common-sense thinking.

The complex relations involved in stereotyping processes demand a more flexible conceptual treatment, with an ear trained on their ambivalences and contradictions, if we are to avoid seeing them as simply inevitable in the symbolic reproduction of social categories and identities. This much, at least, was clear to Lippmann himself: 'if our philosophy tells us that each man is only a small part of the world, that his intelligence catches at best only phases and aspects in a coarse net of ideas, then, when we use our stereotypes, we tend to know that they are only stereotypes, to hold them lightly, to modify them gladly' (1965: 60).

Drawing the difficult line between appreciation of difference and aggressive, destructive stereotyping may thus begin with assessing the degree to which a particular stereotype flatters our individual or collective *amour-propre*: 'To the extent that a stereotype gives us a feeling of superiority over the Other ... it should be immediately suspect' (Hwang, 1989). This is easily said, and it begs the question of all that might obstruct the desired immediacy of making stereotypical inferiority suspect. Yet that is no reason to ignore the injunction. Rendering the naturalising tendencies of stereotypes suspect is the whole point of attempting to understand the operation of their ideological properties.

It is in this light that I think we should take Tajfel's aim, cited in the epigraph to this chapter, of helping to create 'neutral' categories of representation. There may seem to be three immediate problems with this. First, it may appear to invoke an individualistic conception of the subject. However, this does not necessarily follow from evaluation and judgement of someone 'in terms of specific information', for such information could include particularised social as well as personal characteristics, and what matters is the form and quality of the information and our receptivity in working with it. Aside from this, the general effort of examined understanding counselled by Tajfel is happily compatible with the heartfelt request, once made by André Gide, not to judge him too quickly. When people do judge others too quickly, they often do so according to the available stereotypes. Second, to speak of 'neutral' categories may seem to suggest the ideal of a value-free neutrality in the social sciences. In view of Tajfel's own writings, this would be a misconception of what is implied. He quite explicitly rejected this dubious ideal. For instance, in the introductory chapter of *Human Groups and Social Categories*, he spoke of his 'conviction that a "neutral" social psychology is hardly possible', and of such 'neutrality' as often camouflaging 'the implicit taking of a position' (1981: 7; and see Billig, 1996a). The point made in the epigraph to this chapter should therefore be read the other way, with the aim being to *neutralise* pernicious reckonings of the Other, to take the poisonous sting out of their tales. The intention for Tajfel was to seek a broader recognition and encouragement of 'a diversity of social and cultural perspectives' (Tajfel, 1981: 6). This entails a refusal to operate exclusively with general categories – powerful evaluative frames of reference – which tend to homogenise and reduce appraisal to flattened-out similarities. It means attempting to counter this tendency by stressing what is different from category to category without reducing the differences to 'essences' and to negative/positive poles. The aim should be to reveal the fallacy of the final word, for the final word only seems final when we stop thinking about it.

That of course is crucial to the ideological 'effect' of the stereotype in that it tends to freeze-frame our thinking about others. It fossilises representation and excludes alternative ways of seeing and understanding. Attempting to move in the direction of neutralising stereotypical attributions and evaluations cannot be done either from some 'value-free' position or from an allegedly unified theory, for what both induce is an evacuation of the historicality of human thought. Again, this evacuation may seem to be implied by Tajfel's formulation of the aim of social analysis and critique, yet he was, as Billig has put it, 'especially critical of approaches which ignored the particularities of history and which absorbed all social phenomena into general, or universal, categories of psychological explanation, especially those which reduced the social to the individual' (1996a: 341–2). If these three problems are therefore only apparent and not borne out in Tajfel's work, despite leaving certain traces, subsequent applications and refinements of social identity theory have openly *exhibited* them in attempting to unify and universalise theories of psychology, in reducing the social to the individual, in ignoring cultural and historical specificity, and in paying little analytical heed of ideological processes.

Emphasising the historicality of human thought and discourse has a particular virtue in running counter to these tendencies, but it should not be taken as meaning that we can relativise everything that is historical. Historical phenomena are both particular *and* comparative in the way they are subsequently understood by historically located actors. We think conflictually about such phenomena in processes of categorisation and particularisation. These opposed terms indicate the argumentative two-sidedness of thinking, and if inferiorising categorisation leads to prejudice, rendering this process suspect by particularising, by attending to cultural and historical specificities, may lead to increased understanding, if not to greater tolerance. While there is certainly no guarantee of either possibility, keeping these conflicting approaches alternately in view will at least help us in beginning to chafe up against the operation of the ideological properties of the stereotype, to move outwards from the limited and limiting focus on their cognitive 'mechanisms' to a social and historical perspective on their contributions to the creation and maintenance of 'powerful social myths'.

Berndt Ostendorf offers a closer conception of these properties and their always specific operation in defining stereotypes as 'fossilised exorcistic social rituals with a historical basis … proportionate to the sense of alienation which produced them' (1982: 29). In this sense, for example, the racial stereotyping of black people in the imperial context designated, placed and tried to pin down the object evincing 'otherness' so that the Other-who-cannot-be-known became utterly known, utterly visible, in a stripped-down, undifferentiated form, as inferior, disorderly, low. By this means, conduct was rationalised towards those from whom the perpetrators and accomplices of the stereotyping process were alienated. This can be seen to have involved a degree of projection in Gilman's sense – the externalisation of 'our' anxieties, fears and forbidden desires: '"We" can claim that "they" possess the qualities which "we" deny in "ourselves"' (Billig, 1995b: 82). But if stereotypes are always proportionate to the sense of alienation producing them, then they are not absolute or invariant. They always have a historical basis. Stereotypes, and the prejudices they support, are in any case not confined in their use to the fulfilment of universalistic ego-defensive functions. The stereotypical forms and figures with which I shall deal in this book have operated in the social and public domain, and so cannot be seen simply in the individualistic terms of such functions, or even less as some sort of 'autistic information-processing' (McDonald, 1993: 221). These conceptions of stereotyping, as we have seen, define the limits of social cognition research, with its playing down of the 'social', and its recurrent lateral sliding into an identification of cognition with inner mental processes. In criticising the lingering Cartesianism involved, Rom Harré provides a pertinent counter-example: 'Making music is a social, necessarily public process. Just imagine a "psychology" of tuning up before a performance which tried to explain the activity in a Cartesian way!' (1981: 213).

In this chapter, I have shown that the social dilemma of stereotyping has been neglected in academic work. In social psychology, it has been avoided by recourse to the dual strategy of pathologising prejudice and naturalising stereotyping. In media and cultural studies, it has been avoided by recourse to the parallel dual strategy of pathologising stereotypical cultural texts and representations and naturalising the process of stereotypical critique. Psychologists have somehow escaped the taint of prejudice; media researchers and students have somehow never fallen victim to stereotypical values. Professional integrity has been salvaged; moral pieties have been burnished. It is in the light of this situation that I have sketched the basis for rethinking the concept of the stereotype, beginning with the recognition that it involved a socially paradoxical quality right from the very start. Is it not time that we finally grasped the psychological bull of stereotyping by the sociological horns of its dilemma?

In doing so, we shall have to recognise and work with the ambivalent values and contrary themes of everyday culture, for, as already suggested, the rhetorical force of stereotypes depends on the ways in which they seem able to bind contrary features together and banish from view the ambivalent relations which nevertheless underpin them. Ambivalence and contrariety are further manifestations of the categorical mismatches and dilemmas of rejection and attraction which stereotyping seeks to contain but which simultaneously, by this very process, it keeps within active attention. Stereotyping always operates in relation to what is culturally ambivalent and thematically contrary within everyday life, and does so as a common-sense rhetorical strategy of naturalising order and control. Stereotypes operate as socially exorcistic rituals in maintaining the boundaries of normality and legitimacy. It is because they are regarded as common-places in everyday life that they are taken for granted, left unquestioned, and able to attain wide circulation. Yet they do not exist as common-places for all time. They have a historical basis. Despite appearances to the contrary, in common sense, such a basis is prone to change. Rapid and continual social and cultural change may generate the conditions that lead to stereotyping, which is why stereotypes have been such a characteristic feature of modernity, but contrariwise, their rhetorical vibrancy and force is undercut by the contingent historical basis on which they depend. Putting it this way does not mean that we should forget the problem of their resilience or tendency to break out again after appearing to have died away. It is simply to say that stereotyping is always a part of ongoing cultural processes and shifting symbolic relations.

It is because of this that a stereotype may lose its common-sense value when it crosses into a succeeding period or different social group to the one it which it achieved wide circulation. Conflicting meanings may then come to the fore, or its own formerly unquestioned qualities be turned against it. This may help to undermine its previously effective exorcistic functioning, permitting individuals to see stereotypes as stereotypes and so 'hold them lightly', allowing them to do their play rather than applying them aggressively or as absolute truth. It is because stereotyping processes are part of ongoing symbolic life that the ritualistic exorcism of any low-Other is never guaranteed for all time. There is always a danger of discrimination going into reverse: 'the racial/cultural identity of "true nationals" remains invisible but is inferred from … the quasi-hallucinatory visibility of the "false nationals" – Jews, "wops", immigrants, *indios, natives*, blacks' (Balibar, cited in Bhabha, 1996: 55–6). The danger for prejudicial knowledge is that the 'false' being '*too* visible will never guarantee that the "true" are visible enough' (ibid). What is ritually exorcised always poses the *threat* of its return because of being made too visible by the very processes of social exorcism. It is with this conception of stereotyping as a process of symbolic confinement and risk, tied up with self-identity but always within a historical basis, that I operate in this study. In the next chapter, I shall go on to explore its implications further by outlining the related concept of the Other.

Chapter 3

The Concept of the Other

[The] stereotype of the Other is used to control the ambivalent
and to create boundaries. Stereotypes are a way of dealing with
the instabilities arising from the division between self and
non-self by preserving an illusion of control and order.

ELISABETH BRONFEN, 1992: 182

Denying History

In their specific forms, stereotypes are one-sided characterisations of others, and as a general process, stereotyping is a unilinear mode of representing them. While they occur in all sorts of discourse, and can draw on various ideological assumptions, stereotypes operate as a means of evaluatively placing, and attempting to fix in place, other people or cultures from a particular and privileged perspective. This is true also of the process of 'othering'. Over the past twenty years or so, this process and its nominative object, the Other, have become commonplace concerns in the human and social sciences. One result of this is that the concept of the Other has tended to displace the older concept of the stereotype, which by contrast has come to seem 'old hat' and outworn. Even as it continues in use, it does not carry the same critical éclat, the same status of seeming up-to-the-minute.

As I go on to argue, this newer and more fashionable concept is compatible enough with the stereotype, and can be used to revivify and extend its critical applications. One of the purposes of this book is to bring the concept of the Other and the stereotype into analytical conjunction in a more developed sense than seems to apply at present. This is a valid objective because of the ways in which they mutually complement and enhance each other as conceptual items in the critical vocabulary. So, for instance, to designate someone or some group or collectivity as Other parallels what is involved in stereotyping in that it is an evaluative form of naming or labelling which defines someone or some cultural grouping in reductive terms. The Other also parallels stereotyping as a strategy of symbolic expulsion, a mundane exorcistic ritual, used to control ambivalence and create boundaries. Ludmilla Jordanova has defined the process of othering in this way as 'the distancing of what is peripheral, marginal and incidental from a cultural norm, of illicit danger from safe legitimacy' (1989: 109). The stereo-typical act of descriptive compression and assessment as it is serially reit-erated serves to externalise, distance and exclude those so designated. It does so through constructing their 'difference' in terms which diverge from what is taken to be central, safe, normal and conventional. Stereo-typing is in this sense a way of warding off any threat of disruption to 'us' as the 'same together' through the generation of an essentialised Otherness that can then be dealt with from the point of view of this 'same together'. It is a collective process of judgement which feeds upon and reinforces powerful social myths.

The stereotypical Other is a denial of history. It works as an obstacle to change and transformation. In this way it is a component of myth in the Barthesian sense of the term. In demystifying the signs, symbols and images of 'mass' culture in his influential work *Mythologies* (1973), Barthes showed how these function as myth through their evacuation of history. The representation of cultural signs as essential types has a morally normative effect in rendering them as natural, absolute and invariable. To see them in this way is to evacuate history and the possi-bility of change from them and so protect existing structures and rela-tions of power behind the shield of 'safe legitimacy'. When a social category becomes a stereotype it takes on the aura of myth in this sense. Stereotypes are history in drastic reverse. In her study of the aesthetics of femininity and death, Elisabeth Bronfen supports this interpretation in stating that the 'aim of myth is to obscure the ceaseless making of the world by fixating it into an object, to embalm the world so that it can be possessed for ever, to inject into reality some purifying essence which will stop its transformation' (1992: 182). Stereotypes operate through myths because both involve the combined repressions of poli-tics and history. Condensing these repressions in particular representa-tional figures perpetuates social exclusion and economic inequalities, and can serve as a way of rationalising bigotry, hostility and aggression. Yet the damage caused by stereotyping practices applies not only to the objects of stereotypical regard, but also to those who advance any partic-ular stereotype as a definite truth, if only because stereotypes create barriers across their social interactions and relations, over both time and space. Stereotyping is a boundary-maintaining move inward, rather than an emancipatory movement outwards.

As a rhetorical strategy of exclusion, made in the interests of a unified collective identity, stereotypical othering seeks to deny not only its historical basis but also its basis in dependency on that which it casts out to the periphery. It attempts to separate and distance itself from the subjugated Other. The ritualistic process of social exorcism it performs attempts to contain the Other in its place at the periphery. Identity is in this way dependent on the difference that has been translated into Otherness. This gives symbolic centrality to what has been socially excluded, projected outwards onto the Other. Such symbolic centrality suggests either a fear of what cannot be admitted into an ordered identity, or a critical lack, an absence in the presence of identity which demands that the Other be turned into an object of happy assimilation, as a spectacle, an exhibit, a source of entertainment, or as fantasy. The Other can be drawn into fantasies of desire, longing, envy and seduction in the interests of compensating for some perceived deficiency of cultural identity or estrangement from inherited cultural values. Such fantasies solve nothing. They may be very pleasant for those engaged by them, but they only exacerbate the hold over the Other and deny validity and value in their own right to whoever has been othered. The translation of difference into Otherness is a denial of dialogue, interaction and change.

Towards the end of the previous chapter, I stressed the way in which the historically specific processes of the articulation and reception of stereotypes may produce variations of meaning and interpretation, and so lead to the possible amelioration of their prejudicial consequences in social encounters and relations. This suggests that we should try to understand the historical basis of contemporary stereotypes, to understand their contemporary historical character as ritualistic forms of social containment and exorcism, and so begin to see how they have been rendered absolute and immutable. Alongside this we need in many cases to attend to their long lineage and legacy. In order to understand the endurance of certain forms of stereotypical representation we need to trace their roots historically, for although theorisations of the Other are relatively recent, representations of the Other go back much further. It is because they are deeply rooted in the sedimented layers set down by past cultural practices that they have become entrenched as powerful social myths. As I said at the beginning of this book, my intention throughout is to counter the static, ahistorical nature of those approaches to stereotyping which sweep questions of both change and continuity under the surface of a self-referential present. Ironically, this quality is supported and endorsed by the psychological model of a universally individualistic process of cognition that has often been applied to the analysis of stereotypes. The nexus of social categories and relations in which any particular link in the chain of transmission is placed is then lost from view. These categories and relations are caught up in structures of power and control which require a historical as well as sociological perspective if they are to be brought back into the frame.

Ahistorical approaches to stereotyping deal with their objects of analysis as if they had appeared just the other week, in some new TV programme or the recent issue of a magazine. They are insensitive both to transformation and to recurrence. On the one hand, as Ella Shohat and Robert Stam have argued, such forms of stereotypical analysis do not allow for 'mutations, metamorphoses, changes of valence, altered function'. They ignore 'the historical instability of the stereotype and even of language' (1994: 199). They obscure the ceaseless making of the world by embalming it within the present. On the other hand, it is as though such approaches to stereotyping want to inject into historical processes some purifying theoretical essence that will fix it forever as a transparent object. Consequently, they fail to recognise that contemporary racist stereotypes 'are inseparable from the long history of colonialist discourse'. Shohat and Stam provide two pertinent examples. The 'Sambo' stereotype mentioned in the first chapter is but one circumscribed instance of 'the infantalising trope' which endured for so long in colonialist discourse. We shall encounter this discourse in detail in Chapter 5. In the same vein, the 'tragic mulatto' is 'a cautionary figure premised on the trope of purity, the loathing of mixing characteristics' (ibid). This is a trope which has been recurrent in forms of racist discourse across otherwise historically distinct periods.

In emphasising the historical lineage involved in the transmission of such stereotypical figures, I am not suggesting that we can have any transparent or objective view of the various pasts, or the continuities and changes occurring across them, to which this shifting lineage speaks in its passages through time. (For broad elaboration of this point, see Pickering, 1997a, 1999.) Yet there is a historical record, contested though it is, and we are heir to the struggle over its meanings, even though our own perspective is contingent and historically located. What meanings matter, or are made to matter, is what is at stake. We are dealing here not so much with the theoretical question of a knowable social or historical 'real' as with the experientially knowable consequences of symbolic representation. We are dealing with the questions of who is speaking of whom, at what cost and in what terms. In tackling such questions, we need to understand where those terms come from. They certainly do not suddenly spring up like ideological jack-in-the-boxes.

It is important to offset this impression. As a way of doing this, I want to devote the first part of this chapter to a few notes about a primary Other, the white racial phantasm of the Primitive. There are three main reasons for dealing with this construct here. First, I shall discuss examples of more specific forms of primitivised Otherness in later chapters, so it will be useful to deal with it more generally at this stage. Second, particular stereotypical forms of non-European peoples have been based on the generalised construct of the Primitive, in various ways that go back beyond the moment of colonial struggle so acutely examined by writers like Frantz Fanon, whose conception of the Other will be examined in conjunction with that of Simone de Beauvoir. Third, the notion of primitiveness as we have come to understand it is very much a product of modernity and modern imperialism, or rather of the intersections between them. The process of becoming modern and building empires profoundly altered the ways in which people in Europe thought about cultural difference. Western societies classifying themselves as modern and civilised relied heavily on the contrast between their own sense of advancement and the idea of racially backward and inferior societies. Those who were conceived as *inferior* in this way became *interior* to national identity in the West by becoming its Other, its decivilised counterpart. This ideological counterpart of modernity became known by the general name of primitivism, and I shall now outline what it involved and how it changed the Western view of the world.

Constructing the Primitive

The Primitive was a composite, portmanteau figure for Europe's Others, and could be located in various parts of the non-European world, rather than in any particular country or continent. It was nevertheless a racialised object of representation and knowledge, both in its academic and popular forms. The construct of the Primitive came into prominence during the later nineteenth century, although it was prefigured in various ways earlier on, in Columbus's 'cannibals' and figures such as Caliban in Shakespeare's *The Tempest*, in generalised ideas about barbarism and savagery, and in debates about the humanity and human rights of non-European peoples, such as the South American Indians (Montaigne, for example, was a notable exponent of their humanity, and viewed them as living in a state of innocent purity 'unspoiled by the ravages of civilised sin' (Friedman, 1983: 36)). Similar debates cropped up in the later modern period, as for instance in relation to the Australian Aborigines, but in nineteenth-century thought, the composite Primitive was very much a product of progressive evolutionism. This way of thinking was manifest in various disciplines of the human sciences, such as legal studies and art history, but its influence was particularly felt in anthropology, which took primitive society and culture as its special object of study. To a great extent progressive evolutionism displaced Romantic notions of the Noble Savage and a lost Golden Age, although of course it never did so completely. These reappeared at various times, as for instance in Melville's *Typee* of 1844 (1972) or, fifty years later, in Gauguin's *Noa, Noa* (1890), while throughout the nineteenth century, best-selling books by travellers in Africa sometimes depicted different parts of the continent as a sort of lost earthly paradise.

During the nineteenth century, the past and how it could explain the present and offer predictions for the future became a focal concern of western European thought. Especially during the later half of the century, many Europeans felt themselves to be in the throes of a massive transition. This was conceived in terms of a radical break with traditional society. Although this view was crude and exaggerated, its influence on thinking about the transition into modernity cannot be overstated. Among other things, it generated many of the governing conceptual dichotomies of classical sociology. Alongside it, the ideas of Darwin awoke a fresh interest in human origins – what Conrad's Marlow referred to as 'the night of first ages, of those ages that are long gone, leaving hardly a sign – and no memories' (Conrad, 1976: 47). There were various interpretations of this, but many of those who initially investigated these early social origins did so as a set of issues to do with law and the constitution of law. Their research into the development of the family, kinship, marriage, private property and the nation-state was conducted within a framework of legal concerns.

Tracing this development back archaeologically through 'traditional' to 'primitive' society, a whole series of studies by legal scholars like Maine, McLennan and Morgan offered a view of the Primitive that was the conceptual opposite of the civilised subject. The Primitive was nomadic rather than settled into a territorial state; sexually promiscuous by cultural sanction rather than monogamous and grouped in nuclear family units; communal in property relations rather than committed to private property; illogical in mentality and given to magic and superstition rather than being rational and scientific in intellectual orientation. The 'general characteristics of savages were clear enough':

> Dark-skinned and small of stature, unattractive, unclothed and unclean, promiscuous and brutal with their women, they worshipped the spirits animating animals or even sticks and stones – their smaller brains enclosing and enclosed within the mental world described in Spencer's chapters on the mind of primitive man. (Stocking, 1987: 234–5; and see Spencer, 1874)

The underlying assumption was that modern society had evolved from its antithesis, that non-white 'primitives' in the contemporary world were 'childlike, intuitive, and spontaneous', and that because of this they required control and guidance from Europe if they were not to suffer from their inherent physical violence and sexual drives (Kuper, 1988: 5, 231–6; Goldberg, 1993: 156). The justification of such control and guidance was, according to Francis Galton, founder of the eugenics movement, which promoted controlled breeding for the desired, racially inherited characteristics, that the 'requirements of civilisation' had bred into 'advanced' Europeans 'the instinct of continuous steady labour' and bred out the 'wild, untameable restlessness' that was 'innate with savages' (cited in Stocking, 1987: 95).

The evolutionist character of this kind of thought became known as social Darwinism, although somewhat peculiarly in that its basic notions owed little to Darwin's thought and were closer to the major ideas of Lamarck. Darwin himself considered 'hybrid vigour' rather than racial purity to be the key to success in the struggle of different groups for domination over their environment, with ethnically isolated societies being the most vulnerable in this respect (Darwin, 1913: 281–97). The reception and spread of Darwin's theories, however, did lay the ground for a resurgence of evolutionist thought. Social Darwinism posited a racial 'descent of man' and 'was increasingly invoked in attempts to justify the conquest of Africa and discrimination against blacks in Europe and America – the victory of "favoured races in the struggle for life"' (Honour, 1989, IV: 12). In *The Races of Man*, a text to which I shall return, Dr Robert Knox had already argued that racial struggle was all-determining – the singular source of human creativity, civilisation and progress (Knox, 1862; see also Biddis, 1976). This kind of view became increasingly pervasive and fed into the same mind-set associated with social Darwinism. 'Race' governed intelligence and inventiveness and the struggle between different 'races' led to the backwardness and eventual elimination of those who were lacking in the capacity to evolve (see Jones, 1980; Stepan, 1982: 47–110). Thus the Victorian adventurer, John Hanning Speke: 'The African must soon either step out from the darkness, or be superseded by a being superior to himself' (cited in Kiernan, 1972: 215). Social Darwinism proved highly influential in incorporating a static hierarchical model within a dynamic evolutionary system of social development. Western European nations were represented as having attained the peak of this development while 'primitive' societies, in Africa or Aboriginal Australia, remained at its nadir. Such societies had in fact hardly 'evolved' at all. They represented a backward, unchanging, simple form of human existence which the West had long left behind.

In this way, geographical spatial distinctions became temporalised – translated into historical stages of progress towards the culmination of civilisational advance represented by Western society. Primitive peoples in faraway places were viewed as contemporary versions of Europe's own ancestry, the long-ago peoples of its own distinctive space in the world. They were used as a measure for how far European civilisation had developed as a result of its technological prowess and sophistication, and its command of rational thought and behaviour. What had become temporally distant and long superseded at the centre could be viewed at the spatial periphery in the 'living fossil' of the Primitive Other. As an early twentieth-century travel writer imperiously put it: 'The African savage of today serves to indicate to us how much we ourselves have advanced from a similarly primitive state' (Ward, 1910: 287). This was also the conviction of Edward Tylor, whose work was central in the founding of cultural anthropology: 'savage and barbarous tribes often more or less fairly represent stages of culture through which our own ancestors passed long ago, and their customs and laws often explain to us in ways we should otherwise have hardly guessed, the sense and reason of our own' (Tylor, 1913: 388).

Through thinking in this way, time, rather than space, came to divide the world. Time became inverted space. The perception of differences encountered in movement across geographical space turned into the conviction of differences imagined in movement across historical time. In this genealogical production of historical movement, the primitive Other was conceived as historically different on an ahistorical scale of evolutionary development. In anthropology and travel writing, cultural difference was transformed into the historical and the historical into evolution along a unilinear scale that became the key to evaluation of social development and progress. Non-European peoples of the colonial encounter, of the encounter of traveller and 'native', were regarded as both the imaginary long-frame historical penumbra of European peoples, representing the 'then' of European prehistory, and as living 'now' in the shadow of European historical movement forward to the light of rationality, scientific discovery and its technological and industrial application. Yet it was precisely the 'now' of anthropology's object which was refused and turned into its opposite. The time of the Primitive was always distanced as the 'then' and 'there' from the 'now' and 'here' of the civilised West. In evolutionary temporalising, difference became distance in a spatialisation of time: 'evolutionary sequences and their concomitant political practice of colonialism and imperialism ... are founded on distancing and separation', on what Johannes Fabian calls the 'denial of coevalness': 'a persistent and systematic tendency to place the referent(s) of anthropology in a Time other than the present of the producer of anthropological discourse' (Fabian, 1983: 26, 31 and Chapter 2). The construct of the Primitive represented early 'man' in early times, fossilised in the fixed otherness of the long-distant past. *'Beyond* Europe was henceforth *before* Europe ... The non-European Other was a petrified European, and his difference was merely a petrified sameness' (McGrane, 1989: 94; see also Asad, 1973).

The ideological gauge here was progress, which was informed by the historicist set of cultural values grouped around it. For example, Charles Rau, responsible for the ethnological exhibits at the Philadelphia Centennial Exhibition of 1876, felt that 'we should glory in our having advanced so far above' the 'extreme lowness of our remote ancestors', and should 'recognise the great truth that progress is the law that governs the development of mankind' (cited in Rydell, 1984: 24). It was through the application of this 'law' that the otherwise innocuous word 'development' became so value laden, particularly as henceforth, along with 'modernisation', it became necessarily paired with its opposite, which was the realm of 'primitive' existence. Out of this emerged categorisations of differential stages and ages of development, with 'not only past cultures, but all living societies ... irrevocably placed on a temporal slope, a stream in Time – some upstream, others downstream' (Fabian, 1983: 17). Within this historicist schema, Tylor's 'savage and barbarous tribes' represented the originating stages in the long passage from 'our' ancestral past to 'our' contemporary global pre-eminence, 'our' imperial age.

The politics of representation here consisted of what the Other represented for 'us', for what it showed 'us', often more or less *unfairly.* 'Unfairly' because the study of other, faraway peoples was not about them at all. It was about 'us' refracted through 'them', and 'them' temporally excised from the social exclusivity of 'us'. The 'night of first ages' had indeed its sign, its invented memory: the memorialised sign of the Primitive. What the Primitive represented was 'our' historically defined advancement over the ages. History itself was 'regarded as a long-term process of growing fulfilment' with 'the titles of legitimation of political action' bestowed by 'the effects anticipated by plan or prognosis': 'the horizon of expectation was endowed with a coefficient of change that advanced in step with time' (Koselleck, 1985: 278–9). In this stratified historical order, different 'tribes' might represent different levels of advancement, but the Primitive existed in a state of fundamental 'undevelopment', and therefore in 'societies without history', for history as progressive evolutionism belonged to 'us' and was about where 'we' had come to at this pinnacle of social improvement and civilisation. The Primitive Other was in this way divested of his or her 'difference' and petrified into the sameness of 'our' early origins. Whatever is regarded as 'petrified' cannot, by definition, be historical, cannot belong to historical process and change. The Primitive was therefore historicised out of history in order to be made to represent and show 'our' progressive history. In Bernard McGrane's words:

> The concept of progress was what made possible the experience of the *Other-as-primitive*, of the Other-as-fossil ... Without our whole sensibilities being formed and informed by the concept of progress ... we would have never, in encountering and confronting difference, experienced 'primitiveness', experienced our advance over their backwardness ... The resource of 'progress' authorises the transformation of the 'different' into the 'primitive'. If the rather deeply sedimented, institutionalised belief in 'progress' disappeared, the 'primitive' would vanish. (1989: 98–9)

It was through the concept of progress, then, that certain non-European peoples became the primitive Other. The purpose of this figurative construct was always comparative. The interest in 'their' customs and laws was not an interest in what these consisted of in themselves, in their operation and practice, in their ordering of a definite structure of social organisation or in their contribution to a particular pattern of cultural life. The interest consisted in what 'they' 'often explain to us' – 'often' implying 'more often than not' – and not in what they 'often' explained to the people who implemented them in *their* own way of life. The hypostatised difference they exhibited served 'us' with an explanation of 'ourselves', 'in ways we should otherwise have hardly guessed'. What could otherwise have hardly been guessed was the immense scale of this 'difference' from 'our' own culture, the capacity of cultural excellence which we had attained. But once the basis for comparison had been conveniently provided, what needed no guessing, what indeed was abundantly obvious, was 'the sense and reason of our own' customs and laws, sanctified as they were by rational–technical progress. The category of the primitive operated as modernity's repressed Other. Myths of advancement in the West made for a binary opposition between modernity and the non-contemporaneous primitive, with each understandable only through the terms of this opposition as a direct corollary of colonial expansion and domination.

At the same time and in relation to this, the temporalisation of difference was also a racialisation of difference. The Primitive was a general type of racialised Other who, while always amenable to specific application according to case and context, appeared to provide evidence of everything that had, through progressive social selection, led to European global supremacy. It was but one step from this to the confirmation of the inequality of 'races', and then of strength through open competition and imperialist mastery as a natural right. The construct of the Primitive is a classic example of the Other, not least because it was entirely illusory. It was, in Adam Kuper's words, the anthropological version of phlogiston or aether, 'or, less grandly, our equivalent to the notion of hysteria'. Primitive society has never existed. The Primitive as a human type was a figure of fantasy. It was constructed in the first place by speculative lawyers. Yet – and this is what remains a source of amazement – it was endlessly adapted and 'accommodated to virtually any theoretical or political discourse', including Marxism and psychoanalysis. As this capacity for flexible adaptability should make clear, 'the idea of primitive society was never merely an imperial myth, or a charter for nationalism', even though it lent abundant support to the ideologies of nationalism and imperialism (Kuper, 1988: 8–9). To see it simply as propaganda for empire or European national identities is to underestimate its depth and force as an intellectual current. It was within this current that the establishment of anthropology as an independent discipline became swept up. While anthropology did provide ideological ballast for the imperialist project, the role and resilience of primitivism as a powerful idea derived more from its protean character and propensity for continual renewal. It is this propensity which now seems so surprising, for, as Kuper argues, all the theoretical models of primitive social structure developed by anthropologists over the past century or so are simply transformations of the same basic illusion. The illusion turned prototype became an ideal type and then a theoretical model, while all the time acting as an ideological foil for modern society. Primitive society as anthropologists imagined it 'inverted the characteristics of modern society as they saw it' (ibid: 240).

The idea of primitivism was, then, not confined to anthropology, nor indeed to academic research in general. Among other cultural forms, it was manifest in the ethnographic showcases of imperial exhibitions. While these became more frequent during the second half of the nineteenth century, with an expanding European colonialism and the 'scramble for Africa', Africans had been exhibited from early on in the century. Understandably, in view of the public interest shown, and the extreme voyeurism and pathologising of the Other involved, particular attention has recently focused on the sorry case of the Khoi-San woman, Saartje Baartman, who was ignominiously exhibited in life as the 'Hottentot Venus' and dissected in death by Georges Cuvier, the French anatomist who was fascinated by her genitals. Yet this particular and rather special 'specimen' of the primitive Other was followed by many other cases throughout the nineteenth and early twentieth centuries. Increasingly, whole ensembles were put up for visual inspection, and, particularly with reconstructions of 'native' villages, which became a common feature of world fairs from the late 1870s, it was their general 'way of life' which was displayed.

A 'Kaffir Kraal' at the 1899 Greater Britain Exhibition, for instance, was billed as 'A Vivid Representation of Life in the Wilds of the Dark Continent' (MacKenzie, 1985: 104). An earlier example was that of a group of 'Kaffirs' shown in London in 1853, who among other things entertained with a witch doctor 'smelling out' a witch who had brought sickness into the tribe, and with meals eaten with enormous spoons. A contemporary reviewer described the 'howls, yells, hoots, and whoops, the snuffling, wheezing, bubbling, grovelling, and stamping [of a] concert to whose savagery we cannot attempt to do justice' (cited in Honour, 1989, IV, Pt 2: 140.) Small wonder, then, that 'Kaffir' became a term of virulent racist abuse in apartheid South Africa. Such degrading exhibitions – and down the years there were many of them across most of western Europe – appeared to confirm the African's debased position on the racial ladder of living creation. The reporting of one 'troupe' of Bushmen displayed in London represented them as 'benighted beings, little above the monkey tribe and scarcely better than the mere brutes of the field'.

> It was strange, too, in looking through one of the windows of the room into the busy street, to reflect that by a single turn of the head might be

witnessed the two extremes of humanity – the lowest and highest of the race – the wandering savage, and the silken baron of civilisation. (*The Times*, 19 May 1847, and *Illustrated London News*, 12 June 1847, cited in Altick, 1978: 281)

That single turn of the head panoptically encompassed both the fascination with and the dread of these 'benighted beings', at the furthest imagined extreme from silken civility and order. In that single switch of gaze from wandering savage to well-groomed baron, the vast span of ages was neatly swept up, the huge range of 'human types' discursively encompassed. And so:

> When we come to consider the case of savages, and through them the case of pre-historic man, we shall find that, in the great interval which lies between such grades of mental evolution and our own, we are brought far on the way towards bridging the psychological distance which separates the gorilla from the gentleman. (George John Romanes, cited in Brantlinger, 1985: 186)

It is now astounding to think of all that this entailed. In the construction of 'savagery' as spectacle, racial stereotypes were seemingly made real, social Darwinism became 'established in the popular mind', control of the world was 'expressed in its most obvious human form' and 'living proof' was offered 'of the onward march of imperial civilisation' led by the 'mother country' at the head of the colonised 'family of nations' (MacKenzie, 1985: 113–14). So for example, in discussing the Dahomey Village exhibited at the 1909 Imperial International Exhibition at London's White City, the guidebook praised the French for bringing, in their conquest of Dahomey, 'order and decency, trade and civilisation' to a country previously ruled by 'bloodthirsty potentates'. The cataloguers remarked: 'The days of savagery are passing away' (ibid: 116; and see Coombes, 1985). The spectacle of the primitive Other, with its accompanying narrative and commentary, not only proved highly influential in mediating the imagined civilised/savage divide, but also neutralised 'the cognitive dissonance and the threat to Western, middle-class identity constituted by the baffling cultural difference of new peoples' (Corbey, 1995: 72). For cultural difference to be displayed, and temporal as well as spatial distance emphasised, what was seen as strange and exotic could never be totally familiarised by the strategies of exhibition. This would have neutralised the commercial appeal of the primitive Other as a source of awe and fascination, and as trophies of imperial conquest. A fairground-type thrill of fear in the primitive Other was generated by the appearance of 'wild' difference, yet any threat to Western, middle-class identity posed by such difference was at the same time contained by the strategies of exhibition. 'Savagery' as spectacle was 'savagery' domesticated and tamed. The previous exorcism of real threat through tales of horror and images of barbarism became transformed into the delight of decorative exoticism, with the primitive Other not only exploited but also enjoyed, 'enjoyment being a finer form of exploitation' (Pieterse, 1992: 95; and see Chapter 5 on the popular fiction of empire).

Figure 3.1   The 'two extremes of humanity' are graphically depicted in this illustration from a late nineteenth-century Imperial Exhibition. The black as a racially low-Other and the 'silken baron of civilisation' are juxtaposed for the sake of their stark contrast in this animated display of the 'savage' way of life in Darkest Africa
(John Johnson Collection, Bodleian Library)

One and the Other

The purpose of this small case study dealing with the ideological construct of the Primitive has been to sketch out some of the ways in which its long history developed and its attendant notions have been bequeathed to us. It has been offered in order to show the importance of a historical approach to cultural analysis. Differences constructed in relation to myths of advancement in the West during the nineteenth century have cast an extensive shadow. Maryon McDonald has likewise argued that nineteenth-century nationalist and pseudoscientific views 'still tend now to construct the most common mode and means by which differences are drawn and understood' (1993: 226). The question of nationalism, and of 'science' in its production of a supporting racism, will be carried forward into the next two chapters, along with an outline of how racist notions of primitivism spread into popular culture, roughly a century or so ago. Before that, in the second half of this chapter, I want to deal with two writers who have contributed enormously to our conceptual thinking about the Other. These are Simone de Beauvoir and Frantz Fanon.

There are three important reasons for outlining their contributions here. The first is that they show that it is not only certain non-European peoples who have been seen as the Other of white, civilised nations in the West. Within Europe, women have also been constructed as the subjugated Other of their masterful male counterparts. Second, bringing these two writers into conjunction is useful for the ways in which it shows the intersections of 'race' and gender in the cultures of Western modernity. This will prepare the ground for Chapter 6, where these intersections in colonial discourse will be one of my major concerns. The third reason for discussing the ideas of de Beauvoir and Fanon on the Other together is that both of them have been rather ignored by recent writers in cultural theory. Their input into such theory has nevertheless been considerable. De Beauvoir's use of the concept of the Other fed valuably into cultural theory and social criticism during the second half of the twentieth century. The feminist writer, Toril Moi, has also noted this neglect. She adds that while Fanon explicitly invoked Sartre in his *Black Skin, White Masks* (1972), 'the obvious historical connections between Fanon and de Beauvoir' have been played down, and 'present-day colonial and post-colonial critics have done nothing to change this unhappy state of affairs' (1998: 81). In relation to critical discourse on the Other, it is time to move towards the recuperation of both de Beauvoir and Fanon.

In *The Second Sex* (1984), Simone de Beauvoir (1908–86) closely examined the mythical operations of stereotypes that historically men have constructed about women. In interrogating these she built on the concept of the Other in Hegel and Sartre – Hegel's master–slave dialectic and the existentialism of Sartre's *Being and Nothingness* (1969) providing her with a philosophical basis for analysing the condition of women – and turned it into a key term in her analysis of women's oppression. Her analysis centres around two major themes.

First, she argues that in conceiving of themselves as essential beings, as subjects, men have made women into inessential beings, into objects, defined against a male norm: 'He is the Subject, he is the Absolute – she is the Other' (1984: 16). This objectification of women is what has made them the second sex, the sexualised Other. To quote de Beauvoir: 'Although women are not the only Others, the fact remains that women are invariably defined as Others' (cited in Cottrell, 1976: 96). Subsequently, it has sometimes been assumed, implicitly or otherwise, that Otherness is produced primarily or solely by gender. We have already seen that this is not the case, and de Beauvoir herself does not make this claim. She points to various instances of groups being regarded as inferior or abnormal and to the tendency of groups to set themselves up as the One by 'setting up the Other over against itself' (1984: 17). In their subjugation, women have occupied a comparable status as Other to blacks and Jews. 'The eternal feminine' is a stereotypical construct of the Other just as is 'the black soul' and 'the Jewish character' (1984: 23; cf. Sartre, 1962). Black or Jewish women have of course been doubly othered, in racist and sexist terms, but de Beauvoir's main comparison is with black men. In the main, this was due to the influence of the African-American novelist Richard Wright on her understanding of racism and on her conception of the object term of the subject–object relation (Fullbrook and Fullbrook, 1998: 97–8, 121).

In 1947, de Beauvoir travelled for five months in the United States. She was with Wright on various occasions, counted him a good friend and knew him subsequently during his time in Paris. His keen insight on 'the black question' clearly influenced her own views, as for instance when she summarises his account, given over an evening meal in a Harlem restaurant, of the white 'othering' of the black as a stereotypical object of fantasised desire:

These whites define blacks as the antithesis of American civilisation. Magnificently gifted in music and dance, full of animal instincts (including an extraordinary sensuality), carefree, thoughtless, dreamers, poets, given to religious feeling, undisciplined, childish – that's the conventional image of blacks that these whites readily construct. And they are 'drawn to' blacks because they have projected onto them what they would like to be but are not. Those who feel the greatest fascination are people who feel most deeply deficient themselves. (de Beauvoir, 1999: 353)

As forms of 'othering', stereotypes of black men and white women have had similar consequences. Wright's objection to the emergent white hipster of late 1940s New York relates to a relatively positive version of the stereotypical black construct. It was one built out of a sense of certain white people's self-deficiency, or a sense of estrangement from inherited values in the cultural mainstream of white America, in fantasies of envy and desire that could only prove fulfilling by othering blacks, turning them into the antithesis of the cultural order in which they were situated and affirming their low social status. It was because of this that the construct could easily be turned around into a more derogatory version serving a sense of white superiority. This is where the gender parallel strikes home, for the female as Other can induce an attitude of looking up or looking down in a similarly self-serving manner. Black people could be seen as merry, childlike and submissive, which was their preferred image in the deep South, or envied as more free, happy and unrestrained than white people, which is why certain whites in the northern United States were drawn to them. The 'true woman' could likewise be seen as frivolous, infantile and irresponsible, or as caring, dutiful and the 'better half' of men. The black or female as Other have been both denigrated and idealised by white men in comparison with themselves.

Second, de Beauvoir argues that there is no essential feminine nature, that femininity, in whatever version of it, is an artificial construct. To quote her again: 'One is not born a woman; rather one becomes a woman' (1984: 295). The idea that our identities are gendered in the process of being brought up, that gender is socially produced and gender inequalities are not a fact of nature is now readily familiar. It was still a fairly radical claim when de Beauvoir initially pursued it, which she does perhaps best of all in her writing on the formative years (ibid: Pt 4, Chapters 1–2). There she scotches the myth of a mysterious feminine soul or sensibility, and offers a far more satisfactory account of the development of female subjectivity than those focused around the Freudian terms of penis envy or the Electra complex. She attends to some of the biological factors of being female, but her interest lies more in social and cultural factors constraining women and their struggle for independence. According to de Beauvoir, women are not only Other to men but also to themselves in as much as they have accepted male objectifications of them – their essentialist versions of femininity and their conceptions of women's innate inferiority – thus affirming men in their sovereign masculinity. While she avoids presenting women as simply innocent victims of patriarchal oppression, it is not clear whether she sees such collusion as having been done in 'bad faith', or because women have lacked either insight into their condition or the means of resistance to it. Nevertheless, the historical consequence of such collusion in male mastery was that women have existed for men and not for themselves. In this they have been doubly damned: 'Her wings are clipped, and it is found deplorable that she cannot fly' (1984: 616). The purpose of *The Second Sex* was to explore the difficulties involved in women's efforts to redefine themselves, to regain their wings and fly by themselves.

As we shall see in more detail later, a characteristic feature of the Other is an ambivalence of response to it, belying its apparent fixity. In the case of women as a discursive construct of masculinity, this is directly associated with the contradictory stereotypicality of their gender. So, for instance, in being taken to embody Nature, women have symbolised both the source of life and its negation, both purity and innocence and their opposites. These have been manifest in conflicting male attitudes to virginity and sex, and in conflicting standards of female beauty. Male response to woman as Other has also oscillated between requiring an embodiment of their fantasies of women as passive, dutiful, submissive, and a projection of their fears of women as over-assertive, deceitful, narcissistic. 'Woman' is both man's prey and his downfall, everything he is not and everything he longs for. To quote de Beauvoir directly, the category of woman

> incarnates no stable concept; through her is made unceasingly the passage from hope to frustration, from hate to love, from good to evil, from evil to good. Under whatever aspect we may consider her, it is this ambivalence that strikes us first. (1984: 175)

It is in relation to this ambivalence of response that de Beauvoir speaks, in a phrase prefiguring Homi Bhabha's approach to the stereotypical Other, of 'l'hésitation du mâle entre la peur et le désir' (cited in Keefe, 1983: 101). It is here that her argument seems at its strongest. Where it remains somewhat elusive is in relation to specific forms of historical evidence. In developing its highly persuasive case for woman as Other, *The Second Sex* draws on an extensive range of material, but its claim to be an examination of women's situation in the social world is undermined by its excessive use of sources in art and literature, sources perhaps better suited to a study of women's literary and cultural representation. While this makes too clear-cut a distinction between symbolic representation and historical realities, since these continually interfere with and inform each other, the social world itself is largely absent from the book, or present more by inference than empirical evidence. The lack of a materialist grounding of women's oppression is manifest in another way in *The Second Sex*. Through a critical engagement with their writings on women, de Beauvoir rejected Freud's reductive view of gender relations, as she did Engels's economic determinism. For her both are insufficient as explanations of women's historical oppression. Instead she favoured the existentialist categories of immanence, transcendence and the Other, and argued in favour of Otherness as 'a fundamental category of human thought' – 'as primordial as consciousness itself' (1984: 16–17). Consciousness is ever-assertive and in asserting itself it seeks to annul the consciousness of the other by making it Other.

This is a metaphysical argument for consciousness based on aggressivity and conflict, on consciousness as itself imperialistic. Against their better existentialist principles, both early Sartre and de Beauvoir explained human conflict in these essentialist terms – as if the desire to dominate is innate in human nature. This is one of the least satisfying elements in *The Second Sex*. Later, both sought to ground their analyses of power and conflict in material scarcity. De Beauvoir's retrospective view of *The Second Sex* was that it needed to be based more on a political economy of gender and less on a philosophical discussion of the nature of consciousness. She would then have based 'the notion of the Other, together with the Manicheism it entails, not on an idealistic *a priori* struggle pitting each consciousness against every other consciousness, but on the economic reality of supply and demand' (Cottrell, 1976: 105–6). Her rethinking was made in the light of a similar argument in Sartre's *Critique of Dialectical Reason* (1982). It was from there that she took her cue in saying that construction of the Other is a power relationship based on scarcity (Simons and Benjamin, 1979: 345; see also de Beauvoir, 1968: 202). As a corrective, this may have leant too far in an opposing direction, but such a re-grounding for her analysis could also have led to greater clarity in de Beauvoir's use of the concept of the Other, and a sharper treatment of the question of women's complicity in being Other and being morally responsible for this. Her attribution of women's 'bad faith' is clear enough, but the alternative to this of a woman only 'assuming' her situation remains vague. It is not clear what it would involve.

De Beauvoir seems at various points to map the classic Hegelian master–slave relationship directly onto that of men and women. For Hegel, this relationship is a product of an uncompleted struggle for recognition, which can result finally in a switching of roles (Hegel, 1967: Chapter 4). The master defines himself as sovereign and essential, but the slave, initially placed as powerless and inessential, in time comes to realise through fear of death and experience of the work given in service to the master that he is, in fact, *not* inessential and that the master is dependent on him for who he is, rather than the other way round. Only by entering into this conflict is there any possibility of a counterclaim, and a shift in the politics of recognition. De Beauvoir also shows women as historically not within the process of struggle for recognition, which is why they have been uniquely cast as Other in the first place. 'Woman thus seems to be the inessential who never goes back to being the essential, to be the absolute Other, without reciprocity' (1984: 160). This makes the Hegelian master–slave relationship male-centred. Women were not participants in it for Hegel because their self-consciousness was of no interest to him. They did not belong to the public sphere.

Running alongside her emphasis on women's social exclusion, rationalised by the construction of woman as the absolute Other without reciprocity, de Beauvoir suggests an alternative form of relationship between men and women. She refuses any final resignation to the idea of a fateful war of each consciousness against another. This conflict can, in her view, be overcome 'if each individual freely recognises the other, each regarding himself and the other as object and as subject in a reciprocal manner' (ibid). For de Beauvoir, participation in the struggle between consciousnesses raises rather than excludes the possibility that social relations are not always already, forever and forever, conflict-laden. In this she was developing a contrary view to Sartre in *Being and Nothingness*, which by contrast was individualistic, ahistorical and fatalistic. This alternative view could be criticised as either idealistic or as denying the partial, non-essential differences between men and women, but both these objections need to be set against the context of de Beauvoir's broader commitment to a politics of equality. Her socialist belief in the goal of equality fuelled her opposition to the process of symbolic othering, rather than an interest in identity politics or the politics of difference. There is no equivalent *féminitude* as a stage on the way to liberation to Fanon's *négritude* as a radical making over of blacks' own blackness for themselves.

Born into a middle-class family in Martinique, Frantz Fanon (1925–61) fought during the Second World War in Europe and North Africa before training as a psychiatrist and taking up a hospital post in Algeria. There he became actively involved in the struggle for Algerian independence. In his political writings, Fanon developed a penetrating critique of European colonialism. In the process, he first gave Sartre's extensions of the Hegelian dialectic their historical and political appli-cation, rectifying Sartre's abstract conception of alterity by showing that in the colonial context the black is Other to the white, but not the reverse. White is white; white is not 'not-black'. It is a category that is not symbolically constructed by a dependent reverse negativity, as 'black' is for 'white'. Fanon's revision of the Hegelian dialectic hinges on this racist inequality of the black whose struggle for recognition through labour is obstructed, 'walled in', by the colour of his skin. It is the Manichean division between black and white which cut the colonial world in two.

Fanon's perception of the incongruity of racialised forms of recog-nition is acute. Although his analysis of colonial mimicry, of blacks trying to pass for white, does not resolve the dynamics of gender incon-gruity which he registered in the colonial context, his disentanglement of colonial relations is undertaken, as with de Beauvoir's analysis of gender identities and relations, in the interests of 'an ethics of mutual identification', 'a world of reciprocal recognitions' (Fuss, 1994: 22, 29; Fanon, 1972: 155). 'Rather than equate reciprocity with identity, Fanon grounds mutual recognition in the moment of alterity, and calls for recognition from the other, while demanding that it not be a recog-nition that reduces it to identity' (Gibson, 1999: 106). Such a reduc-tive recognition is that of the 'master' imprisoned in his egotism which violently appropriates and deposes the Other. It is in this light that we should understand Fanon's troubled relationship with the *négritude* movement, particularly in the form advocated by his compatriot Aimé Césaire, which sought a regeneration of black cultural values. He regarded it as a provisional but not final step forward, for what he opposed in the end was 'not only "the great white error" of racist stereotyping and reification, but also the "great black mirage" composed of ideas of an essential "African" identity for all black people' (Childs and Williams, 1997: 51). Fanon was clearly aware of the danger of an identity politics where assertive differentiation reproduces through inversion the hierarchical structures of Self/Other relations it seeks to transgress. This is where Fanon and de Beauvoir happily coincide, for both held (contra Sartre) that true reciprocity presupposes difference rather than a narcissistic mirroring of the other: 'Ethical equality implies the mutual recognition of the other as a free, acting subject' (Moi, 1998: 79, 85).

For this reason, the colonialist construction of the inferior Other contradicts the civilising mission of colonialism, which was predicated on making the colonised like the coloniser. The imperial subject's sense of self was a denial of this sense for the colonial Other, who only existed in an incorporated, exterior, racialised form, which he or she was then required to enact. The othering of cultural difference in this way threw into doubt any attempt to prescribe or encourage identification with the coloniser whose identity depended upon this projected Otherness of difference in every confirmation of itself. The colonised subject was thus placed in a chronic situation of double jeopardy. In view of this and the whole history of slavery and imperialism, it may seem somewhat presumptuous of de Beauvoir to have compared women's oppression with black colonial oppression or the black American experience. Maybe, but what is more interesting than the comparison is her stress on the difference. Both forms of oppression depended upon a self-affirming metaphorics of contrast and both were reduced to objects of white male representation. De Beauvoir nevertheless insisted on the specificity of women's oppression. Unlike the essentialised assertive differentiation of blackness in the *négritude* movement, she emphasised the social dispersion of femaleness, cutting across different social categories, classes and communities. For this reason, the 'bond that unites' women to their oppressors 'is not comparable to any other' because they are 'scattered across all social groups', with 'men who are their sons, brothers and fathers when they are not their husbands or lovers' (1984: 19; see also Moi, 1998: 83). The ensuing ambivalence meant that women's lack of freedom could not be squeezed into the Hegelian dialectic, any more than could the black's, and in Sartre's use of this dialectic he imprisons *négritude* in negativity (Moi, 1998: 86). For Fanon, being not 'yet white' and 'no longer wholly black, I was damned' (1972: 138).

The Second Sex was the most important contribution to feminist theory of the twentieth century, prefiguring many similar works of analysis in second-wave feminism. In Dale Spender's estimation, de Beauvoir has been a major source of influence among women, 'with almost every feminist writer since 1949 acknowledging a debt to her' (1982: 512). In preference to other writers, I have concentrated on her analytical treatment of the construct of the female Other as 'not-male', and thus less than human, not only because of its tremendous influence within feminism, but also because I find its more concrete and particular approach in thinking theoretically about the Other more productive than that of both Sartre and Lacan in their existentialist and psychoanalytical treatments of the concept, which are by contrast ahistorical and asocial. It has seemed to me more fruitful to draw on de Beauvoir's more focused work because it helps to counter ahistorical and asocial tendencies in approaches to stereotyping and the concept of the Other, which are very much to their detriment.

We need now to ask how the concept of the Other contributes to thinking about the stereotype. Does the concept of the Other add anything new or extra? In certain ways it does offer more, but as I suggested at the start of this chapter, the two concepts can be taken as complementary. I now want to conclude this chapter by bringing them more closely into alliance with each other.

Stereotypes and the Other

The concept of the Other takes us some way beyond the limitations of the stereotype by bringing more clearly into the frame both those involved in the process of othering as well as the object of this process, and by grounding stereotypical misrepresentations more firmly in the structures and relations of power which give them their binding force. It does not displace or supersede the concept of the stereotype but renders it rather more complex, opening up for interrogation its ambiguities and contradictions of meaning and effect. Analysing stereotypicality through the conceptual lens of the Other allows us to understand more fully how it is implicated in identification as a field of cultural encounter and interaction, how it operates strategically in that field as an 'arrested and fetishistic mode of representation' and provides both a desire for and a disavowal of what it commands (Bhabha, 1997: 75). Compared with the concept of the stereotype, this more complex understanding is a fruit of the fuller theorising of Otherness. While it does not provide a magic wand for solving in their entirety the critical problems of the politics of representation, one of the values of engaging theoretically with questions of stereotypical Otherness is that of deflecting the tendency to be normatively judgemental.

We have seen this as a tendency in the critique of stereotyping when it is considered as something *other* people do, those who are supposedly less intelligent, or who have 'pathological' dispositions. This is an evasion of the dilemma posed by stereotyping of how to negotiate the relation between any tendency towards the fixity of representation and the need to encourage flexibility of thought. It 'others' stereotyping in the interests of professional integrity or a positive self-image. Condemning stereotypes can then be simply a moralistic exercise, based on divisive schemas of 'good' and 'bad' actions and characters which treat 'complex political issues as if they were matters of individual ethics' (Shohat and Stam, 1994: 201). Little else is achieved by this beyond making us feel sanctimoniously indignant and giving ourselves a self-righteous pat on the back of our political correctness. Homi Bhabha makes a pertinent comment on this in saying that: 'To judge the stereo-typed image on the basis of a prior political normativity is to dismiss it, not to displace it, which is only possible by engaging with its *effectivity*' (Bhabha, 1997: 67). At the same time, this effectivity is always lodged within a particular political normativity. We shall see this in Chapter 7 when we examine the ideological construct of the 'normal'. Whatever is taken as normal is usually taken for granted and left unquestioned. The arbitrary nature of its conventions remains unrecognised. This is central to the political effectivity of the stereotyped image.

The particular symbolic work which the stereotypical Other performs in its construction of difference depends upon the illusion it creates of not performing such work. So, for instance, the process which made woman as Other effective was its naturalisation of the difference simul-taneously constructed by this process. Simone de Beauvoir was equally opposed to essentialist conceptions of female difference, as if this is simply a matter of women's anatomical possession of a womb, and the rationalist denial of such difference, as if it is simply a matter of going for a walk with your eyes open. Her rejection of both was central to the political argument that 'woman is *not* the Other, although woman has become the Other' (Pilardi, 1999: 26–7). In becoming Other, the Hegelian subject–object dialectic is frozen; woman is only Other, only object – incidental, inessential, immobile, and never 'for-itself'. To the extent that such difference is established as natural, and thus given and unalterable, so the stereotyping which accomplishes this process is masked, made invisible, and not seen for what it is. Stereotypicality is authorised, and gains in authority, through this repression of the production of difference. The recognition of difference is thereby made innocent, made to appear natural. It is as though this difference is perceived and understood in a purely cognitive way, as if what we see and know in the stereotypical representation is what is simply visible and palpable. What this involves is a spurious equivalence of seeing and believing, so that what is seen is taken to be what the difference is, as we know it in its 'natural' beingness of being different. Through this contrivance recognition achieves its convenient innocence by wearing the mask of primary cognition.

For stereotyping to be effective, it needs not to be seen and acknowledged for what it does. To see a stereotype in this way is to start stepping back from it, to begin unravelling its appearance of being natural, absolute, given, the truth and nothing but the truth of what is represented. But the stereotypical object is always created as object regardless of whether it is given 'positive' or 'negative' value. That is why I have suggested that the concept of the Other is an advance on that of the stereotype. It heightens attention both to the subjugation of the stereotypical Other, and to those who produce the stereotypical object and thereby by implication define themselves as subjects. So, for instance, stereotypical images of black Otherness operate not only with their own externalised constructions of cultural difference, but also with a meta-discourse of 'whiteness' which is either confirmed in its cultural superiority or compensated for in its cultural deficiencies – as, for instance, in the case of the self-serving kind of white attraction to blacks castigated by Richard Wright because it affirmed racist stereotypical values and the American racial divide just as much as the 'Jim Crow' discrimination he had faced in his childhood and youth (de Beauvoir, 1999: 353; and see Wright, 1988). In either case, Otherness exists to subjugate its objects and assign them to their 'natural' place at the behest of those who thereby reconstitute themselves as subjects.

The concept of the stereotypical Other can be used to support a range of different attitudes, from mild condescension to out-and-out hostility. It can involve looking either up or down at an idealised or denigrated object. But the Other is always constructed as an object for the benefit of the subject who stands in need of an objectified Other in order to achieve a masterly self-definition. The relationship between the self and that which stereotypically is othered is a determinate form of relationship predicated on a perception, assumption or evaluative notion of difference existing in the interests of the self who others, downwards or upwards. The external Other in this sense can be quite specific, as in reference to a particular individual, or more generalised, as in identifying a mythic figure or describing a collective group, yet regardless of who is thus defined, a relation of 'me'/'us'/'them' always underpins the definition. At its simplest, 'me' and 'us' are defined in this relation in contradistinction to 'not-me' and 'not-us', the projection and definition of which becomes 'them'. The definition invariably signals some form of trouble at the heart of 'me'/'us'/'them' relations, although of course the trouble may not begin with a particular form of those relations but emanate from the broader social order in which they are constituted.

Appearances notwithstanding, the 'us'/'them' relation which is implicated in the Other is inherently unstable. The ideological function of othering is to attempt to make the relation stable, to give it a static and durable shape and temporally to fast-freeze the configurations of difference and similarity it constructs. This attempt cannot be made once and then forgotten, as if its mapping of the distribution of symbolic configurations is accomplished for all time. It tries to create the illusion that what has been laid down – this is 'us' here, this is 'them' there – is indeed true for all time, but it will only be effective if it is reiterated and worked on, over and over, if not all of the time then definitely at those times when its distancing through selective differentiation is strategically most required. This raises a further paradoxical feature of stereotyping, for what distinguishes the attempt to give a fixed form and durable knowability to its object is its compulsive repetition. As Homi Bhabha has put it, it is 'as if the essential duplicity of the Asiatic or the bestial sexual licence of the African that needs no proof, can never really, in discourse, be proved' (1997: 66). In the encounters and occasions of everyday life, the force of this is felt as ambivalence. This can be manifest in coexisting meanings and values about, or emotions and attitudes towards, stereotyped figures which are contradictory, but it goes beyond this as a general feature, as something inherent in the stereotyping process itself. It is another aspect of the condition of tension in the stereotyping process. Stereotyping is in this way subject to contrary pulls between what is felt to be indubitable and what is felt to be in constant need of reassertion. It is this which leads Bhabha to describe the stereotype as a mode of representation which is 'as anxious as it is assertive' (ibid: 70).

Conceptions of the Other and the structures of difference and similarity which they mobilise do not exist in any natural form at all. There is no pristine, real Other out there, somewhere, yet still to be located. The location of the Other is primarily in language. It is through language that selves and others are mediated and represented. The symbolically constructed Other and the patterns of social exclusion and incorporation entailed by it are distributed in sign and language, discourse and representation. They do not exist primordially or as pre-given states, and in various unrecognised or partially recognised respects they are illusory. The qualification is necessary here because if they were completely founded on illusion and this was clearly recognised, then they would gain very little purchase in people's minds. This should not be taken as a way of resuscitating the 'kernel of truth' notion of the stereotype, for stereotyping involves the stripping down of the manifold characteristics of other people or cultures to such a limited range that any possibility of truth is negated in the exaggeration of this set to cover all of what is represented of other people or cultures in the first place. The name, type-description and perception of the Other is the Other, and that is all there is. You cannot go beyond or inside it to find something prior to its construction. The stereotyped Other does not consist of the misrepresentation of some real or hidden essence – the 'real woman' behind the stereotypical attributes, for instance – and is not a simplification because it falsely represents an already existing reality. 'It is a simplification because it is an arrested, fixated form of representation' (Bhabha, 1997: 75).

In considering the concept of the Other, it is important to remember that those who are 'othered' are unequally positioned in relation to those who do the 'othering'. The latter occupy a privileged space in which they can define themselves in contrast to the Others who are so designated as different, with this designation reinforcing and prolonging the inequalities involved by seeming to confirm and prove them. Defining 'self' in this way confines the Other to the inequalities which allow it. Unequal and asymmetrical relations and divisions, such as those inscribed in discourses of 'race' and ethnicity, gender and sexuality, are thereby legitimated by the ideological constructions of difference that are laid on their back. Naming and defining the characteristics of Others as Others also has as its effect a denial of their right to name and define themselves (although this may be resisted, a point we shall return to later). The process begins with the derogatory terms used to refer to those groups and collectivities perceived as different, as Other – 'pakis', 'coons', 'bimbos', 'poofs' and all the rest – and then goes on to elaborate and justify the prejudicially evaluated difference and symbolic distance thus established. This is a denial of the humanity of those treated in this way because it divests them of their social and cultural identities by diminishing them to their stereotyped characteristics.

In another sense it diminishes those who use and accept the stereotypes. This can be looked at in two ways. On the one hand, once the stereotypical is in the play of discourse, any behaviour which relates to it is seen as a manifestation of a more generalised essence. In this, the stereotypical and the typical are elided. The Other is synecdochically homogenised by this or that stereotypical attribute or trait, while those who traffic in Otherness are themselves richly and diversely individual. On the other hand, those who use and accept the stereotypes narrow their access to forms of difference negated in the narrowness of their own self-identities. Stereotyping not only provides evidence of the poverty of their evaluation of others, but also impoverishes the cultural resources through which their own identities are sustained. This again is why it is important to remember the relations implicated in the question of the Other. Either way, the Other says and reveals far more about the 'self' and its conditioned and self-directed possibilities than about the apparently all-determined Other.

Toni Morrison has spoken of the 'effort to avert the critical gaze from the racial object to the racial subject ... from the serving to the served'. To the analysis of racism, 'contesting the assumption that it is an inevitable, permanent, and eternal part of all social landscapes', needs to be joined another, equally important analysis of 'the impact of racism on those who perpetuate it'. Stereotyping in this way involves using the Other as a means to know yourself, or rather, to have a certain belief about yourself that attains legitimacy by its symbolic exclusion of the Other. In her meditation on the American literary imagination, Morrison argues that an American Africanism, 'a fabricated brew of darkness, otherness, alarm, and desire', 'deployed as rawness and savagery', provided 'the staging ground and arena for the elaboration of the quintessential American identity' (Morrison, 1993: 11, 38, 44, 90). The offsetting of Africanism and Africanist character against, outside, and finally through American national identity is a complex affair, but Morrison's summary of the way it has worked as surrogate and enabler is as good as any:

> Africanism is the vehicle by which the American self knows itself as not enslaved, but free; not repulsive, but desirable; not helpless, but licensed and powerful; not a blind accident of evolution, but a progressive fulfilment of destiny. (ibid: 52)

The European construction of Africanist alterity in many ways shared this self-validating function, but without the benefit of such comparatively close acquaintance with black people. This had various consequences, among which were a divergence between Orientalist and Africanist discourses, with the former alternately evoking 'a powerfully consuming unknown, a forbidden erotic figure, a grotesquely uncivilised world of violence, and a site of incomprehensible difference' (Lowe, 1991: 78), while the latter was burdened with the task of 'reaching out to the most unknown part of the world and bringing it back as language', a process that 'ultimately brings Europe face to face with nothing but itself' (Miller, 1985: 5). In the end, the Otherness of black Africa refused 'to be acquired and domesticated' in the same way as the Orient because it was too 'unknown', too 'different', too 'anterior' to linear European time and so finally resistant to rational explanation. There was always something about the symbolic object 'Africa' produced by the discourse that confounded it and called its terms and conditions of production into question. While writers like Baudelaire and Rimbaud registered this, its first profound expression was given in Conrad's *Heart of Darkness* (1976), 'a self-conscious meditation on misunderstanding … neither colonialistic enough to be damnable nor ironic enough to be completely untainted by colonialistic bias'. As we have already seen, Africa was a 'blank darkness' upon which 'Africa', written in order to fill this emptiness, told a tale of 'supposed incompatibility with time and progress' (Miller, 1985: 170–1; cf. Hawthorn, 1992: Chapter 6).

How this tale was told will be examined in further detail in Chapter 5. What needs to be emphasised here is that in discourses of the Other, their central co-ordinates of differentiation are always implicated in relations of power. The Other is constructed in and for its subordination, in and for its 'inferiority' to the self-in-dominance who has produced it. This is an aspect of power in that those who construct and discursively reproduce the Other are able to do so, are enabled by their power to command the autonomy and means for transforming others into heteronomous, subordinated types who cannot retaliate in kind. In travel writing as in much colonial discourse, such constructions have occurred within and symbolically created what Mary Louise Pratt calls the contact zone 'where disparate cultures meet, clash, and grapple with each other, often in highly asymmetrical relations of domination and subordination' (1992: 4). It is, then, with these kinds of elaboration upon cultural power, subjection and abjection, along with an emphasis on discursive variation, ambivalence and contradiction, and an insistence that analysis focus on both the stereotypical object and the stereotyping subject, that the concept of the Other is often deployed. It is in these ways that it encourages a more sophisticated understanding of what is involved in stereotypicality than is allowed in simplistic notions of stereotypes = 'distortion of the truth'. In theorisations of the Other, the subject of othering is conceived as having been constructed in order to be serviceable to those who are historically dominant (and who have usually been white and male). 'In order to provide this service, the Other cannot be permitted to have a voice, a position, a being of its own, but must remain mute or speak only in the ways permitted by the dominant discourse' (Sampson, 1993: 13). This is not quite so straightforward as it may seem, for although the relatively powerless Other is constructed with the purpose of subordination in mind, the question of whether he or she can speak in any other terms apart from the historically dominant discourse in which he or she is spoken for is a matter of some debate, as we shall see in Chapter 6. Nevertheless, the ideological service of being stereotypically constructed as diametrically *other* to leading conceptions of identity and selfhood should now be clear enough. Being relegated in this way to an essentialised definition seems to smother out any sense of an alternative to it, some distant 'real me' that escapes this servitude.

Susan Zickmund has suggested that prevailing constructions of the Other finally fall into two major categories – those of social contamination and social threat. With the first, the ideological service provided is that of seeming to be socially contained while being metaphorically posed as a cultural disease, 'one whose very presence within the nation is sufficient to destroy the social stability and the special values which made the nation strong at its founding' (1997: 192). Blacks and homosexuals have both been positioned in this way as a fundamental danger to white, heterosexual society. In Britain during the 1980s, for example, immigrant communities were labelled in Thatcherist discourse as an 'alien wedge' driving deep into the national culture. This profoundly *alienating* image left those so labelled with little public sense of themselves outside this representation as a forceful intrusion into a place that denied them any legitimate belonging, regardless of the length of their actual presence in the country. The politics of this kind of exclusionary and allocative strategy will be explored further in Chapter 5.

In the second construct, the Other becomes the source of a threatening power to groups with relatively low social status. The forces of international capitalism which inflict unemployment, job insecurity or high inflation on already impoverished communities are confronted by anthropomorphising particular ethnic groups, generating 'a mythical narrative that converts social problems into conflicts between distinct and identifiable entities' (ibid: 195). Both Jewish and various Asian people have been scapegoated and demonised in this way, and their reification into a 'malevolent Thing-like category' (ibid: 196) has then served as a focus of hatred in displacing feelings of dissociation and anger over social disadvantages, suffering and demoralisation.

This reification into a malevolent Thing is precisely what it means to be othered, generating an experience of yourself as an object, the object of the view that casts you as an Other. The African-American writer, W.E.B. Du Bois, described being marked in this way by a single glance, a glance thrown by a girl who was a newcomer to the schoolhouse he attended as a child. For him, that glance cast him out, 'othered' him because of the colour of his skin. The indelible effect of this recognition of yourself as Other creates a twoness of vision that allows you to see yourself only through the eyes of others, leaving your own, secret striving for a more independent sense of identity bereft in 'a world that looks on in amused contempt and pity'. Du Bois called this a double-consciousness in which there are 'two warring ideals in one dark body', and in which you see yourself 'darkly as through a veil' (1996: 4–5, 9). The veil is the dense shadow cast by 'that crushing objecthood', blocking 'the migration through the Other necessary for subjectivity to take place'. 'Forced to occupy, in a white racial phantasm, the static ontological space of the timeless "primitive", the black man is disenfranchised of his very subjectivity' (Fuss, 1994: 21). This is the violence to yourself of being 'othered' – as in the glance that fires its poisoned arrow of hate: 'Dirty nigger!'; or as in the child's cry: '"Look, a Negro!" … "Mama, see the Negro! I am frightened" … "Mama, the nigger's going to eat me up!"' – when 'I and I' is riven into neither an 'I' nor a 'not-I' (Fanon, 1972: 77–80).

In these dislocating experiences, *who* is this Other that is seen? It is not you, yet you as Other are forced to see yourself as Other because that is the way you have been positioned in the eyes of others, and that positioning seems to be utterly fixed, fastened solidly into its place in an irrevocable scheme. The representation seems to be one and the same as its referent, as if this objectification were *the* truth, the *only* truth, that there is to tell about you. Your heart tells you otherwise – 'my heart makes my head swim' cries Fanon (ibid: 99) – but you are torn in two by this dualistic vision, you as yourself in your strivings for positive self-identity and you as a constructed low-Other. You are torn between yourself in this sense and the racialised object that represents you, so that you hardly know yourself at all. To in any way retain or regain a more positive sense of identity is an intense struggle – not only against external images and representations of you objectified as Other, but also against all you have internalised from those images and representations, absorbed into your own twoness, your own torn self. In the face of this Other who is not-you, but taken-as-you by others, who can you become? This objectification of you is constructed as you as if you must continue to exist in its adamantine mould and shape your own self to it. It is to be imprisoned in an identity that harms you. You are both silenced and spoken for. You are seen but not recognised. You are identified but denied an identity you can call your own. Your identity is split, broken, dispersed into its abjected images, its alienated representations.

Chapter 4

The Politics of Belonging

*Every nation would be richer if
every nation abandoned nationalism.*

BERTRAND RUSSELL, 1939: 494

Symbolic Boundaries

If, to be Other is to be torn in two, to be constructed as an object that denies you as a subject, then where can you belong? Otherness is a denial of belonging; it is the unrelenting sign of not belonging. Before we explore certain historical forms of this in further detail, we need first to examine those positive modes of belonging to which they have existed in counterpoint, for Otherness exists beyond, and is confirmed by, the symbolic boundaries associated with these positive modes. The key focus of interest in this chapter is on the idea of the nation, and national belonging, as the dominant example of such positive modes of belonging. The sense of a national identity and belonging is advanced not only as positive. It is also held up as necessary and right. However, although national belonging tends to subsume other forms of belonging, other popular associations and affiliations, belonging itself is not, in all its various forms, coterminous with a sense of national membership. Belonging has a wider reference. Even in the age of nationalisms, it can be realised and felt in other ways, aside from the idea of the nation. Identifying with a nation is one among other forms of collective identification in the historical anthropology of belonging. I want to begin this chapter with a brief consideration of this broader pattern of belonging before going on to discuss how belonging has come to belong predominantly, across the diverse tapestry of the world's cultures, in association with the nation.

For Anthony Cohen, belonging 'is the almost inexpressibly complex experience of culture' (1982: 16). In this view, culture itself is something we belong to. We carry it with us, like our belongings, when we travel and encounter other cultures. Our culture influences how we interpret and understand what we encounter. We cannot simply discard our cultural being as, if we were disposed, we could our belongings, because while our culture is a property of us, we do not own it in the same way as we do the material effects we may carry with us on a journey. Our cultural properties are constitutive of who we are – they contribute to our growing identity and our sense of where we belong, however inexpressibly complex this may be. To say this does not of course mean that everyone is the same within any identifiably distinct culture, but rather that we inevitably draw on certain cultural resources and repertoires and not others because of where we are and who we are. These resources and repertoires and the ways in which we use them condition the meanings we make of the world. They 'provide the range within which individuality is possible' (Cohen, 1985: 21) – indeed, not only possible but identifiable as such. Our experience of culture is not that of an isolated, self-sufficient being; it is achieved vitally through our complex interactions with a range of other people, in various relationships, scenes and settings. Our experience of belonging is in these ways wrapped up in the culture of our experience, the ways in which our experience is culturally expressed in language and discourse. Cultural experience generates our identity to the extent that it creates an appearance of similarity among those who more or less share it, who seem to belong to it and feel at home within it. Culture is in this way the experience of belonging.

This is to talk of culture largely in the vernacular sense, referring to processes of symbolic exchange in the everyday local milieux that influence and help to shape us in our growing up, in our awkward assimilation into a community and our patchwork acquisition of individuality. While culture in this sense can have a specific reference and application, it can easily lead to various pitfalls. Vernacular as a category can be deployed in supporting a version of cultural essentialism, where each form of it is viewed as separate, creating a social enclave of lived experience which, as lived, generates the reproduction of its 'essence', its immutable difference. A historically informed view of such forms of culture sees the opposite: interpenetration, intermixture, hybridity, movement and transformation, with nothing fixed or pure. This trafficking between cultures is nothing new. It has been occurring for as long as there have been long-distance trade routes, migratory pathways, interaction between languages, cultural crossings and religious traditions linking local communities across broad geographical areas. In our own times cultural trafficking has both quickened and expanded. Along with problems of corporate domination and the threat to particular cultural resources and repertoires, what makes such trafficking characteristically modern is its greater speed, scope and reach, leading to an increased linking of localities across wide expanses of space, and an expanded influence of distant events on local cultural identities and relations.

The vernacular-local mode of sociality is today only one particular frame of reference in modern social life. We now move between many cultural frames of reference, and between many different social milieux. People do not belong to a culture in a single sense at all – they shift between various social worlds and modes of cultural understanding. Various forms of quasi-social interaction are now interwoven within such movement, and become increasingly salient and significant in our late-modern lives, vying for place with our immediate, face-to-face relationships, as our media consumption increases or intensifies. The media play an ever-more important role in contributing to people's sense of themselves and where they belong. This continues to reinforce the ways in which the 'tension – or collusion – between lived and mediated reality is central to the social and psychological processes in which people become socially self-conscious' (Frith, 1999: 21). The third point to note follows directly from this. Modern societies are highly differentiated, large in scale and internally complex in their structures of interdependence. It is because of this that vernacular milieux have themselves become enormously intersected and transformed by a whole range of different cultural experiences, different cultural narratives, styles and repertoires, different sources of identification and allegiance. These have radically changed the relations of belonging.

Cohen cites an anthropological portrait of a Japanese village studied in the mid-twentieth century: 'If you live in Shinohata, the "outside world" begins three hundred yards down the road' (Dore, 1978: 60). The people of Shinohata knew about this 'outside world', but the significant social world for them was defined by the environs of their particular village in the Isokawa valley. This sense of the 'outside world' beginning just outside one's own immediate locality has become, more and more, a minority experience. One of the characteristic experiences of modernity is almost the reversal of this, of our sense of the 'outside world' not only extending, further and further, but also of entering in, more and more, to our 'inside world', the place that we still use, somehow or other, to locate where we belong. This has transformed what it means to belong, or not to belong. Despite wavering between often antithetical ideas in the development of his social and political philosophy, Walter Lippmann saw this early on: 'We are all of us immigrants in the industrial world', he wrote, 'and we have no authority to lean upon' (Lippmann, 1961: 118). In Lippmann's case this bred an anxious fear of extremism and distrust of the 'tyranny of the masses' in modern society. For others it has provided an encouragement to think back nostalgically to times when there were many more 'Shinohatas' still in existence, when everyday social milieux were apparently far more self-contained, and when traditional forms of authority appeared incontestable. Yet no matter how fondly they may imagine the past to have been, having experienced the opening-up of the 'outside world' to them, few people would want to revert to a sense of it beginning just within the range of vision, three hundred yards down the road.

Except for those in command of grand theories, we are still uncertain where this massively sweeping pattern of change has taken us. There is no single, universally accurate balance sheet of what it appears to have brought us. Nor should there be, for we are still in the process of assimilating it all to our cultural experience and relations, of assessing its many consequences for our experience of the world and where we belong. Among these are the altered meanings of our vocabulary for describing it. In English, for example, the word 'parochial' has changed, in its predominant sense, from a descriptive term for belonging to a specific parish to one of negative evaluation where it now denotes a narrowness of view, of belonging to a closely delimited world and of not being able to move with ease to what lies beyond it, somewhere down the road. This new evaluative weight has been externally given to the word; it is not a term of self-description used by the Shinohata villagers of this world. To feel that you belong only to a village, tribe or clan may seem unbelievably constricting to anyone in the West who thinks of themselves as worldly in outlook and disposition, but what is interesting about this sense of belonging is not that it contrasts so much with, say, a culturally footloose style of living that passes for cosmopolitanism, but rather that it gives us a sense of a kind of identity that has now become almost lost to the rest of the world. This is a kind of identity that is not defined in terms of nationhood.

Ronald Dore first visited Shinohata in 1955, and he reported that only fifty years before this, the villagers there 'had never been much aware of being Japanese because no other kind of people had much impinged on their consciousness' (Dore, 1978: 41). It may be that this observation was to some extent a product of Dore's position as outsider in the village, a mid-twentieth-century Westerner awed by the comparative isolation of these 'other kind of people', but the anthropological evidence for such localised forms of belonging, and their gradual disintegration during the twentieth century, is abundant enough. In his study of nationalism, for example, Michael Billig cites various cases of a non-nation sense of identity, including that of rural Slovaks emigrating to the United States around the turn of the twentieth century. These uprooted people possessed no sense of national identity, having previously identified only with their own home village (Billig, 1995b: 62). This other form of identity, of conceiving and talking about relations of self and community, has become more and more attenuated as nationalism has spread out across the world. Its influence over how we think is such that highly localised forms of identity, such as that of turn-of-the-century rural Slovaks, now seem to us archetypally parochial. Our horizons are much broader, and we judge an apparent narrowness of world-view, based on a localised way of life, as inferior by contrast. This is not only to stereotype this alternative, non-national sense of identity. It is also to misrecognise the narrowness of the modern world-view with which it is contrasted.

This world-view sees the world very much through the lenses of nationalism. Nationalism has profoundly shaped our sense of belonging and the symbolic boundaries constructed around it. Nations of course have literal boundaries, where we have to show our passports and maybe a visa if we want to cross over them. The duration of our legitimate stay within these boundaries may be limited, or we may be denied passage over them right from the start. But these literal boundaries do not in themselves define our different identities for us; they only inform our different identities once they have become symbolically defined. Symbolic boundaries are ways of demarcating what is perceived as different from 'us', in our relative sameness, and so of heightening 'our' sense of this sameness by appearing to provide a place for 'our' identity. They are constructs which serve to ensure the identity of 'us' as the 'same together' by symbolically condensing 'their bearers' social theories of similarity and difference' (Cohen, 1986: 17).

Symbolic boundaries may operate at local or regional level – and this is how Cohen and others have applied the concept – but they are manifest as well in how nations communicate to themselves and to other nations, across a world divided and unified by geographical boundaries between nations and symbolically thought into difference as distinct national identities. Craig Calhoun cites the case of the Saami, or Lapps, who do not seem 'naturally' to belong to the constituent Nordic cultures precisely because they have not played much part 'in the history of contentions over the proper constitution of nation-states in the region'.

In this way they confound the sense of a national culture as singular, unified and integrated. He suggests that this sense implies that national cultures are discrete entities and equivalent units. This way of conceiving them obscures interconnections and a sense of the broader world system of which they are a part, and directs attention away from their internal complexity of tensions and antagonisms (1995: 53–5). Directing and organising our empirical observations of the world in this way has meant exchanging a sense of the 'outside world' beginning somewhere just down the road, for a sense of it beginning at our national boundaries. We have moved into another kind of parochialism, the parochialism of national belonging.

In this chapter I want to look at some of the salient features of this transformation of symbolic belonging and boundary maintenance, this heightening of the sense of a national 'we' as the 'same together'. During the nineteenth century, changes in transport and public communications, in taxation structures and patterns of trade and production were among various factors facilitating greater national integration. The growth of newspapers, magazines, journals and novels, for example, helped to foster an understanding of broader links across space than those of neighbourhood or locality. This chapter focuses on the assimilation of this wider understanding within the formation of national identity and belonging, on the ways in which individuals are assumed to be an immediate unit of the larger whole of the nation, with differentiation beyond this identity and belonging being relegated in significance because of the unity of the whole. This is important for the project of making stereotypes part of a bigger story. National stereotypes are often discussed in the cultural analysis of stereotyping, and stereotyping is often mentioned in the political analysis of nationalism, but in the former, the broader question of nationalism is usually left unexplored, while in the latter, the stereotype is rarely addressed in conceptual terms. Both take a crucial element for granted. The task of overcoming these shortcomings is compatible with attempting to place the stereotype within a broader canvas because nationalism has been a key factor in what stereotyping has come to involve within modernity. By developing into such a dominant sense of collective association and belonging, nationalism has deeply affected how we regard and understand other people in the world, in cultures different to our own. All too often this has produced and perpetuated stereotypical forms of characterising 'us and 'them', the multiple Others who do not belong within the exclusive domain of 'our' own nation.

National Belonging

In examining the consequences of this, we need to begin by distinguishing nationalism and the modern nation-state. They are not one and the same. In its recognisably modern form, the nation-state first emerged in Britain (Corrigan and Sayer, 1985; Colley, 1994). Over the nineteenth and twentieth centuries, it developed certain general features, such as a common legal code, a monopoly of legitimate violence by the police and military, a territory-wide administrative machinery over precisely demarcated boundaries, a civic ideology and a set of social and political institutions aiming to bind people together and direct them to a common order and purpose. In all these ways, nation-states have become distinguished from and alongside each other, across the modern world. Nationalism can exist without a nation-state, as the history of the Basques, Kurds and Jews clearly illustrates, although not without some claim to territoriality. The sense of nation as territory, as place, is a very strong nationalist value, which is why people are willing to die for it.

Indeed, in the West at least, national identity has usually been associated with the occupation of a definite territory that has become collectively revered, exalted, even sacralised as a historic homeland, with particular landmarks or memorialised associations of event and place imparting a sense of unity, uniqueness and exclusivity to the people belonging to a nation. These are ways of imagining the nation. Members of a nation do not (and cannot) know each other personally, and so can only be conceived as the 'same together' through a shared cultural history and a shared national territory. Such 'sharing' of territory is only imagined, and can only be imagined, because of the unequal distribution of land and property rights. The imagined sharing of a homeland requires continual ideological work if it is to be sustained. All sorts of stereotypical representations are drawn into this, across all communications media. In British television, for example, they range from the figure of a political correspondent in a parliamentary news item standing against a backdrop of Big Ben and the Thames, to images in the latest historical melodrama of the quilted landscape of rural England spread out behind a lone, love-crossed woman, striding the hills in her windblown shawl. These are symbolic settings, imaginary landscapes. They act beyond immediate situations as a metaphor for the nation itself, giving visible shape and distinction to the way we conceive it. Through a continuous stream of images and visual associations, they provide a daily impulse for feeling that we belong to a nation, adding a powerful emotional charge to the incentive of national belonging, of identifying with the nation.

Narration and nation come together through the visual stereotypes of land and landmark, in an imagined sharing of the national territory.

The need to feel relatively settled, with a sense of cultural location and of social fraternity and solidarity, is a very general one, manifest in all sorts of different societies and cultures. It can, accordingly, take many forms. In nationalism, however, it is deflected away from local communities and networks, and particular sources of affiliation and association. These may be drawn on, but in their deflection they are absorbed into a grander, mythical schema of belonging. This is where the imagining comes into nations as 'imagined communities'. The success of the imagining in the construction of nations is then proportionate to the satisfaction derived from this new ascription of belonging. This new ascription gains its cultural legitimacy, at least partly, from the relative loss and fragmentation of the local, and from the painful experience of new social, economic and political divisions and inequalities as people are swept up into modernity's incessant turbulence of change. In describing the nation as the form of 'modern integration par excellence', Patrick Wright appropriately qualifies this by adding that there is 'no simple replacement of community by nation, but rather a constant – if also always momentary, fragile and partial – redemption of its unhappy remains' (1985: 24). It is not as if nationalism achieves a final, once-and-for-all victory amidst the abandoned ruins of community, but rather that it partially, and yet powerfully, redeems the imagining of communality, or peoplehood, amidst the unhappiness of its debilitation in other forms.

National belonging is a way of imagining a relative sense of 'us' as the 'same together' in the face of this debilitation, wherever it is strongly felt. This does not mean that other forms of belonging and association need to disappear for it to be effective, but rather that its claims upon the sense of collective belonging cannot take hold until local and regional attachments suffer some sort of decline. Sociologically, the classic case of this occurred in the shift from agrarian to industrial society. It has often been noted that nationalist sentiment provided a way of helping people to reconcile themselves to the deeply unsettling experience of migration and settlement in the new, rapidly expanding towns and cities, where industrial waged labour and a regimented work-discipline replaced earlier patterns of work based on sun and seasons. Durkheim's account of the transition from mechanical to organic solidarity, and Tönnies's distinction between *Gemeinschaft* (community) and *Gesellschaft* (society) are typical of how the disruption of face-to-face communities were conceived in early sociology (Durkheim, 1984;

Tönnies, 1963). Ernst Haas's functionalist interpretation of the rise of nationalism continued to operate within the analytical framework developed by Durkheim and Tönnies:

> The nation is a synthetic *Gemeinschaft*. In the mass setting of modern times, it furnishes the vicarious satisfaction of needs that have previously been met by the warmth of small, traditional, face-to-face social relations. As social life has been transformed by industrialisation and social mobilisation into something resembling a *Gesellschaft* based on interest calculations, the nation and nationalism continue to provide the integrative cement that gives the appearance of community. (Haas, 1964: 465)

In some ways it would indeed seem that it was under conditions of internal migration and displacement, following the development of capitalist wage-labour and the centralisation of industrial production through the factory system, that the appeal of a national 'being' first proved compelling. National identity and belonging thus became a source of compensation for the loss of a local, lived community. As Richard Sennett has described it:

> Urban migration and its attendant economics was one of the forces which created nationalism, an image of somewhere fixed, necessary for those who were experiencing displacement. 'A world dissolving into chaos': against it the land stands as a measure of the enduring; its being is set against the trials of one's own becoming. (1996: 195)

This interpretation also suggests something of a general consequence of the development of nationalism. This is that belief in the autonomy of national identity compensates for the lack of autonomy in people's lives, and the more powerful the nation becomes as a source of identity, the weaker will other sources of social identity become. Yet there is nothing inevitable about this, and in some cases the reverse may be true. Structural forces from outside may lead to a greater emphasis on the symbolic affirmation of communities of place or interest, on the symbolic markers of dispersed ethnic groupings or subcultures. Anthony Cohen has argued in exactly this way by saying that the more communities in these senses face the pressures to conform to the broader social structure, the more they reassert their symbolic boundaries of identity and belonging (1985: 44). This is a salutary counter to the polarised dichotomies of classical sociology, such as Durkheim's mechanical versus organic solidarity. To account for the rise of nationalism in these terms, as Haas did, tends to produce one-sided forms of explanation – ignoring, for instance, the liberating experience of city-living for many modern people in contrast to the constrained, insular life of rural or provincial communities – and to reduce the rise and spread of nationalism as a source of identity to a single, overriding cause, such as industrial capitalism, or the advent of 'mass' society.

Nationalism is certainly historically specific in its development, but it is over-schematic to conceive of this in terms of a complete demarcation between 'traditional' and 'modern' social formations, as in the theoretical binaries of classical sociology and anthropology. National identity is not the only result of the development of modern social life. Other forms of cultural identity have arisen or become reinforced in response to the incessant disruption and change of modernity, and not necessarily as a blind reaction or through the creation of a fortress mentality. Particularistic identities such as those of gender, class, religion and locality operate differently to nationalism, and remain part of the same historical process. Nationalism draws parasitically on other forms of identity and belonging, but even in particular cases, it does not have any single psychological mainspring or sociological genesis. And if, in Hobsbawm's words, 'the basic characteristic of the modern nation and everything associated with it is its modernity' (1997: 14), this must not be understood only with reference to Western modernity. Other parts of the world – India, Africa, Latin America – have experienced different modernities, the characteristics of which are defined in distinction from Western modernity. Nationalism, like modernity, has neither one overriding characteristic nor one underlying cause. Other monocausal explanations of nationalism have stressed state formation, political manipulation by social élites, the decline of religious cosmologies and priestcraft, ethnicity, language and the concept of sovereignty. If you range widely enough you will find evidence for all of these, but what this would also show is that nationalism is a diverse, multifaceted phenomenon, and cannot be reduced to a sole dominant factor.

National Identity

National identity does not preclude other forms of identity, rather it is an overarching sense of identity that subsumes, where it can, other, more particularistic, identities. National identity is different to being Muslim, middle class or Mancunian because nationalism, which informs and supports it, has certain constitutive features associated both with its historical development, and with the ways in which these features have been symbolically realised. Overall, they have been realised in terms of the discourse of nationalism, but this does not mean that all forms of nationhood are the same. If a nation is 'an imagined political community' then what distinguishes particular nations, in Benedict Anderson's widely quoted phrase, is 'the style in which they are imagined' (1986: 15). Each nation is assumed to have a specific identity, and to identify with this means assimilating the style in which it is imagined as a nation. It also means distinguishing this identity from others, against which it is divided by the very fact of being construed as intrinsically different. Here we have one of the conceptual paradoxes of the nation highlighted by Anderson: nations are universal because everyone should 'have' a nationality, but 'having' a nationality means identifying with a particular concrete manifestation of it which appears, by definition, to be *sui generis* (ibid: 14). The category of the nation, in other words, is a universal category, but the category of any one nation is particular and unique unto itself and so universally divided off from other people, in other nations, with whom there is otherwise much in common beyond the fact of their 'having' a nationality. The uniqueness and universality of nations reinforce each other.

National belonging and identity mean that whatever divides a people is held to be less significant than what unites them, their common history and destiny, their common land and language. At the same time, what unites a people is held to be more significant than whatever divides them from others in other nations. National identity is both unifying and divisive. Its power to unify depends reciprocally on its power to divide. This is a terrific facility. The ability of national identity to work in these two opposing directions at once – differentiating a nationally defined 'us' from contrasting forms of national identity while simultaneously providing a compulsive substitute for the cultural need to belong – is what makes it both politically dangerous and politically comforting. It creates the illusion that essentially it counts above all else.

What distinguishes national identity from other forms of collectivity is its power of appeal over them. The sense of who 'we' are may, in all sorts of ways, be given shape by a range of other categories of collective identity, but when identity is invoked in the name of the nation its rhetoric politically overrides these other categories. The ideology of nationalism presumes a direct 'I'/'we' reciprocity of identity despite internal differentiation within the nation. In discussing this belonging to a nation as 'an attribute of the individual', and not of intermediate associations, Craig Calhoun has felicitously described its operation in saying that it acts as 'a sort of trump card in the game of identity' (1997: 46). In this game, we may play the cards of other affiliations and other senses of belonging, but when the last deal goes down, nationality throws in its hand and, politically, we are trumped.

An example of nationalism operating as the card of highest value in the ideological pack is shown by the way in which the powerful metaphor of the nation as a family holds sway over the individual family units to which people belong. This is especially the case at a time of inter-state conflict. So, for instance, the British Prime Minister, Margaret Thatcher, claimed that there is no such thing as 'society', the only valid collective unit for her being the family, which she described as 'the very nursery of civic virtue'. She also appeared to contradict herself by saying that family ties 'are at the heart of our society' (*Observer*, 22 May 1988), but as her use of the possessive adjective 'our' suggests, the category of 'society' for her only attains real credibility when conceived in terms of an ideologically shared belonging. Through its very conception, it is easier to imagine a shared belonging to a (unified) nation than to a (divided) society. In other words, society does not exist, but it is useful to think that it does in times of conflict, when the call to unity becomes paramount. It was then against virtually no opposition within Britain that Thatcher rhetorically played the trump card of nationality and national sovereignty at the time of the Falklands/Malvinas War. This was sparked in 1982 when an Argentinian military force contested British ownership of the South Atlantic islands called the Falkland Islands by the British and the Malvinas by Argentina. The Tory government under Thatcher sent a 'task force' to reclaim the islands amid a veritable hullabaloo of righteous indignation, patriotic fervour and stereotypical 'Argie'-bashing in the tabloid press. In the highly charged atmosphere which resulted, Thatcher was able to play the nationality card with relative ease, as for instance in her reference to the Falkland Islanders being 'British in stock and tradition' and wishing 'to remain British in allegiance' (Barnett, 1982: 32).

At such times, we are exhorted to defend the sovereignty of the nation (or nationally annexed territories) as the chief unit of belonging. National identity is then the sovereign identity, and as such it is given further credence by the stereotypical constructions of difference that mark 'us' off against 'them'. These are drawn on as a further way of burnishing the claims of unity, uniqueness and exclusivity that have been made in the name of 'our' nationality. Negative stereotypes of foreigners or outgroups help to shape and endorse such claims, and in this way they are constructed on 'our' behalf.

The trump card of nationality is of course not only played at times of war. The politics of nationalism in New Zealand offers another illustration of Calhoun's point. The indigenous Maori, who refer to their country as Aotearoa, the Land of the Long White Cloud, generally occupy a lower socio-economic status to the white Pakeha population, but unlike the socially dominant Pakeha, they have their own distinctive cultural identity. In the difference game, Maoritanga is a legitimate card to play, but it is relegated in its playing-power to a 'heritage' rating. It cannot beat the ace of national belonging because all peoples inhabiting the two islands, Polynesian, Maori and Pakeha alike, are held to belong to the 'one nation'. The Maori are thus trumped by the nationalist card. The only possible match for it would be the card of decolonised Maori sovereignty, but this card is of course not officially regarded as legitimate, unlike Maori cultural identity (Jesson, 1983; Awatere, 1984). Bill Willmott's claim that national identity in New Zealand is 'only one of the many identities that any individual may choose from' (1989: 8) is therefore naively idealistic and subjectivist. It offers a consumerist conception of both identity and multiculturalism, as if acquiring a cultural identity is the same as choosing what to buy among the many goods on offer in a supermarket. While our identities are multiple and change over time in relation to a variety of forces, circumstances and opportunities, we cannot, as I suggested at the beginning of this chapter, simply discard our identities as a snake sheds its skin. That is the fallacy of individualism.

Anderson's definition of the nation as an *imagined* community does not mean that the nation is *imaginary*, but rather that it is imagined as real and in this way acts as a frame within which lives are lived, and often lost. At the same time, as we have already seen, people have increasingly come to live their lives within and across several different frames, to belong, within modernity, to several imagined communities rather than to one. The question of which will predominate and affect how the others are referred to is never fixed for all time. It depends very much on the situation and context of the time *in* question. What is special about the nation as an imagined political community is its claim as an all-encompassing frame, a frame of collectivity that exceeds all others. Willmott's comment can perhaps be accepted in a modified form, however, if we say that different people within a nation imagine 'the nation' differently, and thus have different conceptions of national identity and belonging. The politics of belonging manifests itself, in part, through the conflict between these different versions of nationhood. For example, whereas nationalism in Australia has been used to produce a white-defined consensus of common purpose, it has been used in an alternative sense by its Aboriginal peoples to challenge the consensus which marginalises them and denies them the specific rights which they wish to claim. This, in turn, may require a modification of Anderson's conception of national identity, for he overstates his case in saying that 'the nation is always conceived as a deep, horizontal comradeship' (1986: 16). If different national identities are stylistically imagined in different ways, then this is true also of difference within a nation and of identifications made with it. National identity is cut across by gender, class, political and regional affiliations, and as Joanna Bourke has argued for the British working class, these can lead to different, and sometimes contradictory, identifications with the 'nation' (1994: Chapter 6).

Nonetheless, the force of Calhoun's point remains. Different identities neither carry equal status nor exert the same pulling power, and they are all – in the end – susceptible to being politically trumped by national identity, with its overriding integrative force for collective unity and self-determination. This is where the notion of a national 'self' is most dangerous – spawning the belief that it has its own inner voice, its own will, its own destiny to which all others are alien. However loosely, it is this belief which animates symbolic acts of flag-waving and flag-burning. These are more potent than any totemic rites and symbols associated with the primitive Other discussed in the previous chapter, 'for nationalism dispenses with any mediating referent, be it totem or deity; its deity is the nation itself' (Smith, 1991: 78; see also Mosse, 1976 and Thompson, 1985). To quote Ernest Gellner: 'in a nationalist age, societies worship themselves brazenly and openly, spurning camouflage' (1997: 57). National cultural pride is the narcissism of small differences writ large, and at its most chauvinistic it is so without the camouflage which political strategy or diplomacy would otherwise require. A self-conception of singularity and uniqueness is then transposed on the broad social plane into desire for a pure and impermeable national identity, with very definite symbolic boundaries between 'us' and 'them'.

One could counter Calhoun's point by saying that national identity, in most Western countries, is built on the tolerance of difference between the various cultures of which it consists. The celebration of regional and local plurality has indeed been a key line of response to the contradiction between manifold cultural diversity within a whole country, and national cultural belonging as a perceived unifying affiliation across a whole country. The problem with this response derives from the way the former is delimited by the latter. The response relies on a consensual view of what such plurality should consist of, thus having no adequate explanation of tension and conflict between different cultural traditions and formations. It fails in the face of the affective force of nationality as an overarching source of identity and attachment. It may celebrate all the other cards in the politically legitimated pack, but it cannot match the trump card of nationality itself.

National identities do not necessarily encourage feelings of superiority over members of other nations, as we may see if we turn to Wales, Puerto Rico or Taiwan. But to the degree that they are involved in worshipping themselves, nations often contrast themselves with other nations, and with the 'foreigners' who occupy them. Foreignness acts then as a means of symbolic differentiation, of defining national identity by dissociative antithesis: what 'x' is consists of not being 'y'. This process of defining 'x' as 'non-y' exaggerates the differences of 'y-ness' in contrast to its lack of 'x-ness' in order to raise 'x-ness' above it (Devereux, 1975). Raphael Samuel gives two examples of this process in the negative stereotyping of the Irish and the French. 'Incompetent where the English were efficient, lazy where they were industrious, impulsive where the English had learnt self-control, they [the Irish] behaved in the manner of weaklings.' Similarly, during the nineteenth century, France was instrumental in sustaining English national conceit by negative example, being regarded as a morally loose, sexually licentious country, 'the paradise of atheists, a place of refuge for the bankrupt and the disgraced', and, regardless of the many cultural interchanges that had occurred, a place breeding foppish vanity, pretentious excess, effeminacy and deviousness (Samuel, 1989, Vol. 3: xxv–xxvi). The English defined who they were by negative symbolic reference to who they were not, making France 'a kind of blackboard on which English character draws its traits in chalk' (Emerson, 1966: 94). Chalking up the virtues of the English character 'was to live up to a stereotype generated in anti-Frenchness' (Newman, 1997: 124). Anti-Frenchness, and anti-Irishness, served to bolster the sense of a superior 'national character'.

These examples demonstrate a particular theme in the discourse of nationalism – the illusion that national identity and national culture develop chronologically alongside each other in a completely independent, self-sustaining manner. Nationalist rhetoric argues for a conception of difference based on the supposed distillate of a nation's independent being. Louis Kossuth's account of Magyar identity is a case in point. In producing this account, Kossuth ignored the centuries-long interaction of Magyars with Turks, Slavs and Germans, which had 'coloured the practice of religion, created a complex cuisine, and altered the structure of the Hungarian language itself'. In presenting Magyar culture as unchanging and self-sustaining from generation to generation, the 'corollary of national time,' was then, according to Richard Sennett, 'the concept of national purity' (1996: 181). The cultivation of a 'national character' epitomises this concept. The idea of a national character emerged in the eighteenth century, and, for philosophers such as Hume, Rousseau and Herder, ideas of national genius and character were considered as expressive of a collective unity and uniqueness. Thus, for instance, David Hume (1974: 208) stated: 'When a number of men are united into one political body, the occasions of their intercourse must be so frequent for defence, commerce, and government, that, together with the same speech or language, they must acquire a resemblance in their manners, and have a common or national character, as well as a personal one, peculiar to each individual'.

For Hume, national character was the consequence of moral causes, and the English were superior to all others in this respect. A century later, Thomas Arnold voiced the same belief in the national pre-eminence of the English (or Anglo-Saxons) in his inaugural lecture as Regius Professor of Modern History at Oxford (1841: 27–41). An anonymous contemporary contributor to the *Cornhill Magazine* (Vol. 4, July–December 1861: 584–98) was rather more circumspect in approach. National character, it was argued, cannot be taken simply as the aggregate of the characters of all of a nation's members at a given time since this is not available for observation and evidence of it could not be gathered. Does national character therefore refer to 'the character of an imaginary person or persons' which is constructed as nationally representative? To say that the English are brave, energetic and persevering does not mean that they all are, but rather that these qualities are possessed by a 'conspicuous minority'. This small élite is then personified as an ideal representative of the English, but such an ideal is 'defective in two respects – in making a part of the character of a part of the population stand for the whole of the character of the whole of the population'. By describing 'the notions which we frame of national character' in this way, the unnamed writer had come to the recognition of a positive stereotype, although this item of critical vocabulary was not available at the time. Hence his or her formulation of a figure operating somewhere 'between a memorandum and a portrait', with an inevitable tendency to 'depreciation, or at least to caricature'. Despite this tendency, the 'very vivid, if not very definite and exhaustive notion' which people have of 'their own national character' was vindicated by this writer on the grounds that there are hereditary, racial qualities – 'peculiarities of temperament, taste and manner' – which represent 'true national characteristics'. So, for instance, 'the assertion that the French are fickle … points to a quality which is common to almost all Frenchmen'. From initial suspicion of the idea of 'national character', either inability or disinclination to argue against this 'vivid notion' led finally to its simple affirmation. The use of the qualifying adverb 'almost' is the only trace of doubt remaining at the end of the article, and this could hardly be regarded as valid ground for denying that the existence of national character 'is a fact which ought to find its place in any sound theory of history'.

Exactly the opposite is the case, yet this is perhaps something that can be said only with the benefit of hindsight. The idea of 'national character' was typical of the kind of essentialist thinking applied to categories of association and identity in the nineteenth century. Being English or French distilled a defining racial essence, given by nature and taken as hereditary. In some ways this may be seen as an anxious assertion of symbolic boundaries in a period when colonisation and expanding trade and economic organisation were leading to increased contact between people and cultures across the world, particularly during the later nineteenth century. It was no accident that nationalist and racist stereotyping intensified at this time, and that the critical term for it soon came into being.

National character was a form of positively stereotyping a collective 'we' through an imagined personification of this identity in its ideal essence. Given its appeal as a stereotypical notion, it is hardly surprising that it remained in common currency for so long. Acceptance of it as a valid notion continued well into the twentieth century. For Edward Sapir, writing in 1924, national character meant 'some peculiar excellence, some distinguishing force, that is strikingly its own', although he did recognise the dangers of this conception. These include mistaking specifically historical features for innate racial characteristics which, as the national 'genius' or 'spirit', is then 'worshipped as an irreducible psychological fetish' (Sapir, 1970: 83–4). In a BBC broadcast of 1930 it was noted that 'we still speak as if England were a single person and France another' (Bourke, 1994: 173), and this same stereotypical habit of expression was criticised by George Orwell fifteen years later: 'Patently absurd remarks such as "Germany is naturally treacherous" are to be found in any newspaper one opens, and reckless generalisations about national character … are uttered by almost everyone' (1984: 411). Books with titles referring specifically to 'national character' were regularly published in Britain from the 1920s to the 1950s, showing how engrained the idea had become. Continuing reference to an essentialised national character shows how difficult it is to defuse and nullify certain stereotypes, especially when the historical accretions built up around them seem to provide evidence of long-term continuities and deeply innate characteristics.

Although criticisms made of the concept were noted, 'national character' even figures as an entry in a much reprinted sociological dictionary of the later twentieth century (Mitchell, 1977: 123–4). During this period, however, the concept retained its currency more under the aegis of 'national type', as for instance in that of the Australian (white, male) national type, characterised by a no-bullshit self-reliance, solidarity and mateship (Ward, 1966; cf. Lake, 1998). In New Zealand, a rather more ambivalently gendered nationality grew up over the colonial period, with the culture of female experience being constituted through a cult of domesticity, and male cultural experience combined in an uneasy alliance of mateship and the less socially disruptive male role of 'family man'. The legacies of the national male 'type' forged in this alliance are still active in contemporary New Zealand society (Phillips, 1987; James and Saville-Smith, 1990: 7–46). National identity is always structured around differently related gender models, although historically the emphasis has been masculine, with the comradeship it idealises being a socially organised form of male bonding (Mosse, 1985; Parker et al., 1992). Nationalisms have 'typically sprung from masculinised memory, masculinised humiliation and masculinised hope' (Enloe, 1989: 44).

The shift from national 'character' to 'type' was part of a wider critical rejection of the morally individualistic, Victorian idea of character, but the idea of identity as stable and continuous, singular, homogeneous and unitary, upon which the idea of 'national character' relied, has also been seriously questioned, over the past century, by new theories of subjectivity and language. While non-national cultures, such as those of the Saami, remain instructive as alternative ways of living in a world mapped by the historically contingent boundaries of nations, the category of the nation has itself come into question. In the West at least, the nation-state as a unifying collective frame has been undermined both from 'inside', by the new social movements and campaigns for regional autonomy, and from 'outside', by a globalising economic infrastructure of finance, trade, market and communications. Its earlier claim of being able to provide a totally incorporating framework of cultural identity is increasingly seen as untenable, and not least in being unable to accommodate the expansion of social diversity following new patterns of diasporic movement, migration and settlement – all that is summed up as 'multicultural society' – which have changed most Western nation-states and enriched them ethnically, linguistically and culturally.

Yet nationalism has by no means disappeared in Western societies. It remains part of the fabric of everyday life in the West, and banally so, as Michael Billig (1995b) has so persuasively argued. It is because it is so integral to how we see the world that it goes unnoticed. It has, in other words, to become banal to be effective in the longer term, to become fully established in our meanings and values. It has to be overlooked on a day-to-day basis for it to become commonplace, interwoven with the lived fabric of everyday culture. Its routinely forgotten existence is itself an indication that thinking nationally has become dyed in the wool of common sense.

For example, we still take it for granted that nations exist in separate territories, and this is very much bound up with the idea of nations having separate languages. Such views have not arisen by themselves, like flowers in an uncultivated field. They are a product of history, and have developed out of struggles over which ways of living, seeing and thinking should prevail in the modern world. These struggles have involved the imposition of particular criteria for what constitutes a national territory and a national language, over and against its particular regions and dialects. At times the imposition of official national languages has involved the suppression or sidelining of other languages, such as the speaking of Welsh in Welsh schools or of Welsh in Patagonia by farming emigrants who, having settled there in order, among other things, to achieve a sense of belonging through freedom to speak, and worship in, their own language, were then faced with the pressure to assimilate in their adopted country (Williams, 1991). The struggle for national hegemony asserts the need for 'us' to speak the 'same together', in the unifying language of the nation, as if languages are, in fact, actually discrete, with fixed boundaries, just like national territories. Nationalist languages are forms of linguistic authoritarianism, transforming a particular dialect into the official and correct language and relegating other ways of speaking, other 'languages', to the status of dialects or some other contrasting category. This is, for example, what happened to Piedmontese when Tuscan achieved ascendancy as the language of Italy. Thinking of language in this way, as if it is a territory with precise and unchanging borderlines, is not something characteristic only of nationalist dictators or 'extremists'. It is characteristic of every form of nationalism. It is integral to the historical common sense of nationalism, which imagines languages themselves as distinct entities (Billig, 1995b: Chapter 2).

Nationalism is a classic case of familiarity breeding forgetfulness. That is why it seems to be confined, as an international issue, to emergent nations or brutal, fascistic political regimes. Certainly, in the so-called postcolonial period, new, sometimes virulent nationalisms have arisen, and not only in those places affected by the breakdown of the old Soviet communist bloc. In these new drives to nationhood, as Stuart Hall reminds us, there is a danger of the older nationalist model being taken up again in the attempt to construct ethnically or culturally closed or 'pure' formations: 'a closure which comes, in Gellner's terms, from trying to realise the aspiration, which they see as the secret of success of the great modernising nation-states of Western modernity, of gathering *one* people, *one* ethnicity, under *one* political roof' (Hall, 1993a: 355–6).

Building the Nation

Ernest Gellner has made a major contribution to our understanding of nationalism. Reading him reminds us that defining identity around the idea of the nation and of belonging to a nation has radically altered the way people see themselves and the rest of the world. This is why nationalism has been one of the most politically significant developments in the modern period. National identity presupposes a culture that supports this sense of allegiance and belonging. This can be seen most readily perhaps in publicly staged rituals and ceremonies, symbols and traditions, but nationalism as a form of collective identification is sustained much more broadly by a set of attitudes and assumptions that accepts the necessity of the nation, of a world of nations, and of the need for belonging to a particular nation. The particularity of 'our' national belonging defines who 'we' are, in the world of nations, but the nation as a source of identity and belonging requires a belief in the inevitability of its existence as an organising form of life. Nationalism is about the modern politics of belonging. It produces and mobilises a way of seeing and speaking about belonging through the discursive formation generated around it. It does this as an ideological process because it makes this way of seeing and speaking seem natural and inevitable, as if, in Gellner's words, we must have a nationality as we must have a nose and two ears (1964: 150). This is not true. It is the obviousness of its appearance as truth, as if it were as obviously true as having a nose and two ears, which is the core problem of nationalism. 'Having a nation,' as Gellner says, 'is not an inherent attribute of humanity, but it has now come to appear as such' (1997: 6).

Making it appear as such is where the schooling of the national subject is so important. Rousseau was one of the first to recognise this:

'It is education that must give souls a national formation, and direct their opinions and tastes in such a way that they will be patriotic by inclination, by passion, and by necessity' (cited in Bauman, 1991: 65). Mass compulsory education with a standardised language and set curriculum has been of primary importance in naturalising the idea of national belonging. As we have seen, nations cannot be defined in terms of shared cultures, because all shared cultures are not nations. But they do define certain cultural 'contents' as national, and the dissemination of a specifically national culture requires the state organisation and control of education. While universal, centralised education is conditional on nationalism, within nation-states a 'monopoly of legitimate education is', according to Gellner, 'more important, more central than is the monopoly of legitimate violence'. During the modern period, 'national culture', educationally sanctioned and unified, has become a new source of attachment with which people have willingly and closely identified as it has taken on the hallowed credentials of political legitimacy, binding the people to the polity and conferring on the state the right to endow culture with its own political roof (1997: 34, 43, 111).

Gellner interprets the development of national education systems as resulting from industrialisation and its more flexible as well as more complex division of labour. For him, nationalism arises from the uneven diffusion of industrialisation and 'modernisation'. These create moral if not physical dislocation, and new structural divisions and inequalities, which are not legitimated by existing ideologies and which lead to social unrest, conflict and potential revolution. This situation is remedied (at least partially) by the construction of a national identity and culture, which act functionally to open up and erode local cultural networks and provide a new sense of belonging, membership and unity that is 'direct, and not mediated by intervening subgroups' (Gellner, 1964: 173). These general shifts are illustrated by the introduction of compulsory school education in Britain in the late nineteenth century. While providing a means of 'reconnaissance into working-class life', the 'acknowledged object of the school was integrative: to "civilise" the children of the poor and to anglicise foreign children – to ensure that the next generation met the needs of the modern nation-state' (Davin, 1996: 214–15; cf. Bourke, 1994: 185–6). At the opposite end of the educational scale, public schools endeavoured to produce the future leaders of what a Harrow headmaster referred to in 1899 as 'the greatest empire under heaven' (Wilkinson, 1964: 101).

There are, however, at least three problems with Gellner's general model. It offers little recognition of 'national culture' as an intrinsically problematic concept, does not deal with opposition to its official versions, and discusses it as something already achieved and fully settled in place as a result of the transition from an 'agro-literate' polity to the nation-state. And while Gellner rightly stresses the role of education in the construction and dissemination of national culture and identity, he plays down the role of the communications media in helping to imagine the nation as community. This is, again, a problem of reciprocal blind-spots, for in communication studies: 'the nation is underconceptualised, whereas in the nationalism literature the mass media are usually quite untheorised' (Schlesinger, 1991: 156).

If national belonging and identity are felt as the sense of a direct and apparently unmediated communion with the nation, the media are obviously important vehicles in facilitating this process. In his study of the origins and spread of nationalism, Benedict Anderson at least partially overcomes the media blind spot which is common elsewhere by discussing the significance of print media for an emerging nationalism during the early nineteenth century. Their significance was in linking people together within a new apprehension of time, where time spent was transformed into time spread, net-like, across the nation. In a process complementing that discussed in Chapter 2, national space became temporalised; spatially dispersed people were conjoined in a national conception of time. For example, Anderson highlights the importance of the temporal structure of the nineteenth-century realist novel for creating a sense of unity in national space, as different events were shown as happening simultaneously, in a sort of 'complex gloss upon the word "meanwhile"' (1986: 31, 122). Newspapers extended this sense of the meaning of 'meanwhile' in creating the impression of a broadly shared simultaneity of involvement in events, episodes and developments affecting or implicating the nation as a whole. 'At the same time, the newspaper reader, observing exact replicas of his own paper being consumed by his subway, barbershop, or residential neighbours, is continually reassured that the imagined world is visibly rooted in everyday life' (Anderson, 1986: 39–40).

This 'directness' of national belonging, this emergent synchronicity of nationality and everyday life, was made more immediate and instantaneous by the mode of public address offered by radio, and subsequently by television. Both monarchs and political leaders have exploited this when, in 'speaking to the nation', it has been assumed that common access to the media of communication creates the potential for bringing the people together as a nation, and creating a 'we-feeling' of national belonging (Scannell and Cardiff, 1991: 277). Television and, earlier, cinema have been crucial for nationalism in other ways, particularly through re-enacting myths of national formation, retelling the stories of significant events in national history, and symbolising national identity, sometimes with strong racist elements, as for instance in D.W. Griffith's film *The Birth of a Nation* (1915). By 'interweaving actions occurring in different places at the same time', the cinema encompassed 'the scope and diversity of the modern nation as a visual narrative', and 'allowed differences of race, class, gender, ethnicity and sexuality to be mapped onto a seemingly homogeneous national space'.

By instituting textual borders which enforced the boundaries of dominant cultural and political discourse, counterpointing the alterity of the foreign and unfamiliar with stereotypical images of self-identity, cinema assumed a key role at the modern intersection of nation and narration. Film's unique capacity to join the representation of space to the experience of time, matching landscape as a nationalist metaphor with the re-enactment of landmark historical events, has made cinema a primary site for establishing the modern nation as a textual unity and imagined community (McQuire, 1998: 205–6).

Antiquity and Invention

Whether manifest in education, the mass media or occasions of state ritual, nationalist rhetoric always involves some form of mystification. A common example of this is its claim to deep-rootedness in a heroic and venerable past. This is mystificatory because, as a distinct ideology and discursive formation, nationalism is a modern phenomenon. It was only from the later eighteenth century onwards that definite forms of national consciousness emerged, at first in Europe and subsequently around the globe. During the nineteenth century, nationalism as a discourse and project spread throughout Europe and began to emanate from there to other countries, particularly those which had been colonised by European nations. Nationalism then served as a source of resistance to colonialism. In a variety of different ways, over the course of two centuries, nationalism became not only a defining feature of modernity, but also internationally distributed as a rhetoric of belonging. It was as a way of establishing its discursive credentials in its emergence and development, and of enhancing the potency of its values, that nationalism drew on older cultural traditions, icons and symbols. These imparted to the idea of the nation a sense of immemorial flow and continuity, although of course these elements from the past were transformed in the process. In this sense the nation was then advanced as the principal source of community, of uniting with others to achieve common goals and purposes, with their legitimacy based on the claim to a primordial lineage of shared origins and shared ancestry.

At times this putative lineage has become racially charged, binding people together nationally in a conflation of blood and history, race and soil, as with National Socialism in mid-twentieth-century Germany. This pernicious mix not only generates a fierce form of social cohesion and patriotism. It also leads to the suppression of domestic social dissent and an acute intolerance of aliens or racially 'impure' elements within the national boundaries. While the twentieth century has thrown up numerous abhorrent examples of such barbarism, these do not cover the diverse ways in which ethnic sources of identity have been drawn upon, across a range of different meanings and values. Such sources of identity are not incontestable. They can become a site of conflict over their significance and the claims they may legitimately make over people's practical action. Certainly, to invoke the name of the nation is to affirm the confluence of civic territory and racial genealogy, albeit in varying proportions from one place to another, but ethnicity and nationalism should not be considered as one and the same. Ethnicity is one source of national identity – a powerful one in Germany from the late nineteenth century, for instance, but less significant in the 'melting pot' development of an American identity as it has developed from that time, unless of course you happened to be born black. Ethnic and national identities do often blend closely together, but ethnicity is not a *sine qua non* for national identity.

Laying claim to a deep genealogical vintage runs counter to the comparatively recent origin of all forms of nationalism. Its subjective antiquity in the eyes of nationalists is contradicted by its objective modernity in the eyes of historians (Anderson, 1986: 14). In many cases, this contradiction is what is peculiar about a specifically national identity. It is generated by a modernising impulse but legitimated by its appeal to the past, to primordial lineage and loyalty. Historical ballast provides a means of stabilising any ideological vessel, particularly when confronted with turbulent times. The highly tendentious sense of the term 'historical' here is entirely commensurate with the mystically resonant appeal of nationalism to primordial ties through blood, language, territory, soil. This appeal continues to resonate because nations seem to be natural, seem to have a long-established and given existence, as if the world atlas has always been divided up into a world of nations, with fixed territories and definitive borders.

There is nothing primordial about these geographical divisions and borders. The rhetorical claim of immemoriality conceals their recent history as a product of modernity, while the claim that national identity represents some perdurable essence of collective being obscures the continuous process of its maintenance and reinvention. National identity is constructed out of selective elements which are historically inherited, but their use in this construction camouflages the ways in which national identity is always historically located. Its historicality may begin to become apparent when it is shown to serve present circumstances and contingencies, rather than passing neutrally into them or in some way standing over against them, but it usually remains hidden from view because of the heavy investment in national belonging. Part of this comes from the conviction of having been brought up into it, of it being a key aspect of people's inheritance, so that 'their' nation appears as if it has always been there, for their forebears in the same way as for them. The idea that 'there'll always be an England' derives its banal conviction from the sense that there *has* always been an England, at least for as long a time as time itself is felt to carry any cultural relevance. That is why it is inadequate to understand national identity simply as the product of a doctrine or political principle. It is rooted in a psychologically more entangled way of regarding the world and one's place within it. It has an affective power, as we see with images of flag-waving and flag-burning in political demonstrations, or ground-kissing rituals on return to a homeland, but its affective power is not necessarily manifest in histrionic expressions such as these. For example, in 1945 George Orwell contrasted extreme nationalists – 'each of them simply an enormous mouth bellowing the same lie over and over again' – with the nationalism that is 'part of the make-up of most of us, whether we like it or not'. This can turn people in a moment from fair-mindedness to vicious partisanship: 'One prod to the nerve of nationalism, and the intellectual decencies can vanish, the past can be altered, and the plainest facts can be denied' (Orwell, 1984: 428, 430).

Contrary to appearances, nations are in certain ways always artificial. This is certainly the case with their putative continuity with a historic past. As Eric Hobsbawm and others have shown, many of the traditions supporting the construction of national cultures are 'invented' by social and political élites in the process of state formation or state transformation (Hobsbawm and Ranger, 1984). David Cannadine (1984) establishes this process very clearly in relation to the ritual and pageantry surrounding the British monarchy. These were largely the product of the late nineteenth and early twentieth centuries. Invented practices helped to fill the voids left by the disintegration of earlier social ties and rituals of social cohesion, following the development of industrial capitalism. Invented or reformulated symbols and social rituals, such as flags, images, ceremonies and music, reminded people of their citizenship and nationhood. National heroes, monuments or annual events helped legitimate new nations such as Italy and Germany, as well as older ones such as Britain and France, where prior to the Revolution of 1789 people did not possess national consciousness – peasants had to be turned into Frenchmen (Weber, 1976). What Hobsbawm and others have critically established is that, just as there is nothing primordial about nation-states, so there is nothing primordial about national traditions. But there are dangers in placing too much emphasis on this dimension of what is involved in the establishment of national cultures and the transition to national identities. In particular, in a clear echo of the binaries of classical sociology, it polarises genuine and invented traditions where distinctions are actually more vague and ambivalent. Three further points follow from this.

First, acknowledging this aspect of national culture points only to the more spectacular manifestations of what become state rituals or calendrical events deliberately staged in the name of the nation. This tends to blur the distinction between social memory and codified official tradition, a distinction which is important in relation to alternative (non-official) accounts of national identity (Schlesinger, 1991: 170). Second, viewing the historical formation of a national culture entirely in the 'invented traditions' mould may exaggerate the degree to which it was intended and preplanned, as if its construction followed a set blueprint and met with general agreement. Third, overemphasising its invented-ness tends to explain it as being only a reaction to the needs of economy or state, as if it could only develop or be sustained in that way. So, for instance, if the sacralisation of cultural achievement and tradition under the aura of the nation was, in the later nineteenth century, a response to the reduction of the world to instrumental reason, to a disenchanted world, this should not be seen simply as a reflex movement against disenchantment. To do so would be to deny an active dynamic presence to cultural processes and practices, and to downplay the ability of cultural and artistic forms to express our deeper, maybe only half-conscious, feelings about the intersecting social worlds we live in. The fact that these can be betrayed by nationalism for other purposes, be they economic, religious or military, only goes to emphasise their connections with more profound responses, on the part of both individuals and collectivities, to patterns of social change and historical development. It is because these connections are often powerfully felt that they can be exploited for nationalistic ends.

The 'invention of tradition' intervention was in many ways a compelling one. What was disappointing about its uncritical acceptance was a widespread misconception of tradition itself and how it operates. Advocates of certain traditions may make claims to primordiality, but this does not mean that all traditions are a manipulative sham. To argue against nationalism entirely in this way does not explain its deep-seated appeal or the emotional power of allegiance it generates. It also ignores the ways in which tradition operates as an enabling framework through which present action is co-ordinated. Tradition as a cultural process fore-structures our understanding and provides an initiating basis for interpretation and evaluation of what we encounter and experience in the world. It is in this way an intrinsic part of our temporal make-up, even as we critically turn against it. Traditions are not simply about the transmission of past cultural content into an acquiescent present. At least when vibrant, traditions are always in the process of being recreated – if you like, reinvented – and subject to evaluation in terms of what they bring to a contemporary situation. Living traditions are not static but always temporally in movement, always in the process of being reshaped in adaptation to the present. This is, again, to signal the danger of any stark opposition between primordiality and 'mere invention', since it 'leaves open a very wide range of historicities within which national or other traditions can exert real force' (Calhoun, 1997: 35).

These important qualifications should not blur our sense of the stress upon continuity which is emphatically felt within nationalism. Commonplace ideas about national identity see it as something relatively static and durable, rather than as continually changing and adapting according to historical circumstances. We live in an age of scurrying social and cultural change, and this increases the attraction of an illusory stability of identity and pattern of belonging. We also live in an age of international connections and interdependencies, but we still think in terms of nations, of 'our' own individual nation as opposed to others. We divide ourselves as citizens belonging to 'our' nation from foreigners who do not belong. The discourse of nationalism operates in order to establish who belongs and who does not, making national identities and cultures more salient and categorically distinguished from each other. This increases the likelihood of those mismatches and misinterpretations which, as outlined in Chapter 1, provide exactly the kinds of condition in which stereotypes flourish. Those who are stereotyped become the natural harbingers of danger and disorder, and national stereotyping must then work that much harder in order to keep them at bay. We support all this, in the name of the nation, with daily reminders of 'our' national uniqueness, exclusivity and integrity. This encourages us to forget the dilemma of prejudice and tolerance under-lying our relations with others, which the rhetoric of stereotyping itself seeks to achieve by attributing prejudice to other nationalities, to foreigners and outgroups. Those who become negatively evaluated as 'them' are made to seem deserving of exclusion, of the ritualistic social exorcism which stereotyping performs. This is also where nationalism connects with racism, for throughout modernity a positively evaluated national 'us' has been contrasted with the stereotypical attributions of other, non-Western peoples, seeking to place and fix them into given conceptions of their distinctive culture or 'racial character'. The next chapter will focus on these stereotypical conceptions, for they have been central to the politics of unbelonging.

Chapter 5

The Politics of Not Belonging

*[The] British Empire ... laid its dictates on us. It was as if we saw
ourselves with the vision of that 'Other', the outsider. Therefore, we
were not the norm; they were. This is to rationalise now, at this
distance of time. Then, one only knew that to speak English (and
not the way we did), to wear English clothes ... to be large, white
and Christian was somehow to be superior.*

SHASHI DESHPANDE, 1993: 105

*I am profoundly convinced that there can be no question but that
British rule has promoted the happiness and welfare of the primitive
races ... We hold these countries because it is the genius of our race
to colonise, to trade, and to govern.*

FREDERICK LUGARD, 1926: 618–19

Methuselah vs Marconi

The inherent danger in any form of nationality lies in the mode of
belonging it generates. To set up and stabilise this mode of belonging
over time, and to defend it when it appears to be challenged by cultural
change and interchange, involves constructing and keeping in public
view its negative counterpart of not belonging, of not being a specific
national or having assigned to you the characteristics of a specific nationality. The question of national belonging is organised and managed
through arguments about these idealised characteristics, but it is nationality itself which narrows the focus of belonging to negativities of exclusion, where what is essentialised as alien is underwritten by what is
essentialised as 'our own'. The production and maintenance of symbolic
boundaries operate by closing off the nationalist core-nation as a
community and culture as if it is exclusive unto itself, as if it should

107

retain or regain some unity of being that has previously been constructed, against all that appears to threaten this, from outside or within. This, as we have seen, creates a dangerous breeding ground for various forms of stereotyping.

The danger lies not only in the nation-centred forms of parochialism this generates, but also in the hostility bred by the force of symbolic closure to other cultures and other peoples. A particular strategy of symbolic boundary maintenance already mentioned in this respect involves defining the constructs of a national community and culture through imagined constructions of difference, the depth and force of which vary from place to place, and time to time. In practice, most formations of nationhood are built up around both 'external' formulations of difference and 'internal' self-characterising features of being putatively the 'same together'. It is for this reason that Giddens defines nationalism as 'a strong psychological affiliation with an "in-group" coupled with a differentiation from, or rejection of, "outgroups"' (1983: 195). The latter has usually provided reinforcement for the former, which is claimed to exist prior to it as the basis for contrast with the outside world, the other nations in the world of nations, and for consequent practices of antagonistic acculturation in the continual process of building the nation. But what counts is the two aspects in their mutual tension. It is this which gives to nationalism its Janus-faced character, producing images of 'self-government, enlightenment, and social justice' alongside 'dreams and images of savagery' (Deutsch, 1969: 53). Nationalism is fraught with its own dilemmas, which stereotypes of the Other seek anxiously to annul.

If this is one irony of the development of nationalism within Europe, another is its historical coincidence with colonial expansionism. Just as the ideological emphasis on the nation as special and unique in its ties to land, language and culture was becoming established, so the reach out beyond the homeland was beginning to accelerate, leading to territorial annexation, culture contact and newly troubling questions for the constitution of national identity. There is a strong tendency in Britain to address these questions by looking only at ethnic conflict since the 1950s, with the increased settlement of people from ex-colonial territories. This is a historically foreshortened view. Cultural flow and interchange which appears to undermine the values and assumptions informing national identities has been one of the key tensions of modernity as a whole. The dilemma created by this tension is felt in the pull towards our relative sense of belonging in the cultural forms that are familiar to us, where we feel at home with their narrative content and symbolic conventions, and in the pull away from this towards a relatively dislocated stage or moment of confronting what is different and strange as a vital source of cultural innovation and change. This dilemma is characteristic of Western modernity because once the historical movement was made outwards, the whole world changed. The consequences of this outward movement, for our sense of how the world is interconnected and for our everyday experience, are central to the modes of life set in motion by modernity. One aspect of this is that, despite rearguard claims of folk purism and essentialist notions of ethnic authenticities, the idea of a culture emerging and forming itself in isolation or entirely out of its own self-originating sources and resources has been seriously eroded. Within modernity, any relatively distinct culture has been and always is being formed and changed in part by everything that comes to it from outside, in the world that was first opened up by mercantile trade, transatlantic slavery, colonialism and imperialism, international capitalist investment, new channels of communication, expanding media markets and endless migrations of peoples and cultures across national borders.

Nationalism always tries to pull us back and keep out what appears to contravene, or for some just simply to complicate, the sense of national identity that has been constructed to define 'us' against 'them'. The elevation of what is culturally close and familiar above what is distant and dissimilar is central to the politics of belonging and not belonging. These necessarily entail each other. They do so both in the sense of territorial attachments and through strategies of dissociation from what is contrasted with national mediations of cultural belonging. Various peoples are then seen as not belonging, not only because they do not have the same nationality but also because their characteristic forms of life are divided from 'ours' by symbolic boundaries which contrastively identify them as inferior. We have already seen what this involved historically in the construct of the atavistic Primitive as a way of anachronistically placing other peoples and symbolically displacing them from where 'we' belong, in the 'civilised' or 'developed' world.

Over the past two centuries, no colonial or potentially colonial continent has been more anachronistically 'othered' in this respect than Africa. Before I elaborate further, later in the chapter, on what this involved, I want to make the point that much of it developed out of two complementary qualities: the profound, but unquestioned sense of superiority of those who produced the stereotypes and their profound, but unrecognised depth of ignorance of those who were so stereotyped. The European approach to Africa over much of the past two centuries betrayed a huge failure of imagination and understanding. So, for instance, its non-representational visual arts went unappreciated in western Europe until modernism, and the rediscovery of the unconscious, created a more favourable climate of reception and recuperation. Its diverse forms of music were lumped together and dismissed as 'those unearthly noises which in Africa pass current for song' (cited in Kiernan, 1972: 204). Its 'magic-laden', 'animistic' and 'superstitious' forms of religion were anathema to those steeped in Christian religious creeds, and particularly its Protestant and Calvinist variants. Its forms of social organisation and polity appeared merely to baffle those who took the category of the nation-state for granted, while its widely varying forms of life were considered to be those of 'people without history'. It was because they were regarded as unchanging that the 'primitive' or 'savage' societies of Africa were conceived as being either without history, in a state of prehistory or belonging only to natural history. Without history they were felt to be, in the words of an Oxford professor, 'blank' and 'uninteresting' (cited in Davidson, 1974: 51). Their 'history' of course only began with the arrival of Europeans and their colonisation. Notoriously as well, the culturally blinkered view of Europeans was applied to physical appearances, with white aesthetic standards setting an absolute yardstick of evaluation, as for instance in this description by Robert Ballantyne of an African chief: '*Unlike negroes in general,* his features were cast in a mould which one is more accustomed to see in the Caucasian race of mankind – the nose being straight, the lips comparatively thin, and the face oval' (1888: 330, my emphasis). The implication is that this 'Caucasian' propinquity explained his chiefly qualities, but it is that initiating minor clause which speaks volumes.

Elsewhere, Ballantyne wrote of the 'human baboons' at an African wedding ritual: 'The men, who were absolutely naked, were engaged in a slow, meaningless dance, which consisted chiefly of stamping their feet, in regular time, while the women, who were nearly naked, clapped their hands in time and sang' (1880: 93–4). His verdict is final and peremptory: 'Truly there is great need for the Gospel's purifying influence here!' (ibid). Both the description and the judgement that accompanies and follows it illustrate perfectly the two complementary qualities I have outlined. Likewise, the Christian *Boy's Own Paper*, in its first year of publication, referred to the Zulu as 'a savage pure and simple, abjectly submissive to the superstitions of the witch-finder and rain-doctor' and settled into 'long-contracted habits of debasing vice'. Its fervent hope was that 'civilisation, Christianity and industry [would] reign instead of ruthless barbarism and savage cruelty' (*Boy's Own Paper*, 1, 10 May 1879: 267, 2 August 1879: 463). Such rhetoric now seems riddled with historical ironies, as does the later characterisation of its readers as 'English lads, with young, free and generous hearts, not yet hardened by prejudice' (*Boy's Own Paper*, 13, 1 August 1891: 696). After twelve years of publication, during which time its readers had been commonly regaled with depictions of primitivist savagery, this was a trifle optimistic. In their initial encounters with all things African, Europeans sensationalised, amplified rumour and hearsay, concentrated on the exotic, and assessed entirely by their own standards and criteria, as if these could and should have been universally applicable. Since they were not, this reinforced the stereotypes of black people, just as those stereotypes themselves made one set of standards and criteria appear valid by not conforming to them. Impression fed upon impression. We have lived with the results of this one-way cultural trafficking ever since.

'Civilisation, Christianity and Commerce' were the watchwords of the most famous missionary to Africa, David Livingstone. Whether imperialist ventures were determined by these interests in that order is debatable, but the idea of a civilising mission was certainly a central bulwark in the justification of imperialism, alongside economic and military interests. This idea was also advanced as a way of reconciling national self-determination with colonial expansionism. To civilise other 'races' regarded as inferior, and without national rights, was a national obligation of the colonising powers, conceived according to their national lights: 'the possession of an empire was the essential precondition for the free development of one's own national culture' (Mommsen, 1974: 126). For this reason, Josep Llobera has recently paraphrased Lenin in describing imperialism as 'the highest stage of nationalism' (1998: 214). The criteria and standards by which civilisation was measured were imposed from outside by the imperialist nations. This was validated by the belief that economic and technological development was globally inevitable; progress and modernisation were the ideological counterparts supporting this development. To quote the widely influential *Boy's Own Paper* again: 'Our behaviour is justified' because 'it is the age of Methuselah touching the age of Edison and Marconi – inactivity must give way to activity' (Dunae, 1977: 96, see also Dunae, 1980: 107–9, 1989: 22–4).

Whether or not this justification was conceded by the countries invaded and subjugated was irrelevant. The same applied to the case for religious conversion, although this raises difficult moral questions about the right to interfere with religiously sanctioned customs, such as that of penal amputation – or in plain language, chopping off the hands of convicted thieves – on the grounds that this would have a civilising effect. To outlaw such customs would certainly seem to be justified in this respect, as is the alleviation of suffering caused by disease, natural disasters and infant mortality. These ethical considerations do not apply to the French or British 'civilising mission' because it operated largely as an ideological adjunct to the economic and military interests of empire. If it had entirely succeeded in its objectives, this would have subverted the project of imperialism itself, which served these other interests. That did not happen because, ideologically, its case was predicated on the racial inferiorisation of the subordinated peoples of imperialist conquest and settlement, a process which generated a whole range of stereotypes othering 'them', in ontological contradistinction to 'us', as part of the basis for establishing and maintaining the symbolic differentiations of belonging and not belonging.

It is perhaps worth picking out one further historical irony involved in the relation between nationalism and imperialism. In the long period of European colonialism and imperialism, the strategy of 'othering' what was conceived as different or alien to the national community and culture has rebounded, not only because the tensions bred by symbolic closure have been played out in one conflict or crisis after another, but also because independence movements have typically adopted nationalist ways of seeing the world. The irony of this strategy is that the models of 'ethnic' authenticity and destiny involved have been taken over from those the movements have opposed. Understandably, the experience of being taken over and administered from outside, of becoming colonial subjects – or as the patronising term had it, 'natives', with all the ideological baggage that went with that – has often driven independence movements towards the nationalist model of their imperial masters. It has been a case of turning around the prescription of 'a nation for us, our colony for you' and redefining it as 'your ex-colonial past and our national future'.

This is not to forget that 'Third World' nationalism has been viewed ambivalently, and that those involved in the anti-colonial struggle have at times been fearful of the dangers of 'reverse' nationalisms (see for example, Fanon, 1970). The difficulties stem from the ways in which the most urgent of political claims in decolonised space are coded within the legacy of imperialism, with nationhood to the fore (Spivak, 1993: 60). Calhoun's neat formula puts the whole process in a nutshell: 'Colonialism drove nationalism forward even while it resisted it' (Calhoun,

1997: 108). Resistance against 'native' nationalisms has first to be seen in relation to the economic dependence of European nation-states on globalised trade and the exploitation of resources in the rest of the world. The opposed propulsions of colonialism and nationalism, of post-colonial nationalisms and accelerating forces of globalisation, run through all the questions of identity and difference that have been negotiated throughout the modern and late-modern periods, with no easy answer available for the problem of what comes after decolonisation. Second, such resistance has also to be seen as a way of resolving the dilemma posed by the Janus-faced character of nationalism by projecting its 'darker' or more extreme versions onto non-Western nation-states. This process often recuperates older forms of 'othering' and the stereotypical notions that accompany them. All too conveniently, Western nations then conclude that nationalism is actually ill-suited to non-Western societies. It is precisely because of the stereotypes associated with them that nationalism is held as 'likely to be abused by Arabs, Zulus, Indonesians, Irish or Jamaicans' (Said, 1994: 261).

In this chapter, I want to look at how ideas about race in the nineteenth century grew into a belief in racial superiority, that 'unquestioning cultural arrogance' which Philip Curtin was one of the first to subject to serious analysis (1971: xv, and see Curtin, 1965). Racial superiority belonged first of all to Europeans, but among them to none more so than the British. 'No European', wrote Francis Younghusband, leader of the first British expedition into Tibet, 'can mix with non-Christian races without feeling his moral superiority over them' (1896: 396), while Joseph Chamberlain declared: 'I believe that the British race is the greatest of governing races that the world has ever seen' (Bennett, 1953: 315). The close ideological affinity of nationalism, racism and imperialism always depended on various forms of stereotypically 'othering' social and cultural differences *in the name of race*. This practice has had a long and pernicious influence. Racism reinforced the nationalist sense of belonging through distinguishing and dissociating it from what did not belong to the category of the nation thus privileged. Ideologically, this worked to seal the symbolic boundaries of identity and difference and enhance the 'purity' of the constructed ethnicity, a 'purity' that was, however, only ever provisional because the threat posed by the Other had been given recognition through the very attempt at boundary-closure. This chapter will add further to the general argument of the book that such Self/Other constructions have to be seen primarily in relation to structures of inequality and power, rather than in terms of cognitive economy. While certain racist prejudices may psychologically be deeply rooted and difficult to eradicate, conceptions of power and domination are indispensable to an anti-racist approach to the problem of stereotypical prejudice.

It is important to begin by clarifying the distinction between 'race' and ethnicity. The category of race denotes a form of labelling imposed on certain groups by those who base their sense of difference from these groups on their self-arrogated superiority. It is an exclusive form of categorisation because it attempts to define groups as inherently inferior to those who command the labelling, and on these grounds to legitimate their social domination. Ethnicity, by contrast, provides a means by which certain groups create their own sense of identity, which they characterise and express in their own terms rather than those used to justify their marginalised status. It is an inclusive form of self-categorisation, and is often used to counter the labelling of racial inferiorisation by putting in its place sources of cultural worth and achievement originating from within the group. From the 1960s, ethnicity has often become politically charged as groups have used their cultural identity as a means of resisting social disadvantages or attempts to contain them under the broader political roof of the nation. Such attempts are often seen as likely to dilute the identity of particular ethnic minorities.

This is to put forward the distinction in too neat and clean fashion. In practice it is not always so easy to tell where the one begins and the other ends. 'Race' is a complex term, and has been used in the past to denote that for which 'ethnicity' is now a contemporary, and apparently more neutral, synonym, as in the example of the 'Celtic race' or even the 'Anglo-Saxon race'. These may now seem ideologically loaded terms, but to some extent at least that is the product of either contemporary meanings overlaying earlier ones, or an equivocal benefit of hindsight, or both. Although it has its inclusive associations and usages, as in the still common term 'human race', which is accepted as all-embracing because paradoxically seeming to override all the connotations of its qualified noun, 'race' has come to be seen primarily as a marker of exclusion, dissociation, discrimination, exploitation – or worse. These senses have developed through the accretion of meanings and values derived from racist ideology and racial theory, and from their now indelible associations with the hell and horror of Nazi genocide and Fascist abuse in the 1930s and 40s, not to mention black lynchings and castration in the American South or the torture and murder of blacks during the apartheid period in South Africa – all twentieth-century atrocities. As a result, the term 'race' is now quite properly discredited. It is, in short, 'a four letter word that hurts' (Fried, 1975: 38). We should nevertheless be aware of the uses of the contemporary alternative 'ethnicity' as a way of smuggling in the older ideological meanings and values, as for instance in the substitution of culturalist (ethnic) for biological (racist) forms of belonging.

We can only be clear about this by understanding racism historically. This shows that racism is neither singular nor homogeneous, even in relation to the same targeted group; that there is no particular main origin of racism since it feeds off various sources and is always inflected by period and place; and that certain forms of racism, such as anti-semitism, need to be understood differently from others, as for instance those developed through colonialist discourse and imperialist ideology. Colonial encounters with social and cultural 'difference' generated forms of racial prejudice that remain part of the legacy of empire. Among other things, nineteenth-century stereotypes of the African have continuing influence, perhaps more than we realise. They remain part of an actively residual 'racial animus' (Childs and Williams, 1997: 74). At the same time that stereotyping was changing as a response to the social dilemmas of modernity, so attitudes to other people, outside western Europe, were hardening and becoming more hostile as a result of colonial expansion and the growth of an imperialist sensibility. The powerful combination of these two processes helped to entrench various forms of the racialised stereotypical Other and ensure their extensive influence. It is because of their enduring legacy that I want to concentrate on some of the racist stereotypes associated with European imperialism, but this should not be taken as a dismissal of other forms of racism which I do not discuss in what follows.

Pride of Race

Early in the twentieth century, the Secretary of the British Anthropological Society, T.A. Joyce, wrote that the 'negro' stood on 'a lower evolutionary plane than the white man', compared with whom he was 'mentally inferior' because of being 'more closely related to the highest anthropoids'. He was also without 'the restless energy which has led to the progress of the white race' (Joyce, 1910–11). Purveying an idea still current at the time, Joyce claimed that an arrested mental development was caused by hyper-sexuality – 'after puberty sexual matters take the first place in the negro's life and thoughts' – and this resulted in a mental outlook and constitution 'very similar to that of a child'. Here we have some of the stereotypical aspects of the black which had become commonplace during the Victorian period. Although some if not all of them have continued to resurface since then, sufficient time has passed since Joyce wrote for the racism underpinning them to seem very much dated. This is true even of the very term of classification used by Joyce, not to mention its entirely male ascription. What is perhaps more striking about these baseless racist slurs today is their appearance in an article written for the 11th edition of the *Encyclopedia Britannica*. Even more so perhaps than the identification of Joyce's place of work as the Department of Ethnography at the British Museum, their appearance in such a prestigious compendium of empirical world knowledge gave them an authoritative status, not to mention a wide readership, at the time this edition of the encyclopedia was published. This does not mean that their sense of authority would have gone entirely unquestioned, but it does mean that the assumptions on which Joyce's views were based were so much beyond question that they could appear in this imperial fount of knowledge in the first place. They were already part of the common sense of readers at that time. Indeed, they had gradually become so during the later nineteenth century and particularly during the period of 'high' imperialism, which was only beginning to draw to a close when Joyce wrote his scholarly article. I shall attempt to sketch the main ways in which they attained such legitimacy and broad consent in order to set out more clearly the historical context in which modern racist stereotypes developed. This is important because of the meanings and values they carry, for while contemporary 'culturalist' racism is clearly different in various ways, it is not clear how different it is from that of the Victorians and Edwardians, which was not in any case as uniform as is sometimes claimed or presumed.

The first such source of these racist stereotypes I want to touch on is what is now known as 'scientific' racism. While its beginnings can be traced to the later eighteenth century, 'scientific' racism only became widely popular from the mid-nineteenth century. A major advocate of pseudoscientific racism at this time was the first president of the Anthropological Society, Dr James Hunt. Joyce not only followed Hunt in this post, but also in his conception of the 'negro', as for instance in reiterating the stock notion of an arrested mental development after puberty (Hunt, 1863–64: see for example 11, 27, 49). The main source of Hunt's ideas about innate racial differences were the writings of Robert Knox, a Scottish anatomist who was already infamous for his connection with the Burke and Hare body-snatching scandal, involving the disinternment of recently buried corpses for medical dissection, even before he published his book *The Races of Man*. In it he declared that 'race is everything: literature, science, art – in a word, civilisation, depends on it ... Look all over the globe, it is always the same; the dark races stand still, the fair progress' (Knox, 1862: v; see also Biddis, 1976; and cf. Disraeli, 1927: 153: 'All is race; there is no other truth'). As for the 'dark races', he asked of the 'negro': 'Does he walk like us, think like us, act like us? Not in the least' (Knox, 1862: 243–4). More broadly, Knox created, according to Nancy Stepan, 'a racial fantasy in which Saxons, Celts, gypsies, Jews and the dark races of the world played out their biological destinies' (1982: 41), destinies of conflict with each other that were fixed in human nature. He even went further than this in openly, and chillingly, endorsing the extinction of 'lesser' and 'troublesome' races. In Curtin's view, Knox was 'the real founder of British racism' (1965: 377), although in view of the ubiquity of race-thinking among Victorians, the origins of post-slavery racism in Britain cannot be laid entirely at his door. The point here is that in following him, Hunt merely reproduced his ragbag of ideas while at the same time giving them wider publicity.

Pseudoscientific racism was not only developed in England. Developments in the biological sciences upon which such racism drew were cross-European. In close affinity with the claims of innate racial inferiority of Knox and Hunt were those based on similar anatomical studies made in France by Paul Broca, a friend of Hunt's and founding president of the Société d'Anthropologie de Paris. Broca was particularly concerned with racial miscegenation and hybridity (Broca, 1864), and his positivist school of ethnology had a considerable influence on French colonial policy and administration. As Patricia Lorcin has put it, Broca's society sought a 'metaphysical confirmation, through the scientific medium of anthropology, of a political fact', this being the existing structures of domination and subordination among the different peoples of the globe (Lorcin, 1995: 154). While social taboos against 'interbreeding' were also being rationalised by anthropological argument, this is an important link, for it was through anthropology's construction of primitivised 'dark races' that 'an explicit political power' presumed 'the authority of a scientific knowledge and vice versa' (Mudimbe, 1988: 15–16). During the early years of the society, however, Broca and his followers were politically cautious, partly because of a disapproving government (Clark, 1984: 20; see also Cohen, 1980: Chapter 8 for 'scientific' racism in France). In the English case, 'scientific' racism, with the Anthropological Society as its institutional front, was used for explicitly political purposes, especially in support of slavery and the Confederate cause in the American Civil War, and in defence of Governor Eyre's use of martial terror in suppressing the Jamaican insurrection of 1865.

It is important to note that many of the typological features identified in such racial categories as the 'negro' drew on already existing stereotypes or aspects of stereotypes which were then reinforced by the 'objectivity' attached to the 'advances' in human biology. The alleged inferiority of the 'dark races' was thus based on a mixture of new 'scientific' evidence, such as that from craniology and phrenology, and revived ideas, such as those of the philosopher John Locke, or his successor, David Hume, in the essay on national character which was noted in the previous chapter. In a footnote to that essay, Hume wrote that he was 'apt to suspect Negroes to be naturally inferior to the Whites', the reason for this being that, in his view, there had never been 'a civilised nation of that complexion' and that black people had developed no technology ('ingenious manufactures'), no science and no art (Hume, 1974: 213; cf. Hunt, 1863–64: 27). In the later eighteenth century, Edward Long had developed far more venomous views about black people, while at the same time giving to their expression a ring of what seemed to be scientific truth. Long was the first pseudoscientific racist as well as a leading advocate of the plantocratic system of slavery in British colonies. In addition to rehearsing pro-slavery propaganda, his influential *History of Jamaica* of 1774 had spread the notion that blacks were biologically distinct from Europeans, having derived from different human origins (the thesis of polygenesis) and being both physically and psychologically close to the animal kingdom. Yet Long was not 'unrepresentative of his time'. His opinions 'were not only public ideology in Jamaica and South Carolina, but were apparently acceptable to an influential minority in Europe' (Davis, 1970: 494–5). More recently, in 1853, Thomas Carlyle had published a notorious pamphlet asserting the superiority of Europeans and the duty that fell on black West Indians, because of their 'innate' racial inferiority, to serve their European masters (Carlyle, 1897). This view was said to have 'matched exactly the opinion of the Colonial Office' (Fryer, 1984: 172).

It was, then, this amalgam of old ideas and new evidence which was significant in the resurgence of racism, following the hiatus marked by the humanitarian and evangelical character of the anti-slavery movement. Certain aspects of black stereotypicality were reproduced by anti-slavery campaigners, but the advocacy of irreconcilable difference and conflict between unequal racial groups only returned after the mid-century, and then as a result of changed historical conditions. Its manifestation in a new form of biological determinism did not meet with a consistent reception, even within the professionalised scientific community. In discussion of the new 'scientific' racism, there were points of disagreement about evidence and degree of inferiority. Thomas Huxley thought of Hunt as a quack and referred to the Anthropological Society as a 'nest of imposters'. Darwin and Wallace likewise objected to Hunt's direction of the Society (Lorimer, 1978: 154, 158, and see 137–45, 148–59 for Hunt). Yet there was little dissent from belief in the validity of race as a determinate category. Racial division and hierarchy were regarded as incontestable. 'Virtually every scientist and intellectual in nineteenth-century Britain took it for granted that only people with white skin were capable of thinking and governing' (Fryer, 1984: 169).

Historians also place varying emphasis on the significance of 'scientific' racism, with Peter Fryer, for instance, describing it as 'the most important ingrediant in British imperial theory', while Douglas Lorimer takes a more circumspect view (ibid: 165; Lorimer, 1978: 144, 160–1). Lorimer suggests that its main influence was on professional men – in Walter Bagehot's phrase, the important ten thousand – and particularly those with aspirations to gentility and social exclusivity. Pride of race offered them what they desired – both a sense of superiority and of *noblesse oblige* 'regarding the protection and governance of the childlike, savage races' (ibid: 159). This may be rather overcautious. 'Scientific' racism was not confined to ethnology. Not only did it spread through various academic disciplines, thus advancing its institutionalisation; it also helped more broadly to corroborate the hostility to different ethnic groups already supported by the transmission of stereotypical views. These in themselves were the outward expression of a pathological fear of the Other.

'The irony of race-theories', as Jacques Barzun once noted, 'is that they arise invariably from a desire to mould other's actions rather than to explain facts' (1937: 284). In general terms, race as a dogma during the modern period has been 'dependent on the validation of a metaphysical concept of identity by "scientific" means and ultimately its vulgarisation into easily accessed images' (Lorcin, 1995: 143). There is no doubt that race attained hegemonic status as a rationale for cultural difference in the heyday of European imperialism and, significant though it was, this was not the result of 'scientific' racism alone. We need to look also at other sources of the development of racism. One of these, evolutionary thought, I have already outlined. Notions of 'lower species' and 'the progress of the white race' drew a good deal of support from such thought, which superseded and discredited the specific claims of comparative anatomy made by Knox, Hunt and their supporters, even though it carried forward and reinforced some of the central assumptions of 'scientific' racism. What was specific to social evolutionism was its explanation of social and cultural development in terms of natural selection. This was then applied in the racialised evaluative scale of 'savage' and 'civilised' societies which was noted in Chapter 2.

Social Darwinism conflated biological and historical accounts in attempting to prove that cultural difference is racially determined. The category of race was transposed to the 'survival of the fittest' schema of evolutionist thinking, with human diversity becoming necessarily reduced as certain races showed greater progress in the battle for survival (being of 'mixed race' was of no lasting consequence since hybridity was felt to lead to sterility – one of Broca's key conclusions). Social Darwinism advanced the view that certain 'races', and particularly those classed as 'negroid', were not as adequately equipped as whites in the struggle over environment and between peoples. The iron law of nature guaranteed the progress of civilisation. In this way Darwinism justified the exploitation of 'inferior' peoples, first through slavery in its prototypical forms, as in the plantocratic rationale, and then through colonialism and imperialism, where, in its distorted and adapted form following its more 'scientific' grounding, it provided 'an ideological prop for empire-building' (Fryer, 1984: 181). Its influence was considerable. To give just one instance of this, Benjamin Kidd's *Social Evolution* of 1894 sold 250,000 copies and 'caught the popular imagination with its praise of the "vigorous and virile" Anglo-Saxon race', against which weaker, 'inferior' races would die out (ibid: 180; and see Hobson, 1895/96 for a contemporary critique). There was nothing new in this presumption of inevitable decline and extinction in the face of racial superiority. Thomas Arnold, in the inaugural lecture cited in the previous chapter, believed that either this would occur – and occur it did with the colonised Aboriginal people of Tasmania – or that assimilation to the language, religion and social organisation of the dominant race would follow. There were no alternatives to these historical paths (1841: 27–41). This became a common view in the later nineteenth century, although with the emphasis increasingly falling on the former rather than the latter. The 'popular imagination' had, then, already been so caught, although Kidd no doubt consolidated for some what was already a growing conviction.

By the 1860s, the philanthropic and evangelical belief held earlier in the century that black people could (and should) be converted to Chris-

Figure 5.1   The servitude of black people naturalised by stereotyping is exploited in this advertisement from the late nineteenth century. The 'nigger' vernacular in the caption emphasises an inherent willingness to please the master, and by extension the British Empire, making this image an idealised version of white stereotypes of the black. The advert is a classic example of imperialist commodity racism in its exploitation of the association of skin colour with commercial product, a common selling ploy employed in relation with other commodities such as shoe polish, tobacco and lead blacking
(John Johnson Collection, Bodleian Library)

Figure 5.2   The specific happy-go-lucky stereotype of the black, intrinsically childlike in character and intellect, along with the more general idea of fixed racial characteristics, are both exploited in this New York advertisement for Payson's indelible ink
(O'Barr, 1994: 114)

tian values, and inducted into a civilised way of life, had considerably diminished. The image of the 'noble savage' had by then been reversed, with the image of the 'cruel savage' predominating. This was part of a hardening of racial attitudes, concomitant with a hardening of class attitudes, throughout the later nineteenth century. But the stereotypes were always contradictory. The 'primitive' black Other, as we have seen, was relegated to infantility on an evolutionary scale, with the white European at the opposite pole, in a position of rational, enlightened maturity. 'Savages' were considered equivalent to perpetual children, who needed to be paternally guided and ruled by 'civilised' whites. Sir Richard Burton (1860: 280) described the 'natives' of East Africa as 'one of those childish races'. David Livingstone spoke of his missionary subjects as 'merely children, as easily pleased as babies', and felt that in exploring African society, 'we are thrown back in imagination to the infancy of the world' (Schapera, 1960: 156). Albert Schweitzer believed that the 'negro is a child, and with children nothing can be done without authority' (1922: 130). The explorer John Hanning Speke (1863: xxx) declared that the average black in northern Africa possessed a 'wonderful amount of loquacity, great risibility, but no stability – a creature of impulse – a grown child, in short', and considered it best to treat 'him'

Figure 5.3   A picture postcard posted from Warrington, 9 February 1904. The absurdity of an African reading a newspaper, never mind forming an intelligent appraisal of its contents, is signified in his posture and broad grin. The stereotypical attribution of a childlike character is abundantly obvious
(author's personal collection)

with 'great forbearance, occasionally tinctured with a little fatherly severity'. Speke's understanding of this tincture of severity often meant a hundred or more lashes (Kiernan, 1972: 215), a sure cure for loquacity and risibility. Vicious cruelty of this kind was common, and it is chilling to read of what occurred, as for instance with the frequent use of the *chicotte* – a whip of sun-dried hippopotamus hide, cut into a long sharp-edged corkscrew strip – in the Belgian Congo under King Leopold II (Hochschild, 1999: 120–3). Such systems of punishment put the projection of barbaric aggression onto the 'primitive' Other in a wholly different light.

The inconsistency between the 'cruel' and 'infantile' aspects of the stereotype was rationalised by white authority and rule, for it was such rule that rescued black people from their 'barbarism' and turned them into deferential, compliant, childlike subjects, but the fear that they would conspire and revolt against their white masters always remained, breeding further fantasies of the grown blacks who white colonialists persisted in calling 'boys'. This view could easily turn into an analogy with social class and its hierarchical ordering of people by rank and status: 'the proponents of social inequality slipped all the more easily into racial rhetoric' (Biddis, 1979: 26–7). What permitted both the rationale and the analogy, making them both seem credible and true, were the inequalities running through the whole of English society.

> Europeans came from a society so permeated by class consciousness, and were so conditioned to the need of having social inferiors to look down on, that they were likely to magnify any analogous divisions in Africa, or to imagine them. (Kiernan, 1972: 214)

Inequality for many was natural and right. In the case of blacks both in America and in Africa, they were given, either by nature or by God, 'strong backs, weak minds, and a placid disposition' so that they could labour effectively under white direction (Curtin, 1960–63: 43). The stereotypes provided what seemed ample support for this orthodoxy. Difference, based on biological racialism, was the sign of inferiority and the source of inequality and, in the imperialist ideology of the late nineteenth-, early twentieth-century period, this way of thinking could be applied to class as well as ethnic position, with a simultaneous emphasis on heredity. In other words, the 'external' Other had its 'internal' counterpart within the nation, which is why the working class was sometimes referred to as 'another race' or 'a race apart'. This interplay of centre and periphery offers one reason, among others, why imperial history is central to understanding modern history more broadly.

Earlier in the chapter, I made the point that Victorian and Edwardian racism was not as uniform as it is sometimes represented. Over the period from the 1830s to the First World War, racist discourse was neither monolithic nor static. I have concentrated so far on tracing the ways in which forms of race-thinking became more solid after the mid-nineteenth century because of the significance of this in the development of the kinds of racist stereotypes which have subsequently endured, but it is important to emphasise that racism at this time was not all of a piece. In a recent essay, as well as in earlier work, Douglas Lorimer has highlighted the variation of opinions on race, and the tensions and contradictions in racial discourse, across the nineteenth century. In many ways, racism derived its potency from these ambivalences and contradictions in that it could adapt to changing contexts and its stereotypes encompass the inconsistencies and discontinuities in white people's views of other 'races'. The 'negro', for instance, was depicted as, among other things, lazy and capable of hard (manual) work, provident and profligate, sinner and patiently forbearing Christian, implacably merry and brutally vengeful. Lorimer notes that evangelicals considered Africans to be both natural Christians and unredeemable savages, whereas 'the advocates of the planting interest thought Negroes were lazy and profligate, yet particularly suited to vigorous physical labour in tropical climates' (1978: 203). Over the Victorian period the difference between various humanitarian causes such as the Aborigines Protection Society and the Anthropological Society, or gender distinctions in attitudes to race and racial supremacism, also show that racist discourse was not a singular or cohesive articulation of ideas, values and beliefs (Lorimer, 1996). Historically, what perhaps has made such discourse appear uniform is the undeniable entrenchment of racist attitudes and their stereotypical accompaniments during the second half of the nineteenth century, with a newly formulated insistence on an indissoluble inequality of races. This insistence on necessarily unequal 'races' was pivotal in the establishment of a deeply formed habit of seeing the world in racialised terms, so that by the early twentieth century, 'a generation had grown up in Europe which accepted without much question the basic racial hypothesis that humankind is divided irrevocably into fixed races' (Fyfe, 1992: 21).

Populist Racism

'Scientific' racism was itself a vulgarised form of knowledge, but the pervasiveness of racist views and attitudes in the nineteenth- and early twentieth-century periods owed more to its easily accessed images. Of greater significance in gaining the widespread acceptance of 'the basic racial hypothesis' were various populist forms of stereotyping. Racist and imperialist views were (in both senses of the term) articulated by journalists, artists, novelists, travel writers, historians, advertising copywriters, cartoonists and songwriters, as well as by scientists and intellectuals. Their ubiquity was such that they were commonplace in the visual images found on such ephemera as brand labels, postcards, alphabet books and cigarette cards. These images conveyed 'a distinct and consistent concept of ascendancy, Empire and military might' and 'evoked pride in imperial race', providing 'the self-confidence and self-conceit needed for world-wide mission' (MacKenzie, 1983: 4). In the remainder of this chapter, I want to discuss some examples of this spread of populist racism and its connections with empire in order to show more clearly how colonial and imperialist stereotypes became established, with their hold over people's perception and imagination lying both in the readily grasped reductiveness of their individual images, and in their underlying ambivalence and the general contradictions between them.

Fundamental to these qualities was the oscillation between the civilising ethos and the constantly reiterated notion of 'innate' racial inferiority as an insuperable obstacle to cultural adaptation on the part of 'native' subjects. This oscillation could occur between the racialised viewpoints of individual whites as they were inflected by greater or lesser degrees of optimism of outlook, but in the following example from the boy's story writer, G.A. Henty, it generates the movement of evaluative meaning from one sentence to its immediate successor:

> Living among white men, their imitative faculties enable them to attain a considerable amount of civilisation. Left alone to their own devices they retrograde into a state little above their native savagery. (1883: 118)

There, in a populist nutshell, is the justification of empire through the civilising mission. Without the ameliorating influence of 'white men', the 'natives' would revert to savagery; only under colonial rule and control could they be brought within the pale of civilisation. Yet note the underlying ambivalence: colonised 'natives' could actually only imitate their masters, and only attain a semblance of civility and order. Beneath this, the repressed 'savagery' always posed the threat of its return. It is this threat which John Buchan exploited in the opening chapter of his widely read novel, *Prester John*, which sees the transformation by night of the respected black clergyman, Rev. John Laputa, to 'a great savage' with 'a great knife', dancing naked round a fire as he practised 'black magic by the sea' (1910: 14). The French narratives of Aniaba and Zaga-Christ relate the same passage from civilised nobility to a debased 'état de nègre' (Miller, 1985: 32–9).

The writers of imperial adventure tales for male youth, the most prominent among them being Marryat, Kingston, Reid and Ballantyne, as well as Henty himself, reproduced in detail the Victorian stereotype of the black African. The characteristic representation was of black people's 'low' instinctual savvy and 'unphilosophic mind' (Reid, n.d.: 17), their live-for-today improvidence, their rudimentary social organisation, their cowardice combined with their irrational tendency to cruelty and violence, their laziness and duplicity and, above all, their childishness: 'The intelligence of an average negro is about equal to that of a European child of ten years old' (Henty, 1883: 117). As we have seen, missionaries, explorers and travellers told the same tale. And if juvenile readers of the 'ripping yarns' of empire did not believe what they were told of the 'native' African, they could always check it for accuracy by consulting the *Encyclopedia Britannica*.

These accounts of the child-like 'natives' of Africa were readily compatible with the happy-go-lucky Sambo figure found in children's books, blackface minstrelsy, imperial advertising and the commodity racism of empire merchandising (Forster, 1989; Pickering, 1997b and the references therein; McClintock, 1995: 207–31). Along with the supine Uncle Tom-type figure, and the faithful-unto-death servant stereotype of imperial fiction (such as those demeaningly named 'Caesar' and 'Quacko' in Henty's *The Fetish Hole*), this was the stereotype at its most desirable so far as whites were concerned, for the contented, jocular, simple-minded black, devoted to the 'massa', posed little threat. To quote again from Henty's *By Sheer Pluck*, 'native' Africans were 'good-natured and passionate, indolent, but will work hard for a time; clever up to a certain point, densely stupid beyond' (1883: 117). These stereotypical attributes drew on the long tradition of racialising the low-black Other, stretching as we have seen from Hume to Carlyle and beyond: Hume (1974: 213) had likened the 'imitative faculties' of the 'negro' to parrots, and this had been more recently endorsed by Winwood Reade (1872: 228).

Yet the stereotype was never monolithic. Its resilience in use was derived from its variable meanings. These could be drawn on as occasion and context required without their contradictions immediately springing back into mutual cancellation. While dark-skinned 'savages' were represented as 'by nature and instinct, very cruel', schoolboy heroes were usually attended with dogged fidelity by black servants who frequently rescue their masters from danger. The same heroes could also express admiration for the courage or even commanding presence of their 'savage' adversaries – in a Jack Harkaway story we are told of his 'thrill of admiration' for the villain's 'eminently dashing and handsome appearance' (James, 1973: 98). As with explorer narratives, the 'savage' stereotype could be undercut by the violent excesses of storybook white heroes, at least imparting a hint of equivocation to their otherwise gentlemanly representation. Traces of doubt may also have been left by the contradictions of common stereotypicality, as for instance in the way the black was both depicted as made for manual labour (in the interests of whites) but naturally hedonistic and lazy. When doubt is raised and then annulled, however, this reinforces the dominant or strategically deployed pattern. Its general representativeness offset the contradictions between different stereotypes, as for instance in the dominant view that without white discipline, 'negroes' were 'naturally' hedonistic and would do only what was necessary for subsistence living. Fletcher and Kipling's widely sold school textbook bore this out by declaring that the prosperity of the West Indies, 'once our richest possession', had declined since the abolition of slavery in 1833 because the black population were, by nature, 'lazy, vicious, and incapable of any improvement'. They were 'quite happy and quite useless', being unwilling to work any more than necessary for the 'few bananas [which] will sustain the life of the negro quite sufficiently' – exactly the premise of Carlyle's specious response to the Caribbean 'nigger question' sixty years or so before (Fletcher and Kipling, 1911: 186, 245).

The white heroes of juvenile popular literature were diametrically opposite in kind, and not only in their 'aristocracy of character' (Smiles, 1911: 449). These gallant adventurers manfully tamed the wild recesses of the world with their pluck, propriety and fair play, their public school ethos and sense of derring-do, and so built the British Empire. They were the strike force, leading the van in the drive to realise the vision of Dilke, Seeley, Chamberlain and the like of a 'Greater Britain' of settler colonies. As a school textbook of 1907 put it:

Well done, Gallant
little Mafeking
The Empire is proud of you

INVESTED OCT. 11ᵗʰ 1899.
RELIEVED MAY 17ᵗʰ 1900.

BADEN·POWELL.

Figure 5.4   Stereotypical British pluck is the basis for this
postcard celebration of the Relief of Mafeking in 1900
(Carline, 1971: 80)

> Of colonies in the real sense of the word, the only ones of importance belong to Britain. They are Canada, Australia, New Zealand and South Africa, which serve as outlets for our surplus population ... Every year they are more and more becoming real 'Britains' over the seas. (cited in Glendenning, 1973: 33)

Other parts of Africa were a rather different colonial prospect, since they involved rule over black people more than the administration of settler society, but in all cases white ascendancy was felt to be guaranteed. To quote Peterkin in Ballantyne's *Coral Island*: 'Of course, we'll rise, naturally, to the top. White people always do in savage countries' (cited in Dixon, 1977: 85).

Imperial heroes in an age of hero-worship combined the self-help ethos and a strident individualism with patriotic racism and a militaristic masculinity. They were both a brasher, more secular version of the earlier, evangelising spirit of Sunday School 'improving' tales, and a smoother, more conformist version of the roisterous, swashbuckling toughs of the 'penny dreadfuls'. From the latter, they extended, as a spice of common appeal, the romance of adventure, and from the former they extended, in an appeal to a common denominator, the sense of 'moral character' which fed directly into British national identity during the later nineteenth-century period of 'prestige imperialism'.

Above all, the imperial heroes represented an anti-intellectual, public-school athleticism, traces of which were still manifest in the 1950s and

"While we were rolling together my faithful coxswain rushed in."

Figure 5.5　British derring-do. Stereotypes of 'savage' violence and treachery and white martial manliness are brought together in this illustration for a late Victorian ripping yarn
(*Boy's Own Paper*, 1 May 1880)

early 1960s in British schools (James, 1973: 96–7; Mangan, 1981: 217–18). This was displayed across the board, from any of Henty's heroes to Buchan's Richard Hannay and Sapper's Bulldog Drummond. Another Sapper hero, Derek Vane, epitomises the stereotype in his personal conceit and national chauvinism, regarding his own country 'as being the supreme country in the world', in his miniscule knowledge of art, literature and music and suspicion of intelligent talk about them, in his bluff, no-nonsense directness – shaking your hand as a man shakes it, meeting your eye as a man meets it – and in his general sporting prowess, with his predilections for golf, horseriding, polo and shooting declaring a definite class orientation and position: 'He belonged, in fact, to the Breed; the Breed that has always existed in England, and will always exist to the world's end' (Sapper, 1919: 42–3). Here, class, race and gender are combined in an absolute hierarchical linkage that is characteristic of empire fiction. In his own novels, Henty intended his male heroes to be exemplary agents of what the Reverend J.E.C. Welldon, headmaster of Harrow, had in 1899 called 'the divinely ordered mission of their country and race' (Wilkinson, 1964: 102), a mission whose spirit was considered to be incarnate in such household names as Gordon, Wolseley, Havelock, Livingstone, Kitchener, and Baden-Powell. So, for instance, Yorke Haberton, in *With Roberts to Pretoria*, was

> a good specimen of the class by which Britain has been built up, her colonies formed, and her battle-fields won – a class in point of energy, fearlessness, the spirit of adventure, and a readiness to overcome all difficulties, unmatched in the world. (Henty, 1902: 16)

The anti-intellectualism of Henty's 'good fellows' is summed up by the one word 'pluck', a quality advanced as the positive obverse of love of learning, bookishness and academic inquiry, the preserve of weaklings and milksops:

> Give me a lad with pluck and spirit, and I don't care a snap of the finger whether he can construe Euripedes or solve a problem in higher mathematics … What do the natives care for our learning? It is pluck and fighting power that have made us their masters. (Henty, 1894:30; MacKenzie, 1985: 209–12, 219–20)

The huge popularity of Henty's novels helped to spread this conception of racial and imperial pride throughout the British Empire. As the introduction to a 1910 edition of *Robinson Crusoe* has it, it was 'Britons who ... have by pluck and perseverance planted colonies all the world over, and turned howling wildernesses into regions of prosperity and plenty' (cited in Pennycook, 1998: 11; cf. Layton-Henry, 1984: 4–5).

Unsurprisingly, Henty's novels were without what used to be called a 'love interest'. According to his biographer, Henty

> had a horror of a lad who displayed any weak emotion and shrank from shedding blood, or winced at any encounter ... There was nothing namby-pamby in Henty's writings. [He] ... never made his works sickly by the introduction of ... the tender passion. (Fenn, 1907: 321, 324)

Henty's novels extolled a world steeped in the stereotypicality of white masculinism. Thus, the 'best thing that could be said about a girl was that she had all the virtues of a boy' (Huttenback, 1965–66: 70). The martial manliness of character and bearing of their white English heroes were part of the broader construction of a repressive masculine identity, built at the intersection of race, gender, class and empire, and deeply distrustful of any involuntary show of feeling as indicative of not only feminine but also racial and cultural weakness. Masculine identity of this kind was widely encountered – the explorer Henry Morton Stanley, made famous for his discovery of Livingstone, is a classic example.

As Jonathan Rutherford (1997) has recently argued, this identity was characterised by a psychologically troubled relationship to maternal love and the figure of the mother, by narcissism and emotional arrest, by varying elements of nationalism and racism, and by deep-seated notions of self-sacrifice. He discusses these aspects of white imperialist masculinity as they were manifest, in variably individual ways, by Rupert Brooke, T.E. Lawrence and Enoch Powell. The sort of masculinity they exhibited had considerable influence over white male sexuality, identity and behaviour during the later nineteenth and early twentieth centuries, particularly in its disidentification with domesticity, its polarisation of masculinity and femininity, its repression of 'weak' emotion and 'the tender passion', and its deeply ambivalent attitude to mother–son relationships. A narcissistic splitting and displacement of confused and unacceptable feelings in this austere form of manliness was manifest as well in a devout attachment to imperialism and war, and a projection of these displaced feelings onto the racialised Other.

Powellism was among the most notable of several last desperate attempts, during the postwar period, to conjure the the phoenix of English nationalism out of the ashes of imperialism, and to recombine nationalism with racist hostility and hatred, and never in a more ill-judged moment than his anti-immigrant 'rivers of blood' speech of April 1968 in Birmingham. While few Conservative politicians openly espoused his political values, they exerted a considerable, shadowy influence on immigration control, institutional racism and the revival of a model of gendered nationalism that was manifest in the 1982 Falklands/Malvinas War. This model was developed during the period of 'high' British imperialism, and the confidence of its reassertion was derived from 'two interdependent forms of essentialism' based on a social Darwinist conception of the immutable being of the nation, and the stereotypical divisions of gender between mother and soldier (Dawson, 1994: 12). Hence Thatcher could claim, in her 'victory speech', that 'the lesson of the Falklands is that Britain has not changed and that this nation still has those sterling qualities which shine through our history'. She went on, in a collective identification of the nation with imperial manhood:

> This generation can match their fathers' and grandfathers' abilities, in courage, and in resolution. We have not changed. (Barnett, 1982: 153)

During the war, the ghosts of stereotypical martial manliness rode through the national media's support for 'our boys'. Graham Dawson rightly comments that military victory in the Falklands 'gave Powell's archaic essentialisms a renewed lease of life, a fresh charge of emotional energy' through which 'an essentialist conception of masculinity was reinstated as a powerful component in the contemporary repertoire of British nationalism' (Dawson, 1994: 15). During the Thatcher years, Powellism also fed a populist orientation into the reconstitution of an 'authentically' white, English national identity against which the black presence in England was posed as a problem and a threat (Gilroy, 1987: 47–8).

As we have seen, nationalism's articulation of people as putatively the 'same together' is a selective unity, generally based on male gender power, and male-oriented narratives and symbols of historical lineage and (mother)land, with women figured as 'inherently atavistic – the conservative repository of the national archaic', as opposed to men's embodiment of 'the forward-thrusting agency of national progress' (McClintock, 1995: 359–60). It is in the light of this that we should recognise the particular form of martial masculinity identified and analysed by Rutherford as, for all its pervasiveness, still a particular strand of *classed* masculinity. Its embodiment was predominantly middle and upper-middle class. The degree and reach of its influence, and representativeness in class or trans-class terms, requires further historical examination. Likewise, its historical analysis requires a more cautious, less generalised application of psychoanalytic theory than is, for instance, shown in Rutherford's rather opportunistic reading of Henty's *With Kitchener in the Sudan* (Rutherford, 1997: 30–2). Such application occasionally becomes strained – as for instance when we are told that the 'narratives of pastoralism, the paganistic celebration of communion with nature, were fuelled by the elusive quality of the phallus' (ibid: 63) – or too easily used as an off-the-peg interpretive device. Despite the symbolic analogies drawn from it, national and imperialist power cannot be reduced to an outward projection of family life, as with the Lacanian Law of the Father, where metaphoric authority suggests an unmediated structural relation.

Although the application of metapsychological theory to historical interpretation has its difficulties, I am not suggesting that it does not have its rewards. Graham Dawson, for instance, draws constructively on Melanie Klein's theoretical work in his analysis of such British soldier heroes as Havelock and T.E. Lawrence, while Frank McClynn draws more specifically on her theory of exploration in addressing the psycho-pathology of Britain's most famous African explorers: Speke, Burton, Stanley and Livingstone (Dawson, 1994; McLynn, 1993: Chapter 16). This works well in revealing the repressed and troubled mentalities of these heroic figures of Britain's imperialist history, some aspects of which connect with those examined among their succeeding generation by Rutherford. Speculative appraisal is always to a degree necessary in developing historical understanding, and at times it can be genuinely illuminating, but equally caution needs to be exercised in applying a priori templates designed to cover common patterns, which are all too easily asserted, whether this is the psychology of fascism, sexuality, nostalgia, or whatever. The danger is of leaping into transhistorical generalisation without first looking into the specificities of people, place and period.

A similar caveat applies to how we treat the mutual affinity of racism and empire. Jose Harris has suggested that, for Britain, 'imperial dominion lent credence to widely disseminated assumptions about the superiority of British institutions and the British race' far more powerfully than 'any explicit racial ideology' (1993: 6). Moreover, Victorian racism did not exist in a direct causal relationship to imperialism and colonial policy. It should not be seen simply as their *ex post facto* endorsement, but rather as centrally informing them and functioning as their 'variable though invaluable adjunct' (Bolt, 1984: 146–7). Particularly in the late nineteenth-century period of 'conscious imperialism', racism closely complemented the imperialist project, for, in Lord Rosebery's rhetorical question, 'what is Empire but the predominance of race?'

(1900: 32). In Curtin's neat summary: 'the golden age of racism was the golden age of the Imperial idea' (1960–63: 40). Yet summaries do not cover the specificities of colonial rule and imperialist ideology, as for instance is shown by Patricia Lorcin's detailed study of the Kabyle myth in Algeria. Algeria was a French colony from 1830 to 1962, first under military and then civilian rule. During this period the French viewed what was actually an ethnically diverse population in terms of a dichotomy between Arabs and Berbers, a mythical binary overlaid with a socio-geographic one of Arabs as nomadic plain-dwellers and Berbers as sedentary mountain-dwellers. The Manichean distinction between these peoples was an assimiliationist device of divide-and-rule colonial politics in that the positively viewed Berbers – and especially the blond Kabyles – were considered, through a three-way comparison, as being closer to the French, whereas as the negatively viewed Arabs were perceived to be culturally more distant and so less amenable to influence from *la mission civilisatrice*. The doctrine of assimilation in French colonial theory gave way to that of association (see Betts, 1961), but this did not substantially affect the Arab/Berber racialised dichotomy in French thinking, being informed as it was by a hostile view of Islam, which was inextricably linked to the Arabs and to its underlying moral themes of 'licentiousness, deceit, indolence, violence, intransigence and immutability'. The Kabyle, by contrast, were described by a member of the Société d'Anthropologie de Paris, in equivalent terms of moral stereotypicality, as 'active, hardworking, honest, dignified, open-minded, and good humoured', with 'elevated sentiments of equality, honour, human dignity and justice'. In other words, the 'exact opposite … to the physiological type of the Arab'. Seen in this way, the attempted co-option of the Kabyles occurred precisely because they were constructed in the mould of Western middle-class virtues and advanced as a means of promoting them in the interests of colonial order and control (Lorcin, 1995: 2–3, 63, 157, 237; see also Ageron, 1968: 267–92, and Lane, 2000, Chapters 4 and 5 for a recent assessment of Bourdieu's celebrated work on Kabylia).

The case of colonial Algeria supports a general argument in this book. The nineteenth-century conviction of European superiority engendered a methodological procedure of contrast and comparison, using nationalist norms at the centre as the evaluative yardstick for conceiving and assessing the peoples of the periphery, sometimes in stark 'them' and 'us' terms, but at others in a triangulating movement that divided colonial subjects according to racialised patterns of similarity and dissimilarity. As Lorcin herself points out, however, in the end 'the racial dialectic can only function within the framework of a positive/negative juxtaposition' (ibid: 196). In the later nineteenth century, the insurrection of the Kabyles, the growth of settler society and the development of the myth of a new Latino-Mediterranean race emerging from the 'melting pot' of settler Algeria, shifted this dialectic to one between European settlers and the *indigène*. Yet Kabyle/Arab stereotypes, anti-Islamic prejudice and racial ideas continued to inform the settlers' outlook. Further propagation of the Kabyle myth, Arab/Berber opposition and the denigratory 'othering' of Islamic social institutions was accomplished and made more powerful through popular fiction (ibid: 218–21). These elements of colonial myth-making have left an enduring legacy, becoming part of the historical memory of both coloniser and colonised, even in post-independence Algeria. For the French, historical use of the racially suffused, negative Arab stereotype as a subliminal Other, originally to reinforce republican values as well as Christian prejudices and colonial interests, continues to exert a strong influence, remaining as a major stumbling-block in prevalent attitudes to Islam (ibid: 233, 243–5; also Cohen, 1980: 256–7).

Cartographies of Unbelonging

This Orientalist stereotype was common in Britain as well, as for instance in imperial fiction where the Arab was generally represented as venal and treacherous, or in contemporary media representations of Islam as a fanatical religion, calling up images of 'bearded clerics and mad suicidal bombers', unrelenting mullahs and 'remorseless turbaned crowds who chant hatred' (Said, 1988: 47, 1985a: 108; Lessing, 1987: 64). Spurred on by response to the Iranian Revolution, the repercussions of such portrayals were readily apparent in the 1990s in the anti-Muslim backlash that followed the Rushdie affair and the Gulf War (Salt, 1998). But populist racism was applied to peoples and cultures encountered in empire-building around the globe as a way of positioning them, across temporalised space, in cartographical relations of symbolic unbelonging to the imperial centre and civilisational present. While the stereotypical mapping of patterns of unbelonging drew on various binary oppositions of Self and Other, it is important to keep in mind the ambivalences and contradictions which ran through them in their mediation of imperial and colonial structures of authority and power. It is now a truism that constructions of the racialised Other tell us more about the imperial centre, about social structures and cultural relations at the heart of empire, than about those at the anachronistic peripheries. In noting this, we should remember that despite the varied ideological strategies for 'fixing' the imperialist Other, spatially and temporally, peripheral unbelonging was itself symbolically variable, and always historically situated, relative to circumstances and context and so subject to change and development over time.

In the final part of this chapter, I want to look briefly at two specific British constructs of peripheral unbelonging and the stereotypical notions around which they were built. The first, China and the Chinese, were geographically far away, and while, apart from the forcefully ceded island of Hong Kong, never colonised by settlement or conquest, were nevertheless subject to Britain's imperial power through coercive trade and military intervention. They were a component of informal empire and their placing in the symbolic cartography of unbelonging was attendant on this. The second, Ireland and the Irish, were geographically close at hand, and for this reason were for a long time not considered in terms of the imperial relation. Ireland was nevertheless an 'internal colony' on the fringe of Victorian Britain (Hechter, 1975), and during the Victorian period the Irish became subject to a process of racialised 'othering' that distanced and dissociated them just as much as if they were far away and utterly alien. In the cross-relations of peripheral unbelonging, the near and far symbolically collapse into each other.

As we have seen, Henty's views on race and empire were predominantly expressed in adventure romances located in places of colonial settlement and conquest. He nevertheless reserved some of his most unpleasant imperialist stereotypes for the Chinese. Although in one of his last books he acknowledged British provocation in the Boxer Rebellion, his racism remained strident: the Chinese were 'treacherous and cruel brutes' (Arnold, 1980: 73). A few writers created relatively sympathetic Chinese characters, E. Harcourt Burrage's Ching Ching, who at one time rivalled Harkaway for popularity, being perhaps the most notable (James, 1973: 97). But wily cunning, insular secrecy, a deceitful nature, an inveterate compulsion to steal, and a bestial cruelty were the more usual features of the 'John Chinaman' stereotype that developed during the later nineteenth and early twentieth centuries. This stereotype developed out of the stage Chinaman of Victorian melodrama, a sinister character with pigtail and drooping moustache, into the Oriental male 'of popular twentieth-century imagination': 'a ruthless, cunning, sabre-toothed, slant-eyed yellow devil, ready to knife anyone in the back' (Barr, 1970: 121). Chinese stereotypes in the West have operated largely through the strategy of blaming the victim, and through the promotion of self-fulfilling fantasies. Both became possible and achievable because of the general lack of knowledge available about the Celestial Empire.

In British school textbooks of the early twentieth century, for example, accounts of Chinese history were worse than threadbare, concentrating on only three recent events, all involving the British themselves: the Opium Wars of 1839–42 and 1856–60, and the Boxer Rebellion of 1900. The Opium Wars were blamed on the Chinese not only because of their 'craft and perfidy' (Glendenning, 1973: 39), but also because their supposed cultural stagnation and introspective anti-foreignism were felt to stand untenably in the path of progress. It was yet another case of Methuselah confronting Marconi – with 'inactivity' needing to give way to 'activity'. What schoolbooks neglected to explain was that the Chinese confiscation of British opium, which led to military retaliation and the occupation of Chinese ports, had been brought about by a continual disregard of the Chinese ban on the import of opium, the huge increase in the number of addicts in China in the early nineteenth century, and the damaging effects of the trade on the Chinese economy. The Chartists had argued that the opium traffic was not a legitimate component of the comity of nations, but this view did not prevail. The treaty which followed Chinese defeat ceded Hong Kong and other major ports to Britain, while ill-judged attempts to repair the Chinese economy in order to pay huge indemnities to the British and compensate for the loss of customs revenue led to the Taiping Rebellion and further British intervention, with massive slaughter of the rebel army. From the 1870s, ensuing poverty among the Chinese peasantry created the conditions for the nefarious 'coolie trade' – a system of indentured cheap labour that recruited Chinese for work in British colonies and led to a diasporic spread of Chinese people around the world. As with the brutal exploitation of black manual labour, the stereotype ran in the opposite direction to reality: 'The coolies are shiftless and stupid, they prefer opium and sleep to dollars' (Ehrenberg, 1976: 52).

This, in brief outline, was the backdrop to the construction of the 'yellow peril' menace, sketched in textbooks very much from the British perspective of how the Chinese 'were brought to their senses' (Glendenning, 1973: 39). The 'yellow peril' scare itself did not usually surface in school texts or juvenile literature, but was given paranoid expression in press attention to the Chinatowns of London and Liverpool, with their mysterious 'opium dens' seeming to threaten a retributive contagion, turning imperial trade back on its perpetrators and subverting British identity from within. The spectre of opium use in the heartland of empire condensed anxieties about racial stock and the sapping of discipline and self-control held to be vital to the 'national character', with so-called tainted or fallen women being the weak link leading to an insidious Orientalisation and an 'unclean spirit of imitation', as Dickens melodramatically staged it in the opening pages of his final, unfinished novel (Dickens, 1961: 9). The same stereotypical elements were still there, fifty years later, in the Limehouse narrative of D.W. Griffith's film *Broken Blossoms* (1919), and of course they endured over most of the twentieth century. At stake in the myth of the 'yellow peril' was not only the dread of miscegenation, vice and crime as associated with the racist stereotype of the 'cunning and artful Chinaman' – the evil feared in the heart of that 'darkness of semi-barbarism', to cite the description of the Chinese offered by one late nineteenth-century apol-

A MALAY.

Figure 5.6 An opium-smoking Malay, portraying the sinister danger and threat of the Orient. Although dressed similarly in a loincloth, he is in marked contrast to the iconic picture of the crucifixion pinned to the wall ('A Night in an Opium Den', *Strand Magazine*, 1891, 1: 91)

Figure 5.7   Orientalist degeneration in the heartland
of empire: Engraving of the opium den which
Dickens wrote about in Edwin Drood
(Doré and Jerrold 1872)

ogist for empire (Wyatt, 1897: 518; see also Berridge, 1978: 14). The myth also purveyed intimations of 'a possible inversion of colonial dynamics' and 'the economic power relations that largely demarcate[d] the centre and periphery of the empire'. It was this which gave rhetorical force to the contemporary characterisation of the 'yellow peril' as 'the plague spreading and attacking our vitals' (Milligan, 1995: 83, 100).

The groundless fabrication of this moral panic amplified its affective force. It was this which Sax Rohmer exploited when he created the stereotypical Oriental villain of Fu Manchu. In diabolically personifying the 'yellow peril', Fu Manchu symbolically focused three racial fears: Asian mastery of Western knowledge and technique, 'occult' Oriental powers, and mobilisation of 'the yellow hordes' (Oehling, 1980: 204). As arch-villain, he provided a foil for the upper-class English hero, Sir Denis Nayland-Smith. The narratively preferred identification with his 'Western acumen pitted against Eastern cunning' was then used 'to convince the audience of the necessity of Empire as the sole guarantee of security' (Clegg, 1994: x, 1–5). Calls for security against 'the yellow hordes' were the outer response to fantasies of miscegenation, with sexual aggression against white women acting metaphorically for the racial threat posed to Western culture by the demonised Other (Hoppenstand, 1983: 174; Marchetti, 1993, Chapters 2–4; Xing, 1998: 55). The strategy of blaming the victim by stigmatising him in self-fulfilling fantasies was reversed in the non-threatening stereotype of the 'good' Asian, perhaps most famously personified by the 'inscrutable' Oriental detective, Charlie Chan. Chan himself was 'devoid of all the traditional masculine qualities associated with Anglo-American males', and has been compared to the 'house nigger' stereotype of African-Americans: patient, submissive, accommodating and feminised (Kim, 1982: 18; Chen, 1996: 62–3; Xing, 1998: 61–2). Like many other racialised stereotypes, the feminised image of Asian men in Western media has its roots in the nineteenth century, from which time it has involved the double articulation of sexist and racist discourses, with symbolic emasculation serving to reproduce ideas of male gender superiority.

Beginning with the musical, *Flower Drum Song* (1961), a more recent variation of the Chan genre has been the 'model minority' narrative image of the Chinese as humble, quiet and successful, an image grounded in white paternalism. Contemporary negative stereotyping continues alongside this in highly selective, sensationalised press coverage involving gangs, extortion, gambling, drugs and crime, in lurid exposés such as Martin Booth's *The Triads* (1990), and in such filmic representations as *Dr No* (1962) or *The Year of the Dragon* (1985). How such stereotyping structures and informs occidental perceptions and attitudes has not been much studied, although Shi-xu's recent examination of the language of cultural representations turns a neat trick in examining how Chinese expatriate academics in the Netherlands think about the Dutch, and how Dutch visitors to China write about the people, places and cultures of China in the travel literature they produce. Shi-xu (1997) is doubly concerned with the ways in which discursive strategies and processes contribute to the construction of the psychological interior, and with the social purposes and consequences of such discursive constructions of mental representations. Talk about self and subjectivity is integral to social process and social relations, and the travel talk and texts he analyses reveal this in the particular cultural Self and Other issues they raise. The talk was generated through informal interviews with Chinese academics working in the Netherlands, which were conducted in Chinese, while the texts are taken from recent Dutch travel literature on China. Evaluation of the cultural Other in informal interviews with Chinese expatriates tends to be mainly positive, whereas in recent Dutch travel writing the balance tilts the other way. Shi-xu's analysis shows how Dutch travel discourse works generally to elevate Dutch/European/Western identity over and above the Chinese and Chinese self-defined identity, with the cultural Other thus becoming excluded, stigmatised and patronised.

These distinctions bear the traces of nineteenth-century processes of racialisation to which the Irish were also subject in order to dissociate and symbolically exclude them from mainstream British society. The 'wildness' with which the Irish were associated, and the social degradation with which 'Irishness' became synonymous, were ways of casting them into the moral wilderness at a time when their manual labour was being increasingly exploited on the mainland, in the docks, rail and building construction, and domestic service, and when, within Ireland itself, a nationalist movement and more positive cultural identity were being fostered, and social and political unrest was increasing. 'Britishness' (orderly, respectable, advanced, superior) and 'Irishness' (disorderly, debased, backward, inferior) became starkly opposed on the grounds of what were considered innate and immutable racial characteristics. The Irish were increasingly caricatured as ugly and ape-like, content to live in social squalor and prone to drunkenness and violence. As with the Chinese, references were made to 'hordes' of Irish threatening to swamp the country. Particularly after the famine of 1845–47 when hundreds of thousands of Irish peasants were forced to migrate, the peripatetic requirements of much of their low-paid work in Britain lay behind this fear, and supported the opposition between their 'rootless' outsiderness and respectable settlement. In Jim Mac-Laughlin's words, as '"masterless vagabonds" it was feared that they might

TWO FORCES.

Figure 5.8   'Two Forces': Irish primitivism and British civilisation. In this cartoon by Sir John Tenniel (1820–1914), Britannia stands firm, planting the Sword of the Law between her and wild, anarchical Ireland, while throwing a protective arm around a cowering Hibernia (*Punch*, 29 October 1881)

go on the loose and create havoc in the very heart of Victorian society', a fear articulated in an 1884 *Report on Poor Removal* which described the Irish as flooding into England with 'pestilence on their backs, and famine in their stomachs' (MacLaughlin, 1999: 57–8). The image of a flood or deluge, offered in terms of a natural disaster, has continued into our own day as a key means of representing migrant flows in the British media (Philo and Beattie, 1999: 181–4). Migration remains a 'threat', exciting general anxiety and fear.

Anti-Irish racist stereotyping, and the core–periphery antinomy which it supported, was not only an expression of such fear. It was also politically mobilised as a way of underwriting the 'unfreeness' of Irish manual labour, the racialised condition of their proletarian status, their relegation to the edges of mainstream society, and state restrictions on their upward mobility (MacLaughlin, 1999: 65). The attributes of such stereotyping closely resembled those associated with Africans in Victorian Britain – childlike, ignorant, sensual, slothful, garrulous, affectionate, excitable and so on – and because of this were found either funny or fearful according to whichever facet of the contradictory stereotypical features were contextually brought into view. The notion of arrested maturity was a similarity in both stereotypes: Fletcher and Kipling's school textbook, for example, referred to the Irish as 'spoilt children' (MacKenzie, 1985: 195) while Mr Punch referred to 'their blighted, stunted forms' and 'brassy, cunning, brutalised features' (Lebow, 1976: 40). Both Africans and the Irish were described as the 'missing link'. Along with the African, the Irish were simianised, being dubbed 'white chimpanzees' by Charles Kingsley (1977:107); classified by Dr John Beddoe, President of the Anthropological Society of London and author of *The Races of Britain* (1885), as 'Africanoid' in their 'jutting jaws' and 'long slitty nostrils' (Curtis, 1971: 13, 119–21; see also Szwed, 1975: 20); and depicted in cartoons as lower-level hominoids in such periodicals as *Punch, Puck, Harper's* and *The Atlantic*. In one cartoon, reproduced by Anne McClintock, an Irish couple are both given ape-like facial features while the scene in which they are portrayed signifies 'the very picture of domestic disarray'. McClintock suggests that this iconography of domestic degeneracy was generally deployed in order to mediate 'the manifold contradictions in imperial hierarchy', with signs of degeneracy linking racial, class and gender categories in a 'switchboard analogy' with each other, and where, as in the case of the Irish, chromatic differences were not available for stereotypical denigration, serving to place those thus linked at their lowermost ranking on the threshold of the racialised divide between white and black 'races' (1995: 52–6).

Figure 5.9   The 'white chimpanzee' stereotype of the Irish is starkly
portrayed in Frederick Opper's cartoon. The simian analogy
between Africans and the Irish is underscored by the title of
this cartoon: 'The King of A Shantee'
(*Puck*, 15 February 1882, 10: 258)

This makes for a fitting point on which to conclude this chapter, for
while I have concentrated mainly on racist stereotyping in order to show
that its roots lie in the power structures and relations established by
empire, it is important to stress that the stereotypes of this kind which
we have inherited from the late nineteenth and early twentieth centuries,
as for instance with relation to Irish Catholics, were not developed in
isolation from other social categories. Indeed, race-thinking at that time
informed how these other categories were considered, with racial classifications themselves operating as points of metaphorical crossover
between them, particularly with respect to class, status and gender. We
shall see in more detail what this involved in the next chapter.

Figure 5.10   A more recent cartoon satirising
Irish and other forms of stereotyping
(Campaign for Free Speech on Northern Ireland,
The British Media and Northern Ireland, 1979: 33)

Chapter 6

The Politics of Postcolonial Critique

*Modern thought and experience have taught us to be sensitive to
what is involved in representation, in studying the Other, in racial
thinking, in unthinking and uncritical acceptance of authority and
authoritative ideas, in the sociopolitical role of intellectuals, in the
great value of a sceptical critical consciousness.*

EDWARD SAID, 1985a: 327

East by Not East

As we saw towards the end of the previous chapter, around the late nineteenth and early twentieth centuries, the myth of the 'yellow peril' made
a classic Other of China, turning the victim of British merchants, military forces and missionaries into the evil and cunning aggressor. Opium
figured as the symbolic key to this threat of retributive contagion
through its connections with exogamous sex, crime, occultism and a
downward spiral of social decay and racial degeneration. As Andrew
Blake has noted, this was a clear case of moral transposition. Evil lay 'in
the "heart of darkness", and not in the heart of the Europeans, unless
(and this is a perpetual danger) they came to be corrupted by it' (1996:
251). From the troubled dreams of de Quincey to the villains of imperialist fiction, the danger of that corruption was shown to be ever-
present, or at least was seen to have been so in retrospect, for it was only
through the Victorian period that an increasing emphasis on the danger
marked a gradual turnaround in attitude from the admiration of Asiatic
civilisation that had existed in the eighteenth century (for de Quincey,
see Lindop, 1981 and Barrell, 1991). The incarnation of that danger in
Fu Manchu and his various successors in popular fiction and film then
reverberated throughout the twentieth century in images of corruption,

147

cunning and cruelty. Along with this kind of oriental figure there developed a stereotypical view of China as socially stagnant, despotic and lacking in disciplined rationality, a view which left unexplained the clear evidence of Chinese scientific development and technological ingenuity and change.

The strategic distancing, projection and transposition represented by the 'yellow menace' discourse provides a particular example of Orientalism. This is a term used to identify a long history and a huge accumulation of mythical representations of the East by the West. The long history begins with the Crusades, and the first clash of European Christianity with Islam. The mythical representations begin with occidental visions of the Orient as a place of darkness where exoticism and barbarism were inextricably mixed together. Whether it was China or the Middle East that was the object of attention, Orientalism was an intellectual and aesthetic response to the East grounded in Western culture, and only ostensibly dealing with its subject. Orientalism was constructed in the interests of a civilisational self-image which was elevated to a position of superiority by its dichotomous contrast with the East. The essentialised conception of the East in Orientalism operated with a particular regime of stereotypical figures and notions, the aim of which was to make Europe and Asia appear to be fundamentally different from each other.

The Orientalist regime of the stereotype which I want to focus on in this chapter is that which developed from the later eighteenth century onwards, as a way of trying to understand what was being newly encountered in a world opening up to western European expansion. Oriental stereotypes emerged as an attempt to control, through a unifying fixity of image, what was diverse and unfamiliar. Their recurrent images of an Eastern Other also defined Europe and the West through their provision of a contrasting idea and experience (Said, 1985a: 1–2). Along with a general irrationalism and backwardness, the stereotypical regime which emerged, in literary and pictorial representations, included corrupt and irrational despotism, fanatic religiosity, exotic mysticism, teeming markets and dreamy harems, sexually predatory and insatiable men, and sensual, decadent and devious women. As with other racially generated stereotypes, those associated with Orientalism can have a positive face, as for example when exotic mysticism is transmuted into the benign transcendental spirituality of Eastern wisdom, but in either case they tend to exaggerate East/West differences as absolute and unchanging. The uniform evaluations they offer are made one-sidedly, with the Orient taken as in need of exterior representation. Orientalism indicates

Figure 6.1   The stereotypical view of China as socially backward and stagnant is portrayed in this corpulent representative of the Celestial Empire being greeted by the nationally iconic figures of Europe and America, including John Bull and Uncle Sam, who collectively point to 'modern ways' (*The Review of Reviews*, 1912, **45**(267): 252)

one of the key ways in which, as suggested at the start of Chapter 4, the whole world began irrevocably to change in a developing imperialist context, for both the West and the Rest. It is the legacy of that change which requires our historical understanding.

In previous chapters, we have seen how Africa became known about almost entirely through Western cultural myths and stereotypes. Although new data was steadily forthcoming, this was continually filtered through European preconceptions, or simply ignored if it did not conform with existing images of what became known as the 'Dark Continent'. As Curtin put it, Victorians 'did not ask, "What is Africa like, and what manner of men live there?" but "how does Africa, and how do the Africans fit into what we already know of the world?"' (1965: 479). Fitting Africa and Africans into what they already knew, and how they already thought, made their image of Africa a largely European construct created to suit European needs. Europeans imagined the African in their own regard, as a non-self standing over against themselves. In this respect, Africa was an absence filled up by the presence of

European discourse about it. Orientalism is a similarly one-sided view of the world, a product of the way in which the modern West gained its sense of superiority in being modern at least in part from the discursive contrasts and coercive evaluations that were made with the rest of the world, with non-European cultures. These were made to fit into what was already known of the world from a European perspective.

Produced initially through learning and scholarship, by the end of the nineteenth century Orientalism had become a specific and pervasive kind of knowledge that had assimilated biological determinism and social Darwinism. It had by then become entrenched in the European vision of the rest of the world. Its fabricated truths helped to realise a will to dominate over an orientalised East and consolidate the interests of Western colonial and imperial power. Orientalist discourse and European material interests were mutual allies. As a discourse, Orientalism has always operated as a general configuration of ideas and images which organise and enact a way of representing knowledge of the East, determining not only the means by which but also the position from which the East is represented. It provides a matrix of meanings into which both older and emergent elements are absorbed, and synthesises these into a regularised pattern of characteristics and a unifying set of values, systematically forming the objects of which it speaks. Orientalism is not disinterested knowledge but knowledge with very worldly affiliations, dealing with ritualised forms of truth designed to produce and reproduce an apparently 'ineradicable distinction between Western superiority and Oriental inferiority' (Said, 1985a: 42).

Edward Said is perhaps the most well-known critical writer on Orientalism. His book on the topic was first published in 1978 as the initial volume of a trilogy dealing with the West's representations of and relations with the Middle East (1979, 1981, 1985a). In his detailed exposition of Orientalism, Said showed that texts which have been informed by the terms of colonial and imperial relations share certain discursive features. These have produced a particular way of thinking of non-Western peoples. They have worked to ensure the 'flexible positional superiority' that was central to European culture and essential for its dominant status both in and outside Europe (1985a: 7). Orientalist discourse created an 'archive of information' which 'explained the behaviour of Orientals' by supplying them with 'a mentality, a genealogy, an atmosphere', and by guaranteeing accounts of them a factual status and objective truth (ibid: 41–2). This archive was a repository of Western knowledge about the Oriental, establishing and reinforcing the place of power from which to speak definitively of those represented. In the case of the Middle East which Said deals with, Orientalism secured a position of dominance for European identity by constructing Arab-Orientals as the opposite of rational, peaceful and liberal Western subjects, with those subjects always existing 'outside the Orient, as an existential and moral fact'. Premised upon exteriority, Orientalism was knowledge of the East for the benefit of the West, and knowledge of the East that was, paradoxically, just as much about knowledge of the West (ibid: 20–1). This does mean that it has just been made up. While the East/West dualistic contrast is always produced by the discourse, it is never 'merely imaginative'. Said warns against assuming that it consists solely of a tissue of lies 'which, were the truth about them to be told, would simply blow away' – a warning echoing the one sounded in Chapter 1 concerning stereotyping and the liberal hope of dispelling it with detailed information. If it consisted simply of lies and distortions, Orientalism would not have become institutionalised in colonial administration and policy. It would not have been able to operate as a material practice embodying active forms of power and authority over the Orient.

Said dealt with a broad range of writing in which Orientalism was variously inscribed. This included historical scholarship, literary texts, ethnography, linguistic and philological analysis, political tracts, journalism and travel books. He touched on the influence of the Orientalist paradigm in the social sciences, but this was more systematically treated in Bryan Turner's accounts (1974, 1978) of such influence in both Marxism and sociology. This influence was perhaps most marked in the dualistic models of the Orient as static, irrational and backward, and of the Occident as dynamic, rational and progressive, but Orientalist categories have surfaced recurrently in the discussion of Eastern questions, with images of despotism, social stagnation, indolence and sensuality showing considerable range and strength, as for instance when Oriental 'excess' was posed in contradistinction to Protestant asceticism in Weber's sociology of religion. Turner singles out two particularly abiding consequences of Orientalist discourse in the social sciences:

> First, it provided a general perspective on social and historical difference which separated the Occident and the Orient. Indeed, in this framework the Orient became the negative imprint of the Occident. Second, it generated a moral position on the origins of modern culture, despite the fact that this social science language was couched in terms of value neutrality. (1989: 633)

Many criticisms have been made of Said's *Orientalism* (1985a), some of them eminently justified, some a form of open learning after the fact, some a form of tendentious reading advanced in pursuit of alternative positions, some intemperate and ill-judged. Bart Moore-Gilbert has recently produced a useful critical synthesis and treatment of them and of postcolonial studies more broadly (Moore-Gilbert, 1997; also Young, 1990). In this chapter I want to take up just a few of the issues raised by Said and other writers associated with postcolonial criticism, yet all of them are directly relevant to the reconsideration of stereotyping which I am concerned with in the book as a whole. The first issue concerns the way in which the diverse stereotypical figurations of Orientalist discourse are represented in critique. Despite his recognition of the flexible positionality of Orientalist strategy, Said assumes a single, systematic and homogeneous colonial discourse rather than various discourses in circulation that related to colonialism and indigenous peoples. For all the sinuous ingenuity of his analysis, in the end Said overplays his hand and makes Orientalist discourse *too* powerful, *too* efficient, as if there was no hindrance to its 'underwriting the authority of overseas empire or arrogating the right to represent what is beyond Europe's borders' (Parry, 1992: 26). Given the need to build up a compelling demonstration of Orientalism's ability to make its stereotypical characteristics and scenarios seem objective and non-contradictory, the inclination to exaggerate its consistency and reach is understandable. While Childs and Williams note that some critics have themselves produced a monolithic Said (1997: 116), the problem is encapsulated by Said in his later observation that the Orient was 'not Europe's interlocutor, but its silent Other' (Said, 1985b: 17).

The 'silence' of the Other is rather an effect of the tendency to focus so closely on the disciplinary functions of Orientalist discourse that insufficient attention is given to its gaps and contradictions, not to mention its finer shades of meaning and nuance. This tendency derives from the influence of Foucault, which Said has subsequently distanced himself from, but it also conflicts with the orientation to individuality and intention which Said has always wanted to retain from the humanist tradition (for example 1985a: 23). The analytical value of drawing on a Foucauldian conception of discourse is that it enables him to bring together his wide range of texts within a single critical framework. This is one of the major achievements of the book, but at the same time it produces a major weakness in Said's argument with everything he deals with being considered within that pessimistic framework. That's why he becomes open 'to the charge of promoting Occidentalism' and contributing 'to the perpetuation of that Orientalist thought which he set out to demystify in the first place', a contradiction which inverts the stereotyping he contests (Porter, 1983: 181). Robert Young similarly refers to Said finding himself 'repeating the very structures that he censures' (1995: 127). The methodological apparatus of *Orientalism* leaves Said with no means to go beyond the terms of its object of analysis. The book has no ear for such forms of resistance as 'sly civility' and the elision of mimicry and mockery within colonial discourse later analysed by Homi Bhabha. Both of these modes of resisting Orientalist stereo-typing were examples of role distance in adapting the script of colonial relations and moving between competing subject positions (Goffman, 1972: 75–134; Bhabha, 1997: Chapters 4 and 5). Much of the subse-quent development of postcolonial studies following Said has attempted to avoid a reverse Orientalism by focusing instead on the semantic slip-pages, elisions, contradictions and ellipses of colonial discourse as a way of estranging its authority and registering, through what it denied and disavowed, the unsettled murmurings within its own unconscious.

The silent Other is silent only when analysis does not listen. It is then that it reproduces the discourse it is designed to critique. In his more recent work, Said has attended much more to the question of resistances, acknowledging that it was never the case that 'the imperial encounter pitted an active Western intruder against a supine or inert non-Western native; there was always some form of active resistance', which of course culminated in decolonisation across the 'Third World' (1994: xii, Chapter 3). But a further aspect of the problem in presenting colonial discourse as a singular, determinist mechanism in the earlier text is that of playing down differences in its localised artic-ulations (or using such a conception of colonial discourse to override differences of approach) both across and within specific historical periods. This has regrettable consequences. For example, the humane and relatively sympathetic writing of scholars such as A.J. Arberry become swept up by the same polemical brush, allowing us to forget that he too recognised 'the chronic and dangerous psychological malad-justment' attendant on the East/West divide (1960: 256). Another such consequence is that, in tendentiously concentrating on French and British Orientalism because these traditions suit his argument, German Orientalism does not figure much in the book. It is 'atypical of a genealogy that defines the discourse as essentially colonialist' (Clifford, 1988: 267; also Beckingham, 1979: 562).

A further shortcoming of Said's critical study is that, while drawing on all sorts of historical material, it is insensitive to changes in discourse over time, tending to present Western discourse about the Orient as if it was historically unified and seamless in its construction of Europe's 'silent Other'. Although his study is concerned with Orientalism as a hegemonic system, it does not deal with hegemony as a historical process. It is in view of this that Dennis Porter felt impelled to ask if a knowledge as opposed to an ideology can actually exist, or is Orientalism 'not only what we have but all we can ever have' (1983: 180). Said takes a hesitant, unresolved stance to this problem, so it's never finally clear whether his critique is conducted in order to provide a counterknowledge based on a demonstrable authenticity (an actual Orient to which appeal can be made in the face of Orientalist accounts) or to refute the terms of a self-enclosed power/knowledge fabrication (the Orientalised Orient). If Orientalism consists of its constructed representations, then it can be appraised on this basis, but it cannot misrepresent what it has only constructed.

Said's *Orientalism* certainly has its lacunae, inconsistencies and contradictions, both methodological and epistemological. Subsequent work has picked up on these as well as the powerful impetus of its general argument in developing and refining the analysis of colonial discourse. While I have outlined what seem to me some of the most significant problems associated with the book, it could be argued that even more serious problems follow from keeping apart the positions Said tries to bring into some sort of relation. His sustained and politically committed study is to be praised for its interrogation of the core intellectual issue of interplay between different cultures, histories, traditions and societies. The purpose of this interrogation is to counteract the clear-cut divisions and distinctions between them that become invidious oppositions ('our' nation elevated through contrast with stereotypes of other nations) and delimit the opportunities for human encounter and exchange. Said rejects the essences and polar distinctions on which culturalist stereotyping thrives, and asks whether the notion of a distinct culture is useful or more likely to generate either 'self-congratulation (when one discusses one's own) or hostility and aggression (when one discusses the "other")' (Said, 1985a: 325). Belonging becomes constricting and repressive in conjunction with the affirmative, uni-focal championing of cultural distinctiveness. The known is then celebrated at the expense of the knowable. In contrast to this, the clear message that comes from Said's book is that cultures are formed by change and interchange, and not by organic patterns of internal continuity and growth. Cultures are not autonomous and histories are not singular. Crucially, for imperial and colonial history, this entails 'rewriting the West's story so that the export of cultural products from Europe is interwoven with the entry of empire into its cultures' (Parry, 1992: 24).

Postcolonial Studies

So far I have dealt with the stereotypical Other as it has been constructed in Orientalist discourse, and with some of the problems arising from its most influential critique. I want to go on now to look at postcolonial studies, the diverse body of work that has developed out of the initial impetus provided by Said, among others. The descriptive term 'post-colonial' may suggest that the period of colonialism is over and finished, even though its legacy lives on, as for instance in stereotypical images of non-Western cultures. This is quite wrong. The prefix 'post' obscures the continuing processes of neo-colonialism and continuing inequities in global power while also reproducing the paradigm of unilinear developing time on which the Victorian notions of progress and primitivism depended. All that the term can sensibly mean is that, coming after formal decolonisation, it stands for a critique of the historical formations of colonial domination and of colonial legacies. The use of plural nouns here is deliberate, for there is no singular period, condition, subject or space of postcoloniality. It takes various forms, and it applies to the formerly colonising as well as colonised societies. Conceived in this way, postcolonial critique has various benefits for our understanding of the stereotypical Other. The first of these follows from Benita Parry's point about the need to rewrite the West's story. If the development of our understanding of stereotyping depends on making it part of a bigger story, this is by no means a unitary story or a story which already exists in some definitive form. The stories are multiple and existing narratives are contestable. Some stories need to be retold in various ways. The emphasis in postcolonial studies on the relations between the imperial centre and its colonial peripheries makes an important contribution to this process.

With this emphasis, there can be no recourse to the pathologising of prejudice on an individualist basis because we are dealing with broad cultural formations based around the unequal axis of the imperial relation. The conception of a stark binary divide separating the dominant and subordinate groups and ethnicities defined by this relation is rendered suspect because the cultural formations involved deeply affected the lives and sensibilities of people at the centre as much as at the periphery of empire. As we've seen already, white people in Europe did often think in terms of binary oppositions between varieties of primitivist and civilisational categories, but the analysis of colonial and imperial discourse obviously needs to do more than point this out. It is because Said's *Orientalism* gains its power from the realisation that 'the fact of empire radically corrodes the claims of Western civilisation' (Varadharajan, 1995: 114), that work which has followed in its wake is concerned with the effects of the periphery within the imperial centre rather than simply the other way round, in the construction of the imperialist Other. This means seeing centre and periphery as multiply interrelated rather than being at opposite poles. It means exploring their mutual influence alongside their inequality of power in order to displace the terms which have been set up in their long opposition to each other. This two-way influence mediated by the power structures and relations of empire permeated through to other categories of difference, such as gender, sexuality, religion and class as well as 'race', and, as we have seen in Chapter 4, informed 'high' intellectual as well as 'low' cultural discourses and the trafficking between them.

The interweaving of centre/periphery relations in empire-building and consolidation led to various ambivalences and contradictions. These arose and continued to exist even in the face of attempts to polarise the relations. An example of this was the feminisation of the colonised male. This was part of the wider strategy of rendering him inferior to the martial manliness of the imperial male. The tightly buttoned, public school English masculinity discussed in the previous chapter did not develop only within a framework of nationalist belonging. With equal significance, it was defined through the symbolic boundaries operating at the mutually constitutive intersections of metropolitan centre and colonial periphery. In India this resulted in the colonial stereotypes of the 'manly Englishman' and the 'effeminate Bengali *babu*' (a middle-class, Western-educated Hindu). The stereotypical contrasts between them underpinned various legislative and administrative controversies in the late nineteenth-century period of the British Raj. Shifts in the political economy of colonialism at this time were rearticulated in the politics of colonial masculinity, substituting 'for a straightforward defence of racial exclusivity a supposedly more "natural" gender hierarchy between "manly" and "unmanly" men'. At the same time, the effeminate *babu* stereotype was twisted around, creating a point of discursive strain, in representations of the Bengali male as sexually insatiable and lacking in 'manly self-control' (Sinha, 1995: 5, 18–19). This ideological contradiction in a particular

Orientalist discourse shows that when circumstances led to it, denigration took whatever form seemed to suit, regardless of the contradictions thus generated.

In Chapter 3 I suggested that one of the advantages of the concept of the Other over earlier ideas about the process of stereotyping is that it brings into critical view the relational force-field between those who stereotype and those who are the object of stereotyping. Postcolonial studies have helped to consolidate this advantage. Such studies see the Other as providing confirmation of self-identity at the same time as satisfying a desire for difference, for different desire and pleasure, with the difference existing safely outside the 'home' culture's bounds of normality. With the Other constructed in this way there is always a potential danger for the self-identity it confirms. In the psychic composition of colonial relations, othering entails the coexistence of attraction and fear, desire and derision. Stereotyping tries to pin down the Other, to govern its psychic value and currency in the economy of stereotyping, but the figures constructed in this process carry with them more than a hint, at times a distinct air and at others even a definite threat, of disorder and licence. In the figure of the Other there arises, like a vengeful ghost, that which is not permitted in the culture which produces it. The Other represents an attempt to make the unfamiliar familiar, to make what is disturbing safe, but the stereotypical Other is thereby set up as a source of contradictory response: providing pleasure in the exotic, say, and reawakening fear or disgust in relation to what is foreign. The stereotype may succeed in making the foreign familiar, in domesticating it at the expense of the knowable, so that contempt becomes directed at what has become incorporated into the already-known. Yet at the same time that new things are seen through the familiar and previously known, what is foreign exceeds this process and sets in motion an ambivalent response to what is new and different which vacillates between its easy intent towards the already-known and 'its shivers of delight in – or fear of – novelty' (Said, 1985a: 59). The stereotyped Other is allowed to approach, and is simultaneously cast out, marking out, over and over, a series of conflicting moments that alternate between recognition and disavowal.

This is to think of the stereotyping process in terms of an intersubjective, self-constituting regard for those stereotyped, and to trace this relation along a tangled chain of signification and representation that invites a mode of psychological identification which is split, interspliced and ambivalent. It undermines the idea of the position and identity of those who stereotype or are stereotyped as unitary, fixed over time, and absolutely opposite to each other. Those among whom a stereotype circulates do not necessarily gain a secure point of identification from it because of the 'difference' and therefore the 'lack' which it invokes. This 'lack' is located in identity defined in terms of what it is not, and what it is not always poses a potential threat to what it is in its own self-definition. Stereotyping attempts to ward off this perceived threat by normalising difference, reducing it to a few putative, metaphoric and metonymic attributes, such as the Jew's 'sleuth-hound instinct for gain' (Russell and Lewis, 1900: 5), and casting out in exaggerated form what is affirmed in acceptable forms of self-interest. Postcolonial theory is often stylistically dense and clotted, as for instance in much of the work of Homi Bhabha, but it repays attention because of the way it challenges us to think beyond the binarisms of fixed identifications – of men as opposed to women, say, or of heterosexuality in strict opposition to homosexuality. Bhabha also shows a sceptical regard for general terms such as race, gender and nation. Such terms tend to lump different people together in one monolithic category. Against unitary classifications and closed dyads, Bhabha's practice is to think in terms of contrary impulses and affects, fractured and stricken identities, unstable certainties, and, as he continually insists, 'forms of multiple and contradictory belief' (1997: 75). So for instance, in the field of the imaginary in which it operates, it is exactly because the stereotype is 'as anxious as it is assertive', because its contradictory form is a 'site of both fixity and fantasy', that it must produce, and go on producing, as if in order to prove what cannot be proved, 'the *same old* stories of the Negro's animality, the Coolie's inscrutability or the stupidity of the Irish' (ibid: 77, emphasis in original). This is what is fetishistic about the stereotypical Other.

But it is a mistake to think of the stereotype in its fetishistic mode as transhistorical. This returns us to the question of the utility of psychoanalysis in historical cultural studies. The fetish, at least as Bhabha uses it, is a psychoanalytic concept and the problem with using the putatively universal categories of psychoanalysis is knowing how they may relate to particular historical and cultural contexts. Bhabha's concern is with the cultural encounters of colonial history and he uses psychoanalytic terms as a way of thinking about these. Such terms within psychoanalysis relate specifically to sexuality, although sexuality generally conceived in an ahistorical sense. Unlike Fanon, Bhabha does not analyse colonialist cultural encounters in terms of sexuality, so it is unclear whether he is using Freudian categories as an analogy in order to prise open what these encounters have involved, or saying that empirically they apply to them

(Young, 1995: 154; and see Fanon, 1972: Chapters 2 and 3). Bhabha universalises the psychosexual dynamics of gender formation in the Western bourgeois family by applying them to colonial race relations. This productively complicates coloniser/colonised binary oppositions, but again in contrast to Fanon's contextualist scruples, Bhabha's work is so highly generalised it is difficult to know how applicable it is in any particular historical case, such as, for instance, the construct of the 'effeminate *babu*'. As historical cultural analysis it is conducted so much in terms of the forms and formations of discourse that discourse itself tends to float free of the specific historical conditions and consequences within which colonial relations need to be understood. Such relations were not the same the world over, but differed from place to place, not only across global colonised space but also, as Mrinalini Sinha's historical monograph makes clear, within the particular colonial context of the Indian sub-continent with which Bhabha has been chiefly concerned. Bhabha criticises Stephen Heath's understanding of the stereotype as 'offering, *at any one time*, a *secure* point of identification' (1997: 69) where the double emphasis suggests not only a concern with stereotypes as an ambivalent and conflicting repertoire, but also a need for attention to changing temporalities, and to the variety of social contexts in which colonial and postcolonial relations have been played out. What we find, as a result of Bhabha's textualist approach and the generalities this produces and permits, is that he tends to offer a unitary conception of the psychic economy of the stereotype and the colonial discourse in which it operates.

In terms of thinking conceptually about the stereotypical Other, Bhabha's conception of it as fetishistic, along with the psychic dislocations this involves, should not be taken as paradigmatic. The Oedipal scenario is not applicable (literally or metaphorically) to all forms of othering. It is not a meta-discourse leading critique to the fount of truth. Nor can discourse be elevated above other forms of action and interaction within which it is implicated, for while implicated in them it is not constitutive of everything about them. The political importance of thinking beyond the fixed binaries of stereotypical constructions of Self and Other – of seeing stereotypes as often contradicting each other and of seeing them as fraught with an underlying equivocation and ambivalence belying their hardened exteriors – should be clear enough. But the creeping formalism in Bhabha's conception of the Other obscures the forces and pressures of social and economic power by privileging ruptures of form and the subversive potential of ambivalence as a political weapon. In a neat turn of phrase, Anne

McClintock describes this as 'a fetishism of form' involving 'the projection of historical agency onto formal abstractions that are anthropomorphised and given a life of their own':

> Here abstractions become historical actors; discourse desires, dreams and does the work of colonialism while also ensuring its demise. In the process, social relations between humans appear to metamorphise into structural relations between forms – through a formalist fetishism that effectively elides the messier questions of historical change and social activism. (McClintock, 1995: 63–4)

Decolonising the Historical Imagination

We have already seen that Said's totalising framework produces an overpowering sense of Orientalism, as if it has operated as a univocal discourse and single monolithic tradition, without variation or alternative. He does distinguish between the more 'scientific' discourse of British Orientalism, as represented by Edward Lane, from the more 'aesthetic' French tradition, represented by Chateaubriand, and does acknowledge sympathetic Orientalists like Louis Massignon, but the significance of such differences is as underplayed as his argument for the stable continuity of Orientalist discourse over long periods of time is overplayed. The latter argument is encapsulated in his claim that Orientalism is 'the doctrinal antithesis of development' (Said, 1985a: 307). If this is one problem in the way Orientalism has been critically studied, Bhabha reveals another in applying ready-made templates across different historical and cultural contexts, and in making cultural forms and discourses appear to have their own volition, as if they were actual historical agents. Although she is directly opposed to this tendency in her comparative study of Orientalism within British and French literary traditions, Lisa Lowe shows that she too is at times prone to it, as for instance when she writes: 'to conform to binary difference is inevitably to corroborate the logic of domination, to under-develop the spaces in discourse that destabilise the hegemony of dominant formations' (1991: 24). In such formalist fetishism and the belief that escape from domination lies somewhere down an endless chain of signification, we face the critical platitudes of post-structuralism at their most jejune.

Such platitudes hide a thorny problem. This is the problem of speaking in general terms of representations of the Other without reproducing the static dualism of identity and difference and the stark

Figure 6.2   Orientalist notions of sensuous decadence and
exotic pleasures are rendered benign in a cigarette
advertisement of the early twentieth century
(*The Orientalist Poster: A Century of Advertising through the Slaoui Foundation
Collection*, Malika Editions, 1997)

Figure 6.3   The Orientalist stereotypes of subterfuge and deceit
are rendered brutal in this contrasting illustration from a
popular boy's comic of the early twentieth century
(*Penny Dreadfuls and Comics: Exhibition Catalogue,*
Bethnal Green Museum of Childhood, London, 1983)

opposition of differentiated identity and homogenised difference which
the concept is intended to counteract. The stereotypical Other can
easily be used as if what is referred to is unchanging and universal, so
flattening out the diverse ways in which othering has occurred, across
space and time, and not only in order to stabilise 'the hegemony of
dominant formations'. Whether celebrated or denigrated, Otherness
entails an erasure of distinctiveness and particularity of self precisely
because it is always placed over on the other side from selfhood. Postcolonial studies have at least brought this problem more centrally to
our attention, and over the last ten years or so, work on imperialist and

colonialist discourse has tried to avoid the recuperation of binary versions of difference by examining their intersection with other discourses, such as those of gender, ethnicity and social class. The gaps, ambivalences and contradictions – their spaces, if you will – arising from the incomplete reconciliation or 'fit' between these different discourses reveal their weak points of instability and lack of closure. The interest in gendering Orientalism is a valuable development, and not only because it helps to offset the generally male-oriented version of Orientalist discourse presented by Said. Its immediate impetus has come from new historical work on imperialism, women's history and gender history, as well as postcolonial theory itself. Together, these have reworked the approach inspired by Said's *Orientalism* by exploring the distinctive experiences of women in colonial contexts and their different contributions to colonial discourse. Along with new studies of imperialism by social and cultural historians, these recent developments have also effectively challenged the paradigm of classical imperial history which was established in the period of 'high' imperialism. Imperial history performed a largely supportive, legitimating role in relation to empire. It was preoccupied with male domains and paid no attention to questions of gender construction or of the relation of women and empire, whether as colonisers or colonised. The feminist challenge to its principles and purposes is an important corrective in recent work on colonialism and imperialism, but the challenge goes beyond this in linking feminist critique to the analysis of relations and representations more broadly.

Stereotypical feminisation is a form of imperialist category-intersection that has long been central to the orientalisation of the Orient. The stereotype of the effeminate Bengali babu was just one particular example of this, but there has long been a more general blending together of romantic images of femininity with images of the Orient as enigmatic and mysterious, suggesting a dark secret behind the veil of both 'woman' and 'the East' in the contradictory stereotypes of corruption and mysticism, exoticism and sexual insatiability. Among other things, stereotypical feminisation shows how nationalism and sexuality operate as sites where each metaphorically plays out fantasies of the other. The 1970s witnessed a cultural reinvigoration in Islamic societies, a strengthening of values that happened at the same time as the Iranian Revolution and OPEC's successful use of the 'oil weapon'. All such developments were seen in the West as a resurgence of militancy in Islam, stirring up the old spectres of fanatic religiosity and irrational despotism, and leading to a dominant perception of Islam as a dangerous threat to the West generally, and North

America in particular. The Arab revolutionary threat was then mapped onto 'a bad kind of sexuality' or sexual 'aberration' (Said, 1985a: 313–15). An example of this surfaced in the portrayal of Colonel Qaddaffi as a transvestite homosexual after the US air raids on Libya in April 1986 (de Mause, 1986: 9). These links between sexuality and a deviant Other of the home nation indicate a need for power relations that support a 'fixed' social *and* sexual order through the projection of repressed desires onto the Other and the investment of masculine virility in Western nationality. Superseding earlier western European versions as Anglo-French imperialism has declined, US Orientalism has developed with the rise of US neo-colonialism in the Middle East. US Orientalism has been supported by negative stereotypes of Arabs in American popular culture as lecherous and deceitful, bloodthirsty and sadistic. The same old, well-worn, binary oppositions continue to operate in the 'absolute and systematic difference between the West, which is rational, developed, humane, superior, and the Orient, which is aberrant, under-developed and inferior' (Said, 1985a: 300).

Another welcome development, following decolonisation, has been the emergence of hidden or suppressed histories behind that of the colonisers. These historical accounts attempt to show the colonial encounter through the experiences of the colonised, and to bring into the frame female as well as male perspectives on the past. The work of the Subaltern Studies Group has exemplified this for the Indian peasantry (Guha and Spivak, 1988). A real strength of this new historical research and analysis also lies in its keen focus on the intersections of gender with class and 'race', in and across the various sites of imperial encounters and interactions, and yet along with their development serious critical reservations have been voiced about their authenticity, about the possibility of representing 'native' voices from the past, and about the project of locating some real history beyond them which remains to be uncovered and retold in some alternative account (Spivak, 1988). This raises again the difficult methodological problem of reiterating the Other in analysing it. In making this problem a central concern, postcolonial studies have offered provocative contributions to both history and historiography. In her essay 'The Rani of Sirmur', Gayatri Spivak provides a rewarding example of this sceptical attention to the narrative fabrication of the 'realist' past where the concern is not with some alternative to imperial history but rather with the historiographical issues involved in the construction of imperial representation. Such representation operates in the dual sense of the word, both *showing* and *standing in* for the 'native' subject, with the analytical task being to dig up the underlying assumptions and values informing the representation, and creating the world that the Other was meant to inhabit by being made Other (Spivak, 1984). As a critical gadfly, the most important consideration for Spivak seems to be avoiding any complicity with these assumptions and values, the positions and affiliations connecting knowledge and power from which they speak of the past. She sees such complicity as a major pitfall of alternative histories, and sets up her task as finding ways of distancing and dissociating herself from them. As in postcolonial studies generally, this leads to close scrutiny of the discursive mechanisms of representation – how truths are produced – and rejection of any 'true' way of reading representation, with Spivak tacking between subject-positions variably constructed through the discourses of gender, class, race and imperialism in her deconstructions of the archival sources which assign the subaltern to her Third World status. The point is not that of resurrecting the past's authenticity – 'there is no "real" Rani to be found' – but of decolonising the historical imagination. That is why she warns against a nostalgia for a nativist past, or what she calls reverse ethnocentrism – an exaggerated admiration of the third-world subject and a piously critical attitude to the imperialist past (1984: 147, 1985: 245).

In the light of this deconstructionist critique, it may seem that vigilant attention to the dangers besetting subaltern histories can only defeat the purposes for which these histories are written. Against various women's studies of colonialism, it may seem to return us only to the leaden silence of the Other (Parry, 1987: 39). This would certainly be as regrettable as a historical narrative which recuperates the Otherness of the marginalised subaltern. For India at least, the ensuing enigmatic silence may then simply echo the mysterious Orientalist stereotypes in such colonial fiction as Kipling's (Suleri, 1992: 11–12). My own view is that the past can be retold in different ways, hidden histories can be uncovered, alternative memories and experiences can be pieced together, even if the result is still a set of fragments. These submerged pasts and perspectives from below are valuable resources of resistance to the legacies of colonialism. To oppose this calls into question the purpose of postcolonial critique. There is at least a fair degree of justification in the argument that postcolonial critique is preoccupied more by philosophical than political questions, and is again using the subordinated Other as a way of rethinking the Western Self (Hall, 1996: 248–9). If the Other is one who cannot speak, who is spoken for, it is somewhat paradoxical to deconstruct Otherness through Western theoretical models and analytical devices, for this ends up speaking for the still silent Other, albeit in a new critical mode. Implicitly at least, an expectation of submission to the authority of the West remains in place.

Added to this we may well ask if we are any nearer to a better history. Constant questioning of the conceptual basis on which texts and documents are examined does not in itself improve the quality of historical writing. Both Spivak's periphrastic style and Bhabha's opaque abstractions attest to this. There is also a danger in any relentlessly sceptical form of reflexivity that you become so self-absorbed in questioning your own position that the whole point of historical cultural analysis is subverted. Spivak does suggest an alternative to such constant questioning and denial of any 'authentic' historical reality in claiming that at times a strategic essentialism may be necessary in countering imperialist constructions of nativism. While this may be true in certain political contexts, it hardly sits happily with Spivak's aspersions against the notion of authenticity. Yet Spivak has certainly offered 'constructive questions [and] corrective doubts' (1987: 258). Her work is valuable in showing that the problem of recuperating the Otherness of the historical Other, and of being complicit with the discourses which are the object of critical attention, cannot be easily dismissed. If she has firmly rejected any nativist Indian version of *négritude*, she has provided an instructive lead in how to approach the politics of colonial and neocolonial representation, and how to go about the task of de-othering the self-consolidating Other without assimilating her to Western ways of seeing, thinking and valuing. In Moore-Gilbert's estimation, after Spivak there can be no unexamined benevolence to the oppressed or 'intrinsically politically correct denunciations' of colonialism or neocolonialism (1997: 112).

It may be useful to consider one particular case where the problem of reiterating the Other applies. This involves attempts to understand the roles and relations of white women in colonial societies and go behind the well-worn stereotype of the racist memsahib. These have been rebuked for reproducing the grounding assumptions of colonial discourse. In citing examples of such attempts, Jane Haggis (1990) distinguishes between colonising gender for white men and women and gendering colonialism as a historical process. She argues cogently against dealing historically with 'race' and gender as if they belong 'to a series of parallel tracks essentially unrelated to each other' (1998: 49). She also addresses the problem of writing non-recuperative history that is informed by a contemporary awareness of the politics of representing difference without being chronocentric and making the past compliant with the present. Her account of research into British women missionaries in south India relates how she has confronted both the missionary stereotype of the *zenana* victim, and her own stereotypical views of the missionary women as uniformly subordinate to Victorian patriarchy, even as she holds, strategically, to her own purpose of writing a feminist postcolonial history. Haggis shows how the complex issues arising from an attempt to avoid complicity in past relations of domination, of which stereotypical representations are one aspect, can be tackled through a post-structuralist discursive approach without this leading to further mystification or obfuscation. Her contribution to historiographical debate is far more absorbing and helpful than the repetition of tired professional pieties such as those levelled by John MacKenzie at Orientalist critique (1995: for example 214). Yet doubts remain. While she exemplifies how to use theory constructively rather than being obstructively used by it, Haggis nevertheless falls prey to the post-structuralist tendency to divisively pit meaning and discourse against experience and voice, thus polarising critically reflexive gender historians and unwittingly complicit women historians (see Pickering, 1997a: Chapter 7). This is rather ironic in view of her fine sensitivity to processes of othering. Examples can of course be cited of historians on both sides of this stark divide. The problem is that there are people who cannot be so easily assigned.

Take Benita Parry, for example. For Parry, Bhabha's sophisticated readings of colonial encounters obscure the antagonistic relationship of coloniser and colonised, rendering the former as comprehensively paranoic and the latter as comprehensively subversive. This can be illustrated by two quite different accounts of the same historical event. Although its narrative leans far more to coloniser than to colonised points of view, a fictionalised reconstruction such as J.G. Farrell's *The Siege of Krisnapur* reveals far more of this antagonistic relationship than does Bhabha's discourse analysis of the 1857 Sepoy rebellion (Bhabha, 1997: Chapter 10). As Parry points out, Bhabha's analysis

> somehow omits to recollect that the rebellion issued as an armed struggle, and was disarmed and repressed by exorbitant military force ... By subsuming the social to textual representation, Bhabha represents colonialism as transactional rather than conflictual – a version which should be distinguished from the study of how the colonised negotiated colonialism. [His] ... elaborations dispense with the notion of conflict; [they are] ... at variance with the audible violence in its many colonialist utterances, and perversely indifferent to explaining the success and longevity of colonialism. (Parry, 1994: 6, 11–12, 16)

We're back with the question of appropriate paradigms for decolonising the historical imagination. In the case of imperialist violence, an analytical model which conceives it as solely epistemic is historically askew. It simply ignores the many incidences of floggings, murder and massacre in the colonial context, as for instance after the Sepoy rebellion or the Jamaica insurrection of 1865, and at Amritsar in 1919.

Abjection and Cultural Analysis

Throughout this book I have been arguing against certain simplistic notions of the stereotyping process. A stereotype is not merely a sort of caricatured effigy, a target of abuse and discrimination that is scapegoated because of the falsity of the image that is set up. Those who are stereotyped can of course become subject to abuse and discrimination, and racist violence in the streets may be supported by forms of institutional racism in state authorities assigned to deal with such problems. To recognise this does not exhaust our understanding of what stereotyping involves. That is why I have attempted to outline the main ways in which postcolonial studies have complicated, extended and enhanced our understanding of stereotyping and the stereotypical Other. We have seen already that stereotypes represent an attempt to control what is unfamiliar and strange by rigidifying the sense of difference of the 'not us' in contrast to 'us' as putatively the 'same together' in our collective belonging as 'race', nation, class, gender or sexuality. Postcolonial theory supports this interpretation and affirms the interactivity of positive and negative stereotypes, but rightly places greatest emphasis on the structures of social order and power underlying their one-sided evaluative positions. It is the Other who is made to stand in need of representation and then made to conform to such representation, yet in being represented the Other speaks to the identity of those who draw up and distribute the representation. Stereotypes are a component of the broader power/knowledge relations which produce and organise the 'truths' of the self-consolidating Other. In this sense they exist for the benefit of the stereotyping group of whom they reveal as much, if not more, than they do of their targeted object. Understanding stereotyping requires us to look at what is being projected, displaced and transposed onto the Other in the interests of particular forms of self-identity. The danger which continually looms up in doing this is of repeating and perpetuating the terms we're trying critically to take apart. To show why a certain discourse is effective and powerful does not necessarily mean that we've moved beyond the politics of its representations. To identify the specific components of Otherness in any given case is not the same as providing an alternative form of knowledge to that which stereotypicality has attempted to fasten in place. The ambivalence of Otherness haunts analysis as much as it does the activity of othering in the stereotyping process.

Postcolonial studies have at least attempted to overcome this problem by opposing the constitutive structures of stereotypical Otherness – its fixed binary divisions between identity and difference, its categorical closures of symbolic representation, its denials of the potentially knowable in preference to the self-affirming known. Postcolonial theory dwells upon ambivalences of meaning and dissonances of identification as key points to be prised open in articulating resistance to relations of power, authority and control. These points are identified as sources of vulnerability and instability within the whole colonial enterprise and the continuing shadow it casts over the present, which is why they are taken as providing an effective space for critique. However difficult and hedged about with doubts it may be, the critical purpose of postcolonial studies is to write back against empire, against the grain of colonial discourse, in order to articulate alternative identities amidst the legacies of the imperialist past. In doing so, it may appear to flout some of the basic tenets of professional academic history, but nothing less should be expected of any serious historiographical critique. Through thinking reflexively of the past in the present and the present in the past – the articulations of cultural legacies and critical responses – the promise that is made is to a future in which the Other becomes fragmented into multiple relations and disseminated into new identifications with difference. This is where attention to the problems of developing non-recuperative readings of the stereotypical Other properly kicks in. It is because of this attention in postcolonial studies that there is such a methodological centrality on multivalent meanings, ambivalence, contradictions and conflicts of value in and between the different discourses and traditions that may be brought to bear on the interpretation of any cultural text.

If in colonial discourse there has been constructed a surrogate or underground 'self' through which European culture has gained in strength and direction, this locates the unconscious Other within conscious identity. Ambivalences and slippages of meaning have then been read for the fantasies and fears of the colonial unconscious they are said to reveal, yet as we have seen, this critical move creates its own analytical dangers, such as applying the universalising categories of psychic structures to historically and culturally specific cases. With Bhabha, for instance, 'it is implied

that the structures of psychic identification and affect which he theo-
rises apply equally in terms of their operations and results to the
Western-educated rajah and the "illiterate" female subaltern' (Moore-
Gilbert, 1997: 150). It is not only a matter of applicability, but also of
supplying historical material for the 'authorisation' of psychoanalytic
theory, rather than using such material as a way of troubling 'its habitual
claims and procedures' (ibid: 146). Further, the fetishisation of discursive form leads analysis away from questions of institutional power and
social process, while focusing on tensions of psychic economy apparent
between the lines of a dominant discourse begs a number of questions
about the kind of evidence that is being adduced.

I want to begin drawing this account of postcolonial theory to a close
by highlighting three further problems in the work of one of its major
exponents, Homi Bhabha. First, Bhabha's conceptual use of ambivalence, mimicry and hybridity shows that the fixity of the stereotypical
Other is never absolutely achieved, never in place for all time, and in
this sense he provides a useful counterbalance to Said's totalising analysis
of the effectiveness and power of colonial discourse. At the same time
he swings too far in the other direction, and rather overlooks what was,
in the main, the relatively durable, stable and effective nature of colonial power, not to mention the willingness to use force in support of
imperialist interests, as Benita Parry has rightly pointed out. Anne
McClintock also reminds us that 'colonials were both willing and able
to foreclose the poetics of ambivalence by resorting to the technologies
of violence' (1995: 66). We should not need reminding of this, but we
do. Try reading Adam Hochschild's (1999) account of the Belgian
Congo after struggling with Bhabha's heady theoretical elaborations. It
is a sobering experience. Second, while forms of stereotypical mimicry
may have been unsettling for colonial authority by being not quite right
and not quite white, we need to ask whether the mimicry involved was,
indeed, 'a strategic reversal of the process of domination', turning 'the
gaze of the discriminated back upon the eye of power' (Bhabha,
1997: 112). Maybe it was just a strategic confirmation and measure of
colonial control in its deferential emulation of the codes and conduct
of those who, in the imperial relation, were by definition socially dominant. There is no general answer to this question. The general sweep of
postcolonial theory nevertheless entitles us to enquire into the ways in
which ambivalence and hybridity attest to subaltern agency, the ways in
which they were actually subversive, and, as Young notes, the political
status they can be accorded (1995: 152). Third, it is never clear whether
the 'apparently seditionary undoings' which Bhabha analytically

uncovers 'in fact remain unconscious for both coloniser and colonised' (ibid). If they were not consciously realised by subaltern subjects, in what way were they strategic? If they can only be 'read' by Bhabha, at this convenient distance of time, in what way were they destabilising for colonial authority? Does the subversion of Otherness exist more in Bhabha's historical reading than in the history that is being read?

Bhabha's approach to the stereotype is not confined to a conception of it as based on an alleged lack of some kind in its departure from a particular norm. It is concerned with the conflictual meanings and ambivalences within the relationship between those who use a stereotype and those who are stereotyped. This welcome complication of the stereotyping process is, however, prone to an obsessive reading of colonial discourse on the Other through the lens of desire and the thwarting of desire. This point is made by Sara Mills, who complains that figuring 'colonial relations through the analogy of the development of the individual psyche, as psychoanalytic analysis does, simply ratifies colonial expansion, seeing it as a "natural" part of the subject's construction of its sense of self' (1997: 126). This echoes the problem identified in relation to Gilman's conceptualisation of the stereotyping process – naturalising it renders it ungovernable and thus invulnerable to cultural critique. The use of psychoanalytic theory in colonial discourse analysis also repeats the facile attribution of pathological disorder, although now at the level of nation-state rather than the individual subject. This is not to deny the paranoic oscillation between fear and desire in the play of fantasy that operated in certain cases and contexts of colonial history, and that can be detected in certain representations of the colonised, but as I suggested in my earlier discussion of Gilman, the play of fantasy, or indeed the 'deep structures' of ego-development, cannot be generalised out as a way of explaining colonial relations in all their forms. It is rather a question of 'the power relations entailed in sexual relations being used analogically for other power relations' and standing in 'for relations between nations' (Mills, 1997: 128). This brings us back more appropriately to the issue of domination and its maintenance that was central to the colonial situation and the imperial relation.

Anne McClintock keeps this issue clearly in mind even as she applies psychoanalytic theory to the articulated historical experiences of 'race', class, gender and sexuality in the centre–periphery interactions of empire. In discussing the construct of the Primitive, we saw that in modern industrial imperialism, certain 'races' are expelled to the edges of modernity, but it has not only been the 'primitive' Other who has been assigned to anachronistic space. Social 'degenerates' at home – the

Irish, Jews, homosexuals, prostitutes, working-class women, militant trade unionists, criminals and the insane – have also, at various times, been pushed out to the boundaries of normality in exorcistic rituals symbolically facilitated by processes of stereotyping. McClintock productively takes up Kristeva's concept of abjection as a means of analysing these expulsions from the heartlands of society. 'Abjection is above all ambiguity' – existing at the boundaries between the social and anti-social, between stability and danger, and between 'condemnation and yearning' (Kristeva, 1982: 9). Abjection can thus be seen as an adjunct or complementary component of stereotyping, for just as I have defined stereotyping as a process of symbolic containment and risk, so the expunged abject, defining the self's inner limit, continues at that limit to haunt, unsettle and imperil the subject. On this basis, McClintock argues that under imperialism certain abject groups are forced out to the social margins – the slum, ghetto, garret, red light district, asylum, squatter camp and colonial bantustan – and yet in inhabiting these threshold zones they return 'to haunt modernity as its constitutive, inner repudiation: the rejected from which one does not part' (1995: 72). It is in this way that she attempts to develop a *situated* psychoanalysis – a form of historical analysis that is psychoanalytically informed but also culturally contextualised.

This seems to me enormously promising as a way of overcoming the tendencies in historical cultural studies to fetishised formalisms and universalised imperatives while at the same time trying to bring the social and psychic back together and develop 'a mutually transforming investigation in the disavowed relations between psychoanalysis and social history'. As McClintock wryly comments, these disavowed relations are themselves 'a product of abjection' (ibid: 72). The concept of abjection, characterised above all by ambiguity, also allows McClintock to explore fetishism as 'the historical enactment of ambiguity' (ibid: 184) in a way which involves critiquing Lacan's masculinism and phallic fetishism, restoring fetish forms to women, and historically contextualising psychoanalytical dynamics in specific social practices, economic conditions and cultural milieux. McClintock develops a rich and nuanced understanding of imperialism and the ambivalence of colonial Otherness. Her superbly titled *Imperial Leather* (1995) is representative of the most valuable recent work on gender, 'race' and social class in studies of British imperialism. She offers cogent readings of particular sites and processes of social ambiguity and ambivalence, such as the racialisation of gender and class, the hybridity of cross-dressing, the politics of domestic service, the poetics of degeneration, and the intermapping of the languages of empire and urban exploration. Through her situated psychoanalytical approach, she makes various fruitful connections, including the inter-relations between feminised domesticity and masculinised imperialism, the confluence of domesticity, the ethos of progress, the civilising mission and consumerist spectacle in late nineteenth-century kitsch advertising and commodity racism, along with the underlying fetishistic matrix in the classically Victorian iconography of soap. The social relations of the imperialist past constitute a fissured terrain for historical cultural analysis, but what McClintock's study makes abundantly clear is that any advance in our understanding of stereotyping demands the mutually transforming perspectives of psychological and sociological analysis, however fraught their realignment may be. The dilemma of stereotyping cannot be negotiated otherwise.

Chapter 7

The Sociology of Censure

Deviant forms of behaviour, by marking the outer edges of group life, give the inner structures its special character and thus supply the framework within which the people of the group develop an orderly sense of their own cultural identity.

KAI ERIKSON, 1966: 13

Infraction and the Drive to Order

I began this book by defining stereotyping as a process for marking, maintaining and reproducing norms of behaviour, identity and value. The point of this was to deflect attention at the start from the stunted figurations of difference in which stereotypes seem most obviously to trade. Those who negatively stereotype others rarely do so to themselves, except perhaps in faux-ironic or self-disparaging ways designed to achieve a counter-effect. This is quite different to forms of action, features of identity or the stylisation of personality resulting from the internalisation of stereotypical attributions made by others in categories opposed to your own. The definition offered at the outset was made in the light of this critical difference between 'self' and 'other' in the stereotyping process, for stereotypes operate as distancing strategies for placing others in such a manner that will serve to point up and perpetuate certain normative boundaries of social conduct, roles and judgements, separating what is seen as threatening and disturbing from what is regarded as acceptable and legitimate.

It is in the light of my subsequent discussion during the course of this book that the question of social and cultural norms stands in need of further elaboration. Norms collectively are part of the more general conception of normality. This conception came into being early in the nineteenth century and has been central to common-sense thinking ever since. Normality implies order, or at least a set of standards and conventions that are prescribed as the way in which people should behave in particular situations. Such standards and conventions are not fixed for all time. They are negotiated in the process of social interaction in relation to what appears appropriate and expected, and of course they can change. Yet normality by definition exerts considerable pressure on the terms of such negotiation, and can always be reinforced by censure. It is often through censure that normality is defined and legitimate order maintained. Normality entails disciplinary power over people, the responsibility not to be deviant or ab-normal, not to cease patrolling the boundaries between legitimacy and danger. Or in other words, to censure themselves. But what is normality? Where does it begin and end? And how is its ideological presence achieved?

In biology and medicine, what is normal can be taken as the functioning of living beings in a healthy state, in which disease is defined in opposition to it and taken as an aberration from a state of health. Disease then stands over against the normal as its inverse concept. This conception of normality was first extended to social and political life in the early nineteenth century, in a new alignment of the categories of normality, order and progress.

> The normal ceased to be the ordinary healthy state; it became the purified state to which we should strive, and to which our energies are tending. In short, progress and the normal state became inextricably linked. (Hacking, 1990: 168)

The equation of the social organism or body politic and the healthy or normal state to which we should strive has been a very powerful one. In becoming sharply distinguished from notions of pathological social behaviour or social development, normality displaced human nature, a key conception of the Enlightenment, and became the desired goal of social progress. The peculiar power of the word 'normal' arises from its conflation of how things are and how they ought to be: 'The norm may be what is usual or typical, yet our powerful ethical constraints are also called norms'. The word thus 'dances and prances' all over the distinction between fact and value; it closes the gap between 'is' and 'ought'. By running together the two senses of normality as eminently typical and eminently desirable, aspiration became integrally tied to being average. In this way, normality constituted 'one of the most powerful ideological tools of the twentieth century' (ibid: 163, 168–9).

Conceiving what is average as the aspired state of normality always sets up a sharp distinction of what deviates from this state. What is set up as an infraction from it may even be considered to be the priority in defining normality in the first place. Social rules and sanctions follow from the infractions that provide them with their reason for existing and being applied. Infraction is, as it were, discursively 'fitted up' in order to give body to the justification of rules and sanctions regulating the borders of normality and deviance. Nothing is normal in itself. What is regarded as normal is 'not a concept of existence, in itself susceptible of objective measurement', and what is regarded as pathological is itself 'another normal' within its own environment (Canguilhem, 1989: 203). This relationship to its sustaining environment is what makes anything normal or pathological and informs any distinction between them. Normality is not only dynamic but also polemical in the sense that it creates its own inversion of terms as a mode of unifying diversity, resolving difference, or settling disagreement. It is never absolute for both reasons, and what it seeks to regulate always poses the possibility of its opposite, that which is expelled from the form of assessment and discrimination of quality produced by the norm in naming itself. This returns us to the idea of stereotyping as an exorcistic social ritual and to the associated concept of abjection that is integral to stereotyping's strategy of symbolic confinement and risk. If the purpose of a stereotype is to endorse the social or cultural norm from which it is alleged to depart, the satisfaction of thus fulfilling the norm is jeopardised by that which is projected outward as the departure from it. That which is made to inhabit the border zones of normality continually poses the threat of arriving back within its heartland as a subversive force, leading to further waves of expulsion as the only way to contain the danger once again. The pathological is the inner repudiation of normality, and what in modernity is taken as normal has always begun with its infraction.

Normalisation is the active process of securing and maintaining the rules and standards of normality. This regulative function is occasioned not by those rules and standards but by deviations from them, for it is only situations and conditions of irregularity which put 'the regulatory rules to the test'. Any human experience which has been normalised entails a representation of norms 'linked to the temptation to oppose their exercise':

> The abnormal, as ab-normal, comes after the definition of the normal, it is its logical negation ... The normal is the effect obtained by the execution of the normative project, it is the norm exhibited in the fact ... It is not paradoxical to say that the abnormal, while logically second, is existentially first. (ibid: 242–33)

Normality became such a key structuring notion of common-sense thinking over the past two centuries by ushering in a host of dualistic oppositions for the regulation of what is rational, responsible and conventional. What is crucial in this are the forms it takes and the cultural, ethical or political consequences it may have. Processes of normalisation are compelling and people often change their behaviour or modify their ideas in order to fall in line and be in order with what is or ought to be. It's because of this that the normal in its conflated senses is 'an even richer source of hidden power than the fact/value ambiguity that had always been present in the idea of the normal' (Hacking, 1990: 168). If someone is stereotyped as in some way abnormal – that is, not in conformity with a particular social or cultural norm – this may create considerable anxiety or stress, and it is then of little consolation to remind the stereotyped victim that norm-construction is endemic. Analytically, it is the relational character of normality and its contextual specificity which should be emphasised. You are or are not normal in respect of a particular category. Normal is not something you can simply be.

Normality depends on deviations from it to call it into being. What is taken to be normal in relation to any situation or circumstances only makes sense through that which departs from it, as sickness or disease represents a departure from a state of health. It is in this way that normality draws into itself its own pre-eminent quality of being positive, reasonable and right, of being what it is through its own normative force and of constraining action by its unquestioned assumption of centrality, as if what it is is simply the way things are, have been, and will continue to be. By closing the gap between 'is' and 'ought', normality mediates the relations between individuality and collectivity. It creates the base marker from which individuals and groups are adjudged to be aberrant. The structure of longevity and continuity attached to much of what is considered normal often reinforces the stereotypical judgements made in its name. So, for instance, as we have seen earlier in the book, the view of both women and colonial 'natives' as inferior, irrational and often childlike was previously, for many, a normal procedure of outlook and evaluation grounded in the consensual legitimations of the time. If the feminist and postcolonial challenge to such stereotypical assessments at first seemed pathological, the now widespread recognition of the sexist and racist values underpinning them shows how normality, despite strong appearances in any given present to the contrary, is always subject to change and transformation. In the same way deviancy, as its ideological partner in the dance of social relations, is historically inconstant, shifting, mutable.

Over the past two centuries cultural diversity has become as much a source of social tension as an enrichment of dialogue between different discourses, traditions and forms of life. Throughout the various periods of modernity, this has clearly been the case when the relativity of values has been handled and explained in terms of group pathology, cultures of poverty, social degeneration or innate tendencies to delinquency and crime among certain ethnic communities or lower-class strata. These forms of explanation, which drew on the claims of cultural evolutionism, were no more satisfactory in grappling with cultural difference than those claims themselves, based as they were on assumptions of invariant, upward development or racially endowed levels of higher intelligence. Yet their rejection has led to various paradoxical consequences.

For example, the effort to avoid having recourse to attributions of pathology has often led to the almost antithetical position of cultural relativism. Cultural relativism conceives of cultural difference as arbitrary, conventional, normal and positive, and is thus theoretically in opposition to the censure and stigmatisation of deviance. Along with an attention to cultural meanings and personal investments in cultural values, this approach to social deviation usually entails an emphasis on the interpretation of experience from within, as it were, attempting to see how self-identity and action are geared to the general expectations and perceptions of response from an immediate culture, and to interaction with those who are taken to be most significant in the affirmation of identity within that culture.

Such an approach can clearly help in countering the social misrecognitions of stereotypical representations, yet it leaves unresolved the problem of how to reconcile an equality of respect with the acceptance of difference. How do we match up the relativistic affirmation of specific identities with discussions and decisions about collective cultural goods and values? Here the politics of equal respect, which argues that everyone should be treated the same, is at odds with the politics of difference, which argues that every individual or group identity is unique. It remains unclear how everyone can be accorded the same treatment if they are fundamentally different, or how differences can be known, never mind assessed, if our uniqueness is what creates them. Moving beyond the culturally specific and contingent is a familiar problem with relativism. It is also a problem undermining the ethos of multiculturalism, since it does not know where to go beyond a general recognition of the multiplication of difference.

This creates a huge impasse. According to the early twentieth-century sociologist, Emile Durkheim, 'the degree of severity of the censure of crime is a crucial index of a society's capacity for progressive change'. A society 'needs a degree of tolerance of the area between crime and mere difference to sustain its flexibility and capacity for change' (cited in Sumner, 1994: 18). The question of tolerance raises, but does not necessarily resolve, the paradoxical difficulties of recognising and living with cultural difference and diversity, for it is in the area between criminality and 'mere difference' that these are negotiated. This area involves moral and ethical values, including tolerance as a desirable goal, yet in approaching this goal we're constantly beset by vacillations of meaning and understanding. So, for example, if awareness of the social construction of norms and deviance makes 'concrete the principle of reflexivity in civil society', there is nevertheless 'a fundamental ambivalence within and about the value of tolerance as a general name for our consciousness of cultural diversity and relativism' (Chaney, 1994: 123–4). In some ways it could be argued that an increasing sense of 'rage against difference is the pernicious consequence of the reflexive arbitrariness of postmodern culture' (ibid: 125). Even without this degree of affective response, it remains more generally the case that the 'consequence of emphasising distinctive cultural identity … has been on the one hand to intensify feelings of cultural diversity, while, on the other, to exacerbate certain forms of an intransigent intolerance of difference' (ibid: 129).

This is not to suggest that there have been no advances or gains in moving beyond a commitment to strict notions of normality and conformity, at least so far as these applied in the middle decades of the twentieth century. This is clear enough in the increased recognition within contemporary culture of the ways in which the very boundaries between the normal and the pathological are secured by the constructions of deviant Otherness. It is through the stereotypical rhetoric of Otherness that normality is constituted, and the use of such rhetoric ensures that normality itself – or rather, common-sense notions of it – are naturalised and rendered self-evident. Through such assumptions of unquestioned position, normality operates as a regulative construct, providing a way of ordering and managing what people do or say in specific social practices, whether this is in teaching, social work, psychiatry or the legal system:

> The judges of normality are everywhere present. We are in the society of the teacher-judge, the doctor-judge, the educator-judge, the 'social worker'-judge;

it is on them that the universal reign of the normative is based; and each individual, wherever he may find himself, subjects to it his body, his gestures, his behaviour, his aptitudes, his achievements. (Foucault, 1977a: 304)

Yet in the face of Foucault's sweeping assessment it can be argued that the contingent nature of normality is more commonly seen as such than used to be the case forty or fifty years or more ago. One of the consequences of this is that when the view from within a particular group or community shows a way of seeing the world at variance with socially prevailing norms and values – the general 'standards of society' – this may now help to call into question the degree to which such norms and values are collectively shared, which in turn invites questions about interest and ideology. To which ends do they work and why is their partiality made invisible by claims to common agreement and applicability? In this way we return to the relativity of normality and the unstable terrain of moral judgement in a pluralised world.

Like the mythical components of national identity, the 'standards of society' which a normative framework invokes tend to be nebulous precisely because they are advanced as a set of universally shared moral principles and precepts. Along with an increased unwillingness to accept the claims of professional expertise and moral authority without question, there is now an increased scepticism of claims for collectively shared and approved values and beliefs. This scepticism draws strength from the recognition that the norms, rules and standards invoked by such claims are rarely spelt out or inspected. They remain vague and taken-for-granted, and as such may serve the interests of particular groups rather than others, while also obscuring the real conflicts between meaning and value systems among different groups in society. It is, again, the infractions of order and deviations from norms which not only come first in the invocation of consensus, but are also by contrast far more clearly delineated and defined. As C. Wright Mills once put it, in discussing the ideology of social pathology: 'There are few attempts to explain deviations from norms in terms of the norms themselves, and no rigorous facing of the implications of the fact that social transformations would involve shifts *in them*' (1963: 532, emphasis in original). Yet the spectre of normality always stands over and against any assigned presence of deviancy in the midst of the socially untransformed.

Normality implies stability, order and integration, but as Mills clearly recognised, the basis of these conditions is rarely given any serious consideration, even though some conception of what is socially 'healthy' is involved in determining what is 'pathological'. Mills refers to a variant of the pathological attribution which was still common in the early postwar period: 'maladjustment'. The remembered categories from my childhood in this period of 'maladjusted child' or 'maladjusted youth' – who were usually by implicit reference working class – still carry echoes of strong yet vague fears. It was as if what was referred to was a rather terrible condition which you would catch unless you, or your parents, were very careful. It could 'rub off onto you', in one of the anxiously assertive phrases I remember being used. At best what 'adjustment' meant was acceptance of 'the goals and means of smaller community milieux', whether this was suburban America or the English shires. What such 'adjustment' ignored was 'whether or not certain groups or individuals caught in economically underprivileged situations can possibly obtain current goals without drastic shifts in the basic institutions which channel and promote them' (Mills, 1963: 548–50).

To be 'adjusted' has generally meant conforming to white, middle-class, heterosexual ideals, and socialisation from this perspective amounts to being successfully inducted into these ideals. This perspective also shows up socialisation as a classically functionalist concept, premised as it was in the 1950s and 60s on an integrative social system from which any serious deviation was adjudged as 'maladjustment', or incomplete and inefficient socialisation. Clearly, on this basis, entire groups or categories of people can be adjudged as incompletely adjusted or worse, and their particular form of so-called deviance stereotyped accordingly. Deviant stereotypes legitimate dominant norms and control over their alleged subversion in a vicious ideological circle. The only way to break out of this circle is to deny the validity of the misplaced, and, by historical derivation, medical binarism of normal and pathological attributions, however these may be dressed up or whatever substitute terms may be used. The issue, instead, is to do with difference and censure, and the stereotypical or stigmatised forms of difference through which, at least partly, instances of censure are accomplished. The initial questions which follow are therefore to do with the constitutive recognition of difference and the social grounds on which censure operates. Once we begin to talk in this way, deviance at least begins to lose its regulative force, and discrimination may be forced to show its face. Colin Sumner has claimed that 'there can be no science of social deviance where the judges of normality use only the norms of the white male middle-class, where groups live in worlds apart, and where the relativism, factionalism and cultural bigotry intertwined with modernity's moral judgements constantly undercut its drive to order' (1994: 195–6). This is true, but it helps to know what you are up against, and which values are at stake. With discrimination openly revealed, rather than normatively cloaked, that at least is relatively clear.

Yet in attempting to formulate some kind of answer to the question 'what is normality?', the situation we face is one of insecurity and irresolution. The start of a new century finds Western societies beleaguered by ethical uncertainty and political pragmatism, as for instance in relation to institutional racism, even as, at least ostensibly, they embrace cultural diversity, assert the right to choose an individual lifestyle, and refuse the old habits of social deference and meek acquiescence to authority. In the face of the difficulties these new values appear to generate, there is a strong temptation to hark back to a time when whatever was happening in the wider society, somewhere down the road, seemed not to impinge on lives that appeared relatively settled, secure and at one with themselves. Conservative commentators often point to the early postwar period in this respect, creating a mythical time of social inclusion, consumer affluence and moral conformity in contrast to the alleged damage caused to the social fabric by the cultural revolution of the 1960s and early 1970s. As with any myth, there is a residual basis of truth in its claims, both with respect to the identified damage and the relatively more composed social life that preceded it, but the claims are greatly exaggerated. The exaggerations stem from the situation we are in where rules and standards are accepted without resolution as pluralistic and relative, and we lack – even eschew – the means for agreeing about the cultural goods we should seek. The only thing that is clear is that there is no going back, and that the historical jury for assessing the shift from modern to late-modern societies is still out.

Folk Devils

Despite inconsistencies between them and the regressions sometimes entailed, there is no doubt that many of the challenges to the apparently absolute values and consensual certainties of the mid-twentieth century – as for instance from feminism, the civil rights movement, anti-racism and gay politics – have been liberating and progressive. In a range of fruitful ways, they directly inform and sustain any critical analysis of the stereotyping process. But as we move away from the older inequities and discriminations, other previously stable sources of identity, in neighbourhood, family and work, have become severely unravelled. The working class has fragmented. Collectivist ideals are in disarray. Different social groups and strata are increasingly divided into fewer winners and ever-more losers, while many white-collar workers and people in professional occupations as well as those in manual trades are in insecure employment, uncertain about the future of their livelihoods. The rest are impoverished, unemployed and marginalised. In these conditions, it is the socially excluded and dispossessed who stand in greatest danger of being stereotyped and scapegoated, of being represented in ways excessively charged with negative symbolic value. This danger is increased by unreflexive moral reactions to the blurring of distinctions and the increasing ambivalence of values which undermine the very idea of normality. These involve an attempt to return to moral absolutism and a rigid demarcation between right and wrong.

One example of this tendency in recent years has been the resurgence of psychologistic and psychopathological ways of explaining and moralising crime and deviance. This is evident not only in the academic world, but also in media journalism and TV punditry, where ideas associated with 'adjustment' have been revived and, more disturbingly, conceptions of innate human evil and even of the Devil incarnate in human conduct have once again begun to surface. This return to kinds of thinking last prevalent in the 1950s concentrates on 'the criminal type' and 'criminal mentality', on 'pathological wickedness', or on 'mental sickness' conceived in a highly individualistic, asocial framework. Such representations of deviancy overturn virtually every tenet in earlier labelling theory and conflict theory while, at the same time, vindicating the concept of scapegoating. Scapegoating involves the symbolic identification and isolation of a social problem in a single individual or stereotyped category of person. The pathologisation of those scapegoated and their expulsion from the social body reasserts the boundaries of normality within which moral judgement wishes once more to sit pretty. Whether they are single mothers, drug addicts or gays, those who are scapegoated are regarded as having departed from a given set of norms, in these examples those relating to marriage, the nuclear family, heterosexuality and the work ethic. Rather than being a real incarnation of an imaginary Devil, those who are scapegoated are more commonly imagined as folk devils whose ideological value lies in deflecting attention from real social problems and contradictions.

'Folk devils' are one half of a conceptual couplet. They are the object of derogation created by a 'moral panic', a term initially referred to by

Jock Young (1971: 182) in relation to public concern over drug abuse, but then more thoroughly deployed by Stanley Cohen in his highly influential study of media, political and judicial responses to the mods and rockers of the 1960s (Cohen, 1973; see also Cohen, 1971 and Cohen and Young, 1973). The concept of moral panic refers to a perceived threat to socially dominant values or interests, the main protagonists of which are represented by the media 'in a stylised and stereotypical fashion', resulting in a spiralling escalation of the perceived threat, a manning of 'the moral barricades' by 'right-thinking people' and the pronouncement of 'diagnoses and solutions' by 'socially accredited experts' (Cohen, 1973: 9): 'tougher laws, moral isolation, a symbolic court action' (Weeks, 1985: 45). After the legitimately appropriate responses have been made, the panic then recedes until another overtakes it, in successive waves that build up, peak and crash on the shores of normality, slowly thinning out before disappearing, apparently without trace, into the sands of time. Those targeted as posing such threats are represented as contemporary 'folk devils' and met with suitably righteous indignation and moral rebuke. A now classic example of a 'folk devil' constructed through the signification spiral of a moral panic is the African-Caribbean 'mugger' of the mid-1970s: a 'personification of all the positive social images – only in *reverse*: black on white' (Hall et al., 1978: 161–2). Through such constructions of deviance, the media tell us much 'about the normative contours of society ... about the boundaries beyond which one should not venture and about the shapes that the devil can assume' (Cohen, 1973: 17).

Panic is a psychological condition. Its metaphorical value when applied to sociological phenomena such as a clash between opposed interests and values, or an orchestrated upsurge of public concern over a particular issue such as a youth subculture or so-called asylum-seekers, lies in capturing something of the short-lived intensity and over-inflated anxiety that is involved. Such qualities derive from the ways in which media-induced panics generate deep unease in areas of moral ambiguity. These areas lie between given norms and actions which transgress, upset, disturb or challenge the standards they are believed to set. As we have already noted more generally in relation to the material insecurities and moral uncertainties of late modernity, perhaps the most typical solution offered for the social malaise identified by moral panics is a revival of the old ways, based on clear-cut standards of behaviour, a return to the days of moral absolutes and cast-iron rules when 'people had respect for authority', 'everyone knew their place' and rectitude reigned. This fond look back to a mythical past and the melo-dramatic character in which moral panics are expressed act as ways of giving clarion symbolic significance to the norms and values which moral campaigners wish to see reasserted and enhanced, particularly at a time of perceived fear, anxiety and risk. They are also a response to the swirl of constant social change characteristic of (post) modernity, for it is this as much as the increasing pluralism of contemporary societies which creates the sense that 'the moral compasses by which to steer are increasingly uncertain' (*Observer*, 27 October 1996 cited in Thompson, 1998: 2).

Incidences of moral panics can be seen as periodic reactions to newly perceived threats to the moral and social order, but they are better explained as symptoms of broader changes and developments in social and economic structures, in communications technologies, and in forms of cultural interchange, identities, lifestyles and value-systems. These changes and the anxieties they produce are integral to the 'at-risk' character of modern or modernising societies, but as Kenneth Thompson suggests, in his recent handbook on the topic, what makes Britain particularly inclined to the generation of moral panics are the intensely competitive structure of its national press and the decline of earlier forms of élite authority, along with doubts and anxieties about questions of national identity 'in the face of increasing external influences and internal diversity' (1998: 141). In an ideological climate dominated over the past twenty years by the New Right combination of neo-liberal economics and neo-conservative moralism, there has certainly been no shortage of cheap sensationalism and reactionary moral campaigning, that mounted by the *Sunday Times* against a new 'underclass' being but one example. Thompson traces the ways in which moral panics about sexual promiscuity, AIDS, youth violence, 'video nasties' and so on have been whipped up at various times in the 1980s and 90s, and notes that such panics seem both to be on the increase and more all-pervasive in their identification of social threats rather than focusing on specific single-target groups such as Hell's Angels or muggers.

These changes are important, but they need to be set in a broader context of social and cultural change. Thompson operates with a remarkably foreshortened historical view, with all his cases and examples being taken from the second half of the twentieth century. It was reasonable enough for the first pioneering studies of moral panics in the late 1960s and 1970s to focus intensely on a particular temporal frame, for they were concerned primarily with developing an understanding of their immediate social dynamics. But it is now abundantly clear that moral panics were not confined to the period in which they were first studied or have subsequently been noted. Thompson's overview of moral panic theory exemplifies the obsessively present-centred view identified in Chapter 1 as a major weakness of far too much work on the politics of representation. A leading purpose of this book has been to counter this tendency by relating such politics to a perspective which re-centres the question of change and continuity over the wider historical span necessary for its consideration. To examine the discourse of moral panics without such a perspective is not only to neglect the accretions and sedimentations of meaning and value in representations of deviancy which I have attempted to highlight right from the start. As a peculiar consequence of consequences, it also reproduces one of the central ideological aspects of moral panics themselves. This is the inducement of historical amnesia.

A central feature in the episodic waves of moral panic is their reiteration of alarm over the same cause of concern, such as the feckless poor or welfare cheats, yet with little if any reflexive reference backwards. The absence of any consideration of this feature of moral panics is symptomatic of Thompson's historically impoverished framework. It leads to a failure to appreciate the significance of work which does attend to the weft of continuities in the broad canvas of historical movement. For example, Thompson pays scant attention to Golding and Middleton's (1982) study of media and public reactions to welfare 'scroungers' and 'cons', thus adding another brick in the wall of its unwarranted neglect compared with other studies of postwar moral panics. *Images of Welfare* shows the resilience and recurrence of popular stereotypes and myths in the long English tradition of hostility to the poor, tracing this back to its taproots in the treatment meted out to such 'undeserving' types as vagabonds, sturdy beggars and 'masterless men'. Unlike Golding and Middleton's work where a historical dimension informs the general analysis, Thompson's book barely glances back beyond the period in which the concept was first advanced. Fortunately, this neglect of longer-term continuities in modern fears about alleged threats to 'the moral fabric of society', as the beguilingly simple phrase has it, has been recently offset by John Springhall. His study of the roots of such fears, published in the same year as Thompson's handbook, develops the kind of longer-term perspective which I have adopted in my approach to the social analysis of stereotyping. Both moral panics and the stereotypes of folk devils on which they feed share a similar pattern of prevalence, dormancy and recrudescence over time. Forgetfulness or lack of awareness of the deep tentacular roots of certain ethnic or gender stereotypes contributes to their perpetuation in the same way as wave after wave of moral panics occur as if they were each a new response to a newly alarming situation. As Springhall puts it in his conclusion: 'Western societies which refuse self-knowledge by succumbing to more or less continuous "moral panics" ... are hardly well-equipped to withstand the upheavals of the end of the century' (1998: 162).

Although he touches on it only obliquely, Springhall's study complements Geoffrey Pearson's earlier myth-debunking 'history of respectable fears'. Pearson examines the ways in which claims about moral deterioration among contemporary youth have, as already acknowledged, been consistently made in contrast to an earlier halcyon period of social harmony and moderation. As you look back in an attempt to locate this period, it appears to recede further back into the past at each historical stage you reach. Similar fears and anxieties about 'kids today' appeared in the early postwar years, in the 'long weekend' between the wars, in the Edwardian age, and even in Victorian times, when moral order is imagined as having been strong and secure. Victorian Britain was, indeed, especially prone to moral panics, whether these were about garotters, scuttlers or hooligans (Pearson, 1983: Chapters 5 and 6; Sindall, 1990; Davies, 1998). To give just one example of such panics, it was noted by one commentator that while 'gangs of young roughs and thieves are no new thing in London and other large towns ... something like a scare has been produced by paragraphs in popular newspapers' (Trevarthen, 1901: 84).

Moral panics over women's sexual morality have also resurfaced in successive waves of alarm at various times when women have been seen to gain perceptibly in opportunity and independence, whether this was in the two world wars or through work outside the home in factory and field during the early nineteenth century. The implication in this 'fixed vocabulary of complaint' (Pearson, 1983: 230) has always been that social or sexual manners and mores were distinctly better at some blessed time in the past. As Pearson comments, in these 'successive waves of anxiety ... we appear to glimpse a series of "golden ages" nestling inside each other like a set of Russian dolls' (ibid: 156). The idealist reference backward disappears in the very past from which it seeks a normative locus.

Other historians of crime and deviance have productively drawn on the concept of moral panic, and revealed the ways in which scapegoating has been recurrently related to normative social values. For instance, Richard Evans questions stereotypes of the orderly and obedient nineteenth-century German in his study of the 'underworld' beneath 'respectable' society and their differential operation of power. In his final case study, he examines the diary of a young middle-class woman who fell into the 'half-world' of prostitution in the 1890s. Her ironic narrative of decline and fall showed up the 'heartless rigidity' of the conventions of 'respectable' society and graphically revealed 'the hypocrisy at its core'. The moral panic over pimping and procuring in the early years of that decade in Germany made a regular 'folk devil' of the pimp, who was 'increasingly portrayed as a racially degenerate or even alien figure' (Evans, 1998: 9, 192, 209) through a process of moral transposition similar to that achieved at roughly the same time in Britain by the quite different panics over 'hooligans' and the 'yellow peril' (Pearson, 1983: 75 and see Chapter 4 above). Although he is weaker when dealing with broader historiographical issues, Evans productively uses his subterranean micro-studies to reveal more broadly 'the ambiguities of criminality in modern German history, and the complexity of the relations between deviance and control', as well as providing a series of commentaries on Foucault's theoretical propositions (Evans, 1998: 215; and see Evans, 1997).

Springhall's own historical focus on moral panics is directed at popular entertainments and scares about their consequences for juvenile morals. These are traced to nineteenth-century anxieties about the 'ill effects' of new commercial amusements on 'children of the lower classes'. Such children were considered by the judges of normality to be doubly vulnerable because of their age and social location. These two categories were classified from the standpoint of the white, middle-class adult male as an immature, less rational psychological stage of individual development, and a set of debased social and cultural conditions. Because of their vulnerability, the threat posed by immoral influences from the new media was to any hope of saving lower-class children from damnation among the pathologised masses. Springhall focuses on moral panics about the new media through a series of case studies: penny theatres in the 1830s, 'penny dreadfuls' and 'dime novels' of the later nineteenth century, Hollywood 'gangster movies' of the 1930s, the 'horror comics' of the late 1940s and early 1950s, and (more briefly) 'video nasties' and computer games in the 1980s and 90s. Each of these panics has been conducted as if the issues raised were quite novel, yet the debates about them reveal many common features. In particular, targets of generationally specific forms of cultural consumption, assumptions of a direct relay between media experience and social behaviour, attempts to reassert age and class relations of power and authority, along with the general rhetoric of condemnation, run consistently through the criticism of youthful cultural tastes and affiliations all the way from early nineteenth-century penny gaffs to late twentieth-century 'gangsta rap'.

These continuities should not be allowed to underwrite the ahistorical use of the concept of moral panic. The scares and panics which Springhall deals with show a long lineage of cultural pessimism, but the pessimism they express emerges from particular constituencies which are always culturally and historically located. In playing to these constituencies, however, the media have, from the mid-nineteenth century onwards, repeatedly dramatised challenges to social order or infringements of common-sense values, framing certain issues as social problems and stigmatising certain groups as folk devils in order to preserve certain rules or bring new rules into moral or statutory existence. This process can of course be fuelled by publicising and lobbying on the part of campaign or pressure groups. Their stark oppositions of what is right and wrong and the media's sensationalist treatment of the identified social problem may have different motives – the struggle to gain a public voice and credibility on the one hand and the battle for revenue or ratings on the other – but they work happily in combination to produce the problem and folk devils they wish to target. The alarmist narratives and appraisals which the media purvey in these cases provide the tinder for the ensuing moral conflagration. Yet these cases are not unusually reported – they are reported in ways which derive from everyday run-of-the-mill news construction based on the usual criteria of newsworthiness, such as negativity, impact, dramatic appeal and ease of symbolic assimilation – Lippmann's 'line of least resistance'. As the authors of an excellent study of news organisation put it: 'journalists join with other agents of control as a kind of "deviance-defining élite"', providing 'an ongoing articulation of the proper bounds to behaviour'. In their view, 'deviance is the defining characteristic of what journalists regard as newsworthy'. Visualising deviance allows them to bring the normal into relief and to police social life 'for deviations from their conceptions of the order of things' (Ericson et al., 1987: 3–5).

In what remains a rewarding study of drug use, Jock Young identified the formula which seems so often to be followed in media treatments of moral or social conflict. As he had it, events are selected which are atypical, presented in a stereotypical fashion and contrasted against a backcloth of normality which is overtypical. This diminishes the significance of habitual social life while constantly playing on people's conventional worries so that 'the stereotypical distorted image of the deviant' stands in stark contrast to 'the overtypical, hypothetical "man in the street"' (Young, 1971: 179; cf. Reinarman, 1994: 96). It is worth quoting an example given by Young for the way it fused the atypical, stereotypical and overtypical:

> HIPPIE THUGS – THE SORDID TRUTH: Drugtaking, couples making love while others look on, rule by a heavy mob armed with iron bars, foul language, filth and stench, THAT is the scene inside the hippies' fortress in London's Piccadilly. These are not rumours but facts – sordid facts which will shock ordinary, decent, family-loving people. (*People*, 21 September 1969)

This headline and narrative lead-in to the news story condensed both the chosen folk devils of the day and the backcloth of decent normality against which their shock value was exploited. The story attempted to stir up a moral scare out of the contrast between them, and it began to do so, as Young wryly noted, in two magnificent sentences. These two sentences reveal a fascination with as well as fear of the object of moral indignation. The suspicion that deviant others may be realising the covert desires of 'ordinary, decent, family-loving people', and unde-servedly enjoying a lifestyle secretly coveted by those locked inside their own idealised ordinary decency, provides the attraction of such prurient sanctimony.

The one-dimensional stereotypes of drug users which Young dealt with in his study said much more about those who used them as a way of projecting their own fears and desires rather than confronting them, while the media, in attempting to arouse moral indignation, accentu-ated the scapegoating process that affirmed the rules on which it was based. In analysing how this happens, Young supports the perspective on the transgression of norms which I outlined at the beginning of this chapter: 'There is little point in having rules if you have no rule-breakers; norms occur where there is, at least, a perceived possibility of infraction occurring' (1971: 105). Yet if regulation requires disruption, who installs, inspects and maintains the regulation is a matter of social power. As Cohen noted, moral panics are rooted in 'conflicts of inter-ests – at community and societal levels – and the presence of power differentials which leave some groups vulnerable to such attacks' (1973: 198). These conflicts have continually been caught up in the constant upheavals and disruptions that characterise modernity, transforming given norms, networks, traditions and other benchmarks of social exper-ience. Uncertainties in the face of new cultural encounters and clashes between various values and standards create the need to put things back in their place, fasten them down again and redress the moral disequilibrium that has seemed to ensue from new media, new cultural forms or new social opportunities, particularly as they have become available for the up-and-coming generations. Both stereotypes and moral panics have long been implicated in these reactions to change and transformation and the discourses attendant on them.

Among others, Kirsten Drotner has noted how the stereotypical objects of moral panics are relegated to the shadows of acceptance once the panic passes and a new object of panic arises. The graded cultural absorptions which this involves are closely linked to the historical amnesia that afflicts both moral panics and the resurgence of stereotypical attributions in appropriate contexts. If, as she says, 'everybody must learn the fundamental lesson of modernity – the need to live with the possibility of social, cultural, and psychological change', then the attention to new media, new cultural forms and avenues centres on their use and exploration among young people because of the ways they challenge the parameters of normality established in their upbringing. This perceived challenge has been countered in relation to popular music, dance, comics, cinema, television and so on through the stereotypical construction of certain youth groups or subcultures within the folk devil syndrome. As Drotner puts it, 'the social claims and cultural competences that the young often gain as spin-offs of their media use pose a potential threat to existing power relations in social as well as in cultural and psychological terms'. Through scares about sexual depravity, mindless hedonism, cultural decline or whatever, attempts are made 'to re-establish a generational status quo that the youthful pioneers seem to undermine'. In her astute summary of what is involved in moral panics about new media, Drotner suggests that they act as cultural seismographs that 'reveal broader problems of modernity', and operate through one or more Others who 'through their very absence [remain] … central sources of renewed attacks. It is impossible to speak "about" these Others. On the other hand, without them it is impossible to speak at all' (Drotner, 1992: 52–60). This neatly sums up the paradoxical nature of moral panics as a form of public discourse that betrays an inherent inability to engage in discourse between differential publics. But what of the stereotypically targeted folk devils? How have they been affected by the moral panics arising out of the contradictions of modernity?

The paradigmatic explanation offered by the sociology of deviance was that of the amplification of deviant identities. This can be roughly recapped in the following way. The stereotypical identification of a form of behaviour, social philosophy or lifestyle as 'deviant' depends on an interactive process of perceived action by the identified source, and declared reaction on the part of those with a vested interest in existing moral, social and political order. Media involvement in this reaction helps to generate a spiral of signification that dramatises and escalates the initial cause of concern through the combination and diffusion of 'folk devil' stereotypes. This increases the degree of perceived deviancy, and those who are targeted may then react to the social reaction against them by introjecting the stereotypical constructions through which they have been publicly portrayed, yet inflecting the identified features with positive values so that they become normative for the deviancy involved. This in turn increases yet further the social reaction against them in such a way that, as a self-fulfilling prophecy, the originating stereotypes are confirmed in a manner now writ large in public opinion. As Jock Young put it in relation to drug taking: 'the stereotypes may reach such a degree of public currency that individuals are recruited into drug use. In all these instances the fantasy stereotypes of the powerful and the reality of the illicit drug user become identical' (1971: 115–6).

This kind of development has been explained both in terms of imbalances and asymmetries of social power and resources, and of the capacity of deviant individuals and groups to make meaningful the ways in which they have been labelled and turned against by mainstream society. In both these ways, it seemed clear that the prior infractions created and affirmed the normality whose boundaries they were said to transgress, thus deepening the imagined gulf between the twin constructions of normality and deviancy. The problem with this conclusion is that it was generally drawn from the further reaches of the amplification spiral, leaving unclear how usual such extensions actually are. Examples of weekend forms of deviancy are legion, where departures from otherwise accepted conventions are a more or less socially accepted leisure-time pursuit. Deviancy in these ways acts as a temporary diversion coupled with the adoption of conformist behaviour and identity. This is a further source of moral ambivalence concerning difference and sameness, tolerance of diversity and commitment to particular cultural norms and values. It leads us on to a consideration of some of the shortcomings of moral panic theory.

Flaws in the Moral Panic Model

Moral panic theory was successful in describing certain symbolically laden public scares of the 1960s and 70s, particularly in relation to some of the youth subcultures of those decades and to specific forms of crime, especially, but not exclusively, 'crimes without victims'. There is no doubt that it identified a common right-wing political strategy and revealed the operative modes of construction, by the media and various agents of social control, of common-sense consensuality and 'moral majority' rhetoric. Moral panic theory also gave the lie to the absolutist criteria of behavioural psychology in dealing with deviance and 'juvenile delinquency'. It formed a major component of some of the best work in communications research during the 1970s and early 1980s (see Halloran et al., 1970 and Barker, 1984 for two further examples of such research) and contributed to the development of a critical lexicon in what has become known, in its relatively settled educational form, as media studies. A more sophisticated understanding of ideology resulted from this work. It is part of its legacy that notions of stereotypical formation as simple distortion of an otherwise readily knowable reality have given way to a focus on the broader social connections and structures of discursive othering that I have tried to develop in this book.

The analytical model developed around moral panic theory would also seem more or less adequate when applied to certain subsequent amplification spirals, such as the early 1990s' hue and cry over youth crime and media violence, lone mothers and moral decline, following the murder of two-year-old Jamie Bulger, or the mid-1990s' vilification of the drug Ecstasy following the tragic death of Leah Betts at her eighteenth birthday party. Yet at the same time the model does not happily accord with other cases of moral panic, such as the Cleveland scandal of 1987. This involved claims of widespread sexual abuse within families in this area of north-east England. In the ensuing moral panic, ambivalence and uncertainty were much more to the fore, with opposed stereotypes of the incestuous father and the interfering social worker (Nava, 1988; Jenkins, 1992: 16–17). Viewed retrospectively, the model can be seen to have various shortcomings, and it is important to touch on at least some of these as they relate to the issue of stereotypical representation and amplification.

First, moral panics are more varied in form and development than the earlier model suggests. They are also far more routinely and systematically contested than used to be the case. This is a main point raised by Angela McRobbie. The folk devils targeted by moral panics are now 'fiercely defended by any one of a range of pressure groups which have emerged as a key force in opposing the policies of the new right during and after the Thatcher years' (1994: 199). She adds that while moral panics deflect attention from complex social problems and encourage people either to retreat into a fortress mentality or to adopt a gung-ho 'something must be done about it' attitude, the targeted 'folk devil' is now less morally isolated and the social reaction less monolithically articulated and aligned. This is not only related to the expansion of new campaign organisations skilled in countering attempts to stereotype and stigmatise the groups they represent, in providing soundbites and adding their own spin to media stories. It also needs to be understood in the light of media expansion and diversification in the late twentieth century, and, in contrast to the early postwar years, the socially more segmented and culturally more sophisticated character of their audiences. This second set of developments exists in tension with the increasing competitiveness of the mainstream press, at least in Britain, which remains the chief generator of moral panics and offers some of the most stark forms of moral stridency in the cultures of postmodernity. The moral panic model nonetheless needs to be overhauled and revised 'precisely because of its success' (ibid: 217).

The earliest work on moral panics in British sociology was concerned with youth subcultures, but these appear to have ceased developing in the sort of formations in which they coalesced in the third quarter of the twentieth century. The terms 'moral panic' and 'folk devil' have meanwhile become absorbed into the modishly ironic discourse of so much journalistic treatment of youth style and pop music, while references to subcultures signify not the attempt to realise 'magical' solutions to unresolved contradictions in the parent culture or to real problems of unequal social position, but instead to manifest 'the endless attempt to create popular interest in each new commodity being thrown onto the youth market' (see also Taylor, 1999: 75; Hall and Jefferson, 1975: 30–3; and Cohen, 1997: 57). The accusation of whipping up a moral panic is now a standard media debating point and interview ploy, while the incidence of moral panics has rapidly increased. They are now a routine rather than irregular occurrence, without the same sequential pacing of stages and cycles that was advanced in the earlier analytical model. Further, whereas moral panics are said to generate nostalgia for a 'golden age' of social stability and moral discipline as a form of ideological cohesion, contemporary youth are themselves said 'to have overwhelming nostalgia for the days when youth culture was genuinely transgressive', with earlier youth 'folk devils' forming part of the folklore of celebrated figures in 1990s' youth culture:

> Moral panic can therefore be seen as a culmination and fulfilment of youth cultural agendas in so far as negative news coverage baptises transgression.

What better way to turn difference into defiance, lifestyle into social upheaval, leisure into revolt? (McRobbie and Thornton, 1995: 565; see also Thornton, 1995: 120, 132–7)

Moral panics have long been commercially as well as morally exploited. From rock 'n' roll to acid house, deviance and calculated moral outrage have been used to sell youth products. Although he concentrated on its implications for 'social control', Stan Cohen clearly recognised how the mods and rockers phenomenon fed into the marketing of youth style. As an extension of a central theme in this chapter, we can point to the commercial *necessity* of infraction from given cultural norms in youth consumer markets. As Phil Cohen notes, mock confessionally, 'moral panics ... deal in self-fulfilling prophecies and it's an open trade secret that the supply of a particular kind of provision tends to stimulate the demand for that type of service' (Cohen, 1997: 193). For example, McRobbie and Thornton note with regard to the promotion of acid house music: 'Moral panics are one of the few marketing strategies open to relatively anonymous instrumental dance music. To quote one music monthly, they amount to a "priceless PR campaign"' (1995: 565). For this reason, a tabloid page, however distorted, 'can turn the most ephemeral fad into a lasting development' (Thornton, 1994: 183). Of course, the use of scandal, controversy and tragic news has been the mainstay of market promotion since the commercialisation of popular entertainment, whether this was yellow journalism or the cinema, but it is perhaps only in the last thirty years or so that the commercial exploitation of infraction has become routine practice, a development which, somewhat perversely, makes normality itself seem less monolithic and incontrovertible, even when (or even because) the marketing involved is niched and specialist and directed towards self-consciously 'alternative' readerships and audiences.

As already noted, a further drawback with the moral panic model is that certain kinds of public vilification do not conform to it. Simon Watney has shown how the representation of gay men and lesbian women, as well as sexuality more generally, entails not so much an episodic as a *'permanent* ideological struggle over the meaning of signs'. Moral panic theory 'is unable to conceptualise the mass media as an industry which is intrinsically involved with excess, with a voracious appetite and capacity for substitutions, displacements, repetitions and signifying absences'. In the world of the media, heterosexuality is normality, with other forms of sexual identity proving its sanctity by their devilish aberrations from 'decent human nature', by being, as Watney says of homosexuality, continually constructed as 'intrinsically monstrous'. In the face of such representation, it is not the discontinuity marked by a moral panic which counts so much as the relentless continuity and incessant pressure of sexual and gender normality bearing down upon 'sexual deviants'. Any particular moral panic 'merely marks the site of the current front-line in such struggles'.

For Watney the key ideological function of the communications media is the production and reproduction of a unified 'collective mutual complementarity' – the social fantasy of being the 'same together' – with any threat to its 'internal cohesion', such as that constructed around gay men, becoming a deterrent icon of Otherness (Watney, 1987: 41–3). The significance of the AIDS crisis of the 1980s was that it provided an opportunity to call into question the 'three main strands in the moral and sexual shifts of the past generation: a partial secularisation of moral attitudes, a liberalisation of popular beliefs and behaviours, and a greater readiness to accept social, cultural and sexual diversity'. (Thompson, 1998: 84–5). The residues of anxiety and fear left by these changes were exploited by the AIDS panic in an effort to restore a conception of the prior moral and social normality of the 1950s. But the 'policing of desire' is a continuous and more complex process than moral panic theory comprehends. It involves the kinds of ambivalence of exclusion and attraction, regulation and fantasies of transgression, that I tried to highlight in the previous chapter.

Finally, and briefly, moral panic theory is a product of modernist sociology. It is at least partly because of this that it has such a remarkable paucity of explanatory power in historical terms. It tells us virtually nothing about the longer-term generation of moral panics as opposed to their apparently sudden efflorescence, and it sheds little light on their disappearance and on processes of deamplification. Why moral panics flare up at certain times and not others is hardly addressed. Are the conditions for this utterly contingent and immediate, or prepared for through a much longer concatenation of events, episodes, changes and conjunctures? We hardly seem to know. Moral panic analysis offers a sociological snapshot at a particular time, yet in relation to temporal dynamics and movement, it is pretty well illiterate. Despite the efforts of writers like Pearson and Springhall to rectify this by tracing the historical lineages of moral panics about youth deviance and popular entertainments, why they appear to share similar characteristics, why they serially recur and how they connect over time, effectively channelling images and values in processes of cultural transmission, and linking up past resources and meaning-making in the present, remain largely unanswered questions. It is precisely because of its conceptual design that the notion of 'moral panic' is limited in its analytical focus to the hazards of surface discontinuities. Such hazards cannot be properly understood without a way of theoretically embracing the broader movements of historical change from which they spring, and the broader structures of continuity and tradition, conformity and normality, against which they are viewed. The censure of perceived threats to social cohesion does not arise from short-term events, yet it is the immediate response to these which dominates the frame of moral panic theory. It is as if it has always been transfixed by the glare of an incessant headline.

Normality and Stereotypical Censure

For a long time within sociology deviance in itself and in its specific constructions were considered as objective and coherent categories rather than terms of discipline and reformism integral to normative systems of representation. At best they were subject to few attempts at demystification beyond noting the moral entrepreneurship involved in the deployment of stereotypical categories of moral and criminal condemnation. In the 1960s, when social deviance began to be understood in some cases as an intended expression of disaffiliation from mainstream society, this clashed with previous conceptions of social deviants as in some way deficient or aberrant in relation to normality. Once normality is relativised, deviance loses its apparently objective character. The contrary pull between disaffiliation and deviancy presented the sociology of deviancy with a difficulty it was never able to resolve. In moving from an early emphasis on social degeneration and social pathology, through sociopathy and labelling theory to conflict theory and deviancy taken as a form of ideological critique, the sociological study of deviancy completely undermined the basis on which it was established. Since every sphere of life contains 'its own normality and deviance and as we move from one sphere to another we regularly cross the border of normalcy/deviance', we are all potentially objects of such study (Sumner, 1994: 228). This recognition unravels the very rationale of deviancy studies. Deviance began to be seen as a category of attribution and judgement, generated by conflicts between different value-systems, and thus as an ideological category, not, as Becker once emphasised, 'a quality of the act the person commits but rather a consequence of the application by others of rules and sanctions' (Becker, 1966: 9). In the end there was nothing left to study apart from the social attribution and judgement of deviancy.

It is only with hindsight that we can say this is where the sociological study of deviancy should have started from in the first place: not with the apparently objective category of deviancy, but with its socially and historically relative attribution. The lesson can nevertheless be learnt, and in the sociology of censure all the old priorities must be overturned, with attention always given in the first instance to infraction as the basis for stereotypical judgements, rather than simply the assumption of conformity to a social or cultural norm. This is important in so far as judgements do tend to proceed on this basis rather than through a more tentative and circumspect negotiation of the relation between norms and the politics of representation and legitimation. In the 1970s and 80s, while some attempts were made to demystify its key categories (for example, Hall et al., 1978; Box, 1983), there was a strong tendency in the sociology of crime and deviance to economism and class reductionism, translating the relative autonomy of moral judgement into an overly directive strategy of interest and leaving the ideological character of legal censure untheorised (Sumner, 1990: 24–5). In attempting to move beyond these tendencies, Sumner suggests that the concept of social deviance did not 'so much provide us with a conceptually strong way of understanding moral ambiguity as with a new way of organising the censure and administration of groups who posed "social problems" for the state'. The concept was undermined by the 'painfully obvious moral judgement needed to establish the existence of any deviance and by the contingency involved in the whole process of getting stigmatised' (1994: 310). It is for this sort of reason that Sumner argues for a sociology of censure. Through denunciation and regulation, the signifying function of censures is to demarcate 'the deviant, the pathological, the dangerous and the criminal from the normal and the good' (1990: 27). He goes on:

> Because they signify worth and correctness against wrong and danger, they simultaneously form a justification for repressive action against the offender and for attempts to educate the recipient into the desired habits or way of life. Their frequent appeal to general moral principles gives them inherent political potential in the constant struggle for hegemony. (ibid)

Our understanding of stereotyping needs to be situated within the broader field of social censures. This is a further move in making it part of a set of bigger stories. The approach taken by Sumner sits happily enough with the way I have been treating stereotyping, particularly in emphasising the discursive features of its particular forms, their social and historical specificities as well as continuities, and the social relations and cultural contexts in which they occur. Stereotyping is clearly one among various other practices of censure, yet Sumner himself glides over it as if what it involves can simply be taken for granted. Even though he uses the term 'stereotype' quite frequently, it is not included in the index to his zestful obituary of the sociology of deviance, an oversight which is indicative of the problem of its conceptual neglect. It is because I oppose this neglect that I have paid prolonged attention to it as a strategy of moral closure. Moral closure is a prerequisite of consensual belief. The invocation of consensus relies on the assumption of a commitment to shared values and beliefs. In the face of clear evidence showing that the claims of what is socially shared and accepted are greatly exaggerated, belief in such claims may still be strongly advanced and supported. The sociology of censure needs to attend closely to the construction of social deviance which symbolically validates the evaluation and condemnation involved, and it must do this without reproducing the binary divisions between the authority of judgement and whatever is stereotypically positioned by it as socially deviant. It must, in other words, operate with a clear sense of moral judgement as inherently ambivalent.

The base term 'deviance' is neither sociologically nor ethically valid when that which 'deviance' departs from is what brings it into existence, at least in the self-fulfilling form in which it is then discussed and evaluated, whether this is cast as either abnormal individual psychology or aberrant group behaviour. If what is defined as deviant is defined as such because it breaks with a normative consensus, then what needs to be studied are the judgements made in the name of consensus, the relations between particular norms and particular breaches of them as these are represented, and the structures underlying the conditions in which such norms are considered normal. The question of these more pervasive and stable norms is related to the problems of how moral consensus is sustained over time, of how cycles of episodic recurrence speak to both continuity and change, and of how particular conjunctural situations generate such recurrence in resurgent forms of stereotyping and newly reasserted symbolic boundaries when, as always seems to follow, difference and diversity are re-articulated as deviancy and danger and, as a last resort, criminalised. Yet if, in focusing on socially defined deviance, we want to retain a distinction between crime and certain activities which have become criminalised because of their 'difference' from given norms, in what way does this impart to what has thus been defined as deviant any conceptual clarity or coherence? The answer has to be: very little. The activities and their associated evaluations in the particular social, cultural and historical contexts which are potentially involved are so variable and diverse that there can be no specifically definable kind of behaviour which is 'deviant', and therefore no generalised object that could form the core of a theory of deviance. Deviant is not something you can simply be.

The great nineteenth-century socialist writer and activist, Karl Marx, once wrote a superbly ironic passage in order to ridicule typical bourgeois proprieties about decency and depravity, and heroic bourgeois myths about innovation and progress. He noted how the criminal 'produces not only crimes but also criminal law, and with it the professor who gives lectures on criminal law and in addition to this a compendium which this same professor throws onto the general market as "commodities"' (Marx, 1988: 306–9). Indeed, he went on, the criminal 'produces the whole of the police and of criminal justice, constables, judges, hangmen, juries etc', not to mention all the art, journalism, dramatic tragedies and the like which, in focusing on forms of social transgression, engage our moral and aesthetic faculties. The criminal, in short, keeps bourgeois life free from stagnation and provides a vital stimulus to productive forces (ibid). Insistence on the priority of infraction applies a similarly wry corrective to the moral sanctimony of normality, the way in which it forces the light of what appears indubitably objective and right to fall exclusively on itself, after rather than before the fact of its 'logical negation' in 'the execution of the normative project' (Canguilhem, 1989: 243). In many cases of course, norms and infractions, limits and transgressions unevenly coexist, in a relationship of conflicting yet mutually constitutive recognition: 'a limit could not exist if it were absolutely uncrossable and, reciprocally, transgression would be pointless if it merely crossed a limit composed of illusions and shadows' (Foucault, 1977b: 34). The study of stereotyping nevertheless demands that we attend closely to what has been pushed into the shadows, to 'what has been rejected from our own civilisation in terms of its systems of exclusion [and] refusal, in terms of what it does not want, its limits' (Foucault, 1989: 65). What is symbolically rejected defines the limits within which the centred, normative subject is located and naturalised.

While commitment to the notion of normality and integrative structures has certainly weakened over the past half-century, ideas about normality remain consensually powerful when complacently endorsed by any evaluation of perceived departures from it as inferior and low. Stereotypically identified forms of deviance are then the rhetorical components of moral closure. The censure involved in this has always been built into their very definition, whether it has been the juvenile delinquent, the drop-out, the mugger, the prostitute or the scrounger who has been the target of stereotypical attention. As a particularly revealing example of such censure, what were perceived as the socially deviant actions of the Greenham Common peace campaigners in the 1980s produced numerous images in the media of filth, squalor and pollution (they were described as 'smelling of fish paste and bad oysters'), animated various forms of symbolic boundary-maintenance, and generated ritually exorcistic strategies – soldiers bared their backsides to the women, and in a sort of latter-day charivari, local vigilantes threw buckets of excrement, maggots and pig's blood into the women's benders (their home-made shelters) (Gellhorn, 1989: 381). As Stallybrass and White astutely commented, the women's perceived 'transgressions of gender, territorial boundaries, sexual preference, family and group norms [were] ... transcoded into the "grotesque body" terms of excrement, pigs and arses' (Stallybrass and White, 1986: 23–5). In this way, the symbolic grotesquerie of low-Otherness in the politics of response to the Greenham women was not only 'an overt reminder of patriarchal dominance', but also became 'a primary, highly charged intersection and mediation of social and political forces, a sort of intensifier and displacer in the making of identity' (ibid; see also Cresswell, 1996: 97–145).

Normality calls itself into being by posing the transgression of its exclusionary limits and then makes social judgements on this basis. But what lies beneath or beyond an imposed limit troubles the act of judgement itself, so that deviancy not only calls normality into being but also draws it into danger, the danger of reflexively toying with the relativism of normative judgements. As we have seen in discussing both colonial discourse and social deviance, fear and fascination are 'the twin poles of the process in which a *political* imperative to reject and eliminate the debasing "low" conflicts powerfully and unpredictably with a desire for the other' (Stallybrass and White, 1986: 5, emphasis in original). It is because of this 'constitutive ambivalence' of hierarchical judgement in the politics of representation that what is socially peripheral is often symbolically central: 'The low-Other is despised and denied at the level of political organisation and social being while it is instrumentally constitutive of the shared imaginary repertoires of the dominant culture' (ibid: 5–6; also Babcock, 1978: 32). Understanding these centre–periphery interrelations of the social and symbolic means 'shifting the focus of theoretical attention' away from the binary evaluative categories they involve and onto 'the process of classification itself' (Hall, 1993b: 23). The sociology of censure in late-modern culture is thus, inescapably, an interrogation of the symbolic classifications of its constitutive social forms.

Chapter 8

The Sociology of the Stranger

*The settled man says: 'How can one live without certainty about
the day to come, how can one sleep without a roof over his head!'
But an accident threw him out of his home forever, and he spends
his nights in the woods. He cannot sleep: he is afraid of wild
animals, of his own brother the vagabond. In the end, however,
he entrusts his life to contingency, starts living the vagabond's
life and even, perhaps, sleeps quietly at night.*

Lev Shestov, cited in Bauman, 1991: 81

The Stranger and Modernity

From the figure of the deviant it is appropriate to turn to the figure of
the stranger, for both call given cultural norms and standards into question. These two figures cannot of course be simply equated, for they are
generalised categories and there are important sociological distinctions
between them. Both are of interest for the ways in which, among other
things, they subvert modernity's drive to order and compulsive
normality, but in terms of their more particular presence, strangers are
disturbing figures in quite a different way to the figures of deviancy.
They can of course be subject to attempts to define or label them, in
the same way as with social deviancy. For example, differentiations are
commonly made between immigrants, foreigners, asylum-seekers and
gasterbeiter. These are terms for non-national groups that try to fix them
into unambivalent categories. They may seem quite benign, at least
when compared with more repugnant terms for such groups, but this
depends very much on the context in which they are used. For example,
asylum-seeker has now become a racist epithet in Britain because of
hostile coverage of the refugee issue in the tabloid press during 1999
and 2000. The way in which the term stranger is used is also context-
dependent, but as a general category it has a different set of meanings

and associations to those used for non-national groups. I want to begin this chapter by exploring what they involve and how they have developed during the modern period.

Strangers are disturbing because of the difficulty of conventionally placing them, of deciding exactly where they're at. They are neither socially peripheral nor symbolically central, but somewhere peculiarly in between. It is through their anomalous, hybrid position that they may upset any settled pattern, any assertion or appearance of fixed social arrangements. The stranger is inherently ambivalent. The relations of belonging and unbelonging are unsettled and confused by the figure of the stranger because he or she exists in a continual contact zone between belonging and unbelonging. It's because of this that responses to strangers are divided between seeing them as like 'us' and unlike 'us', here and yet still elsewhere, welcome newcomers and unwelcome interlopers, 'fitting in' and being marked with the symbolic brand of the 'enemy within'. Strangers are ambivalent not in the sense already examined in relation to Otherness, but ambivalent because they are neither Other nor not-Other. That is why they upset the normative structures of assessment and censure. They become a target of stereotyping because they are by *definition* elusive to definition.

Definitions are useful, and we couldn't get by without them, but certain forms of defining can become too hard and fast, and lead us into inflexible ways of thinking. That's exactly what a stereotype attempts to do. It tries to create a tight knot of attitudinal thought by attaching a rigidly fixed definition to a social category. Stereotyping exploits the mismatches between different categories and category systems in order to make existing symbolic boundaries seem more absolute, more tightly set in place. We have seen that stereotypes can be charged with either negative or positive values, but the distinction this sets up is an illusion. 'Good' and 'bad' stereotypes are closely interwoven – they are part and parcel of the same process of evaluation and judgement. Stereotyping attempts to translate cultural difference into Otherness, in the interests of order, power and control. At the same time this hides the dilemma of how to enter into open dialogue with cultural difference. As I have argued throughout, seeking to annul this dilemma is a crucial function of stereotyping. It refuses the challenge of moving with the contrasting grain of difference by transforming it into what is always one's own, so affirming and protecting what is constitutive of one's own from ever being 'othered' in itself. The significance of strangers lies in their challenge to the effects of stereotyping. They call such effects into question by exposing the apparent clarity and stability of stereotypes, by making them more equivocal, less absolute and 'natural'. They deny the binary oppositions of 'good' and 'bad' categories which stereotyping sets up and show them as arbitrary and conventional rather than as distinctions that can be flexibly negotiated and, if necessary, reconceived. That's why I have chosen to finish this book with a discussion of strangers.

The stranger has been an abiding preoccupation within the socio-logical tradition. This is primarily because the phenomenon of the stranger is a central feature of modernity, the characteristics and conse-quences of which are central to sociological enquiry and theory. Various aspects of this preoccupation will be discussed in this chapter. All the work that has been done on the stranger within sociology extends back to the German sociologist Georg Simmel. It was Simmel who first artic-ulated the stranger's significance for our understanding of modern society. He was interested in the stranger because what he called socia-tion – that dense web of social interaction and relations involving specific cultural forms and values – was a key focus of his approach to understanding society. In attending to the constitutive forms of socia-tion, Simmel's fascination was with what he called 'the wonderful indis-solubility of society, the fluctuations of its life, which constantly attains, loses and shifts the equilibrium of its elements' (cited in Swingewood, 1984: 141). Simmel's sociology was in this way characterised by its sensi-tivity to ambiguity and ambivalence. His interest in the stranger derived from an alertness to those moments outside of the attainment of sociality when the equilibrium of its elements begins to shift. For him, the stranger is sociologically valuable because of acting as a catalyst of such moments, opening up a gap of ambivalence and irresolution in the taken-for-granted social relations of everyday life.

Simmel treated the stranger as a social form at the centre of structures of interaction characterised, from a perspective of belonging, by being both remote and close at hand, mobile and yet somehow settled, feared and yet desired. For the stranger's part, being 'here' does not betoken any sense of belonging, for that which is germane to this sense is generative of their loss, their unbelonging, their dislocation from what gives cohe-sion and solidarity to ingroups, even though this dislocation may bring new opportunities in its wake that were not previously available in some anterior time or experience. The stranger stands incongruously within those patterns of sociation based upon collusive antagonisms, the inter-dependent divisions between 'us' and 'them'. It is because the stranger is someone who 'comes today and stays tomorrow' (Wolff, 1964: 402) that there is such a compound of negative and positive features, such an admixture of antinomies in the insider/outsider relations by which strangers are characterised. This remains the case despite the conflictual nature of those relations and the relative lack of power wielded by those classified as strangers. Their lack of power is only in extreme cases a total lack because the quality of ambivalence – of 'being strange' but not starkly unfamiliar, of being close and yet distant – allows strangers some degree of leverage over those who see or speak from the asymmetrical perspective of belonging, of being 'at home'.

For Simmel, the figure of the stranger was symbolically tied up with the unsettling experience of modern metropolitan life. When your own presence seems fleeting and social forces seem to overwhelm you, how do you retain a sense of individuality and autonomy? While this problem interested other sociologists of the period, such as Weber, Tönnies and Durkheim, Simmel had a distinctive angle on it. His preoccupation was with the interiority of experience – the internalisation of external forces into people's lives, the filtration of the structures of social organisation into their personal identities. His observations were based on Berlin in its phase of rapid expansion during the late nineteenth and early twentieth centuries. As with other metropolitan centres such as Paris, London, Chicago and New York, Berlin was at that time developing into a new kind of social environment, which Simmel referred to as 'not a spatial entity with sociological consequences, but a sociological entity that is formed spatially' (cited in Frisby, 1984: 131). While particular groups could still be located in specific areas, and thus at a distance from each other, in the new crowded urban centres diverse social groups were being brought openly together as an indiscriminate collection of unconnected people.

For some people experience of this has created an exhilarating sense of personal freedom. They have felt liberated from the claustrophobic morality, petty philistinism and hidebound prejudices which can hem in the small town or village inhabitant. But the price for this new-found freedom is the cold instrumental approach to social interaction characteristic of life in big cities. For Simmel, this 'inconsiderate hardness' in social relations is entirely compatible with a mature money economy in which people are pitted against each other in the struggle for gain and advantage. Preference is given to a calculating rationality in our transactions and dealings. Relationships between people are predominantly mediated by the 'unmerciful matter-of-factness' or impersonality of market forces (Wolff, 1964: 411–12, 420). An increasingly specialised division of labour is co-ordinated by 'the cold and heartless calculus of the necessary money exchanges' (Harvey, 1991: 26). As Simmel put it: 'Money is concerned only with what is common to all [phenomena]: it asks for the exchange value, it reduces all quality and individuality to the question: How much?' (cited in Wolff, 1964: 411). What, Simmel asked, is the characteristic form associated with this quantitative calculus of social relations?

The answer, in short, is objectification: treating people like objects or commodities, approaching them alike with a calculating attitude of 'how much?' and 'at what profit?' This accelerates even further the transformation of cultural variety into social dislocation. These conditions of urban life become characteristic of the interiority of its experience. Simmel's defining approach to modernity centres around a distinct mode of experiencing which consists of psychologically turning the external social world inwards, experiencing that external world as an inner world, in specific forms of subjectivity that are a characteristic response to the proliferating objectification of modern culture. For Simmel, a new sensibility has developed in which social reserve and a blasé manner operate as defence mechanisms against living in the metropolis. As the urban sociologist Robert Park once put it, in the modern city 'the art of life is largely reduced to skating on thin surfaces and a scrupulous study of style and manners', while the segregation of the urban population establishes 'moral distances which make the city a mosaic of little worlds which touch but do not interpenetrate' (1915: 608). A preoccupation with the surfaces of style and manners becomes paramount as a way of maintaining a sense of individual identity amid the continuous visual bombardment of signs, images and stimuli in the social milieux most affected by rapid urbanisation, with, in Simmel's own period, their 'dream worlds' of the department store and arcade, and their 'phantasmagoria of commodities and architectural construction' (Buck-Morss, 1983: 213; see also Williams, 1991, and Geist, 1983). What Simmel referred to as 'an element of coolness' (Wolff, 1964: 406) in everyday interactions across the mosaic of cultural worlds in the modern city acted as a way of preserving social distance where, in crowded urban spaces, this has materially dissolved. Cultivating a blasé outlook and disposition as a means of self-preservation against all that the modern city hurls pell-mell at the experiencing individual is, for Simmel, a specifically urban form of sophistication.

The 'inconsiderate hardness' of this form of sophistication is stylistically interiorised as the state of being 'cool'. A 'cool' front, maintained in the face of 'the big, booming confusion and excitement of city life' (Park, 1915: 608) is a stylistic complement to the process of stereotyping. Both operate as a means of keeping others at a social distance, locked into the label that a stereotype provides, kept in their place across the boundaries which stereotyping attempts to maintain. It is not simply a historical coincidence that this inconsiderate hardness of view comes to distinguish a form of identity and mode of social interaction at the same time that stereotyping was first crystallised as a moment of moral and political concern. The distinct echo of Park's 'big, booming confusion' of the city in Lippmann's 'great blooming, buzzing confusion of reality' derives precisely from the confluence of urbanism and modernity in the early years of the twentieth century. It was this confluence which created the conditions for stereotyping to take on the features which now most distinguish it.

The basis for the urban sensibility identified by Simmel was laid by the growth of a new attitude towards strangers. From the mid-nineteenth century, there was an increasing acceptance of the 'notion that strangers had no right to speak to each other'. The sense that everyone 'possessed as a public right an invisible shield, a right to be left alone', a right not to 'become a participant, enmeshed in a scene', meant that detached observation gained ascendancy over involved social intercourse (Sennett, 1986: 27). At the same time, 'cool' observation in a world of strangers cannot be direct without risking hostility. Avoidance of any breach of the right to avoid each other demands skill in the technique Erving Goffman called civil inattention. This consists of the pretence that one is not looking and listening or even caring in the midst of our daily lives among strangers (who include ourselves). And as Bauman has noted, it is 'but a short step from civil inattention to moral indifference, heartlessness and disregard for the needs of others' (1990: 70). Indifference, heartlessness and disregard for others' needs form an ideal breeding-ground for stereotyping. Stereotyping was part of the complex response to metropolitan life as a world of strangers, and to the cold, impersonal relations of economic rationality and the 'cash-nexus' which characterise that life and which at times strangers are held to personify – none perhaps in more vicious historical stereotypes of 'calculating rationality' than the Jew who, not accidentally, has often been represented as an archetypal form of the stranger.

The condition of metropolitan strangerhood is closely related to the development of consumerism as a distinctive style of social living. Cool yet commercially animated indifference as a mode of being and behaving in city life corresponds to the pseudo-use value in commodities that are rapidly appraised and rapidly passed over, in a perpetually mobile cycle. In modernity consumption becomes a basic source of self-expression, and a basic source of dissatisfaction. The experience of continual postponement incurred by commoditised pleasures generates a search for the experience that truly counts, so that beneath the surface manifestation of blasé urbanity there lies a frantic yearning for the lasting or authentically meaningful experience, 'a pointed event in which extreme impressions are concentrated' (Nedelman, 1990 : 233). The twist of pathos in this is that the dynamic of consumption demands that what is articulated as the sense of identity people wish to express to others can only be short term. An instability of self-expression is inherent in the very resources of cultural consumption. This instability has led to culture's 'inward turn', the growing preoccupation with psychological experience in the modern period, and then for redemptive therapies for a self under siege. These are further manifestations of the increasing 'estrangement between the subject and its products' (Simmel, 1978: 459).

Such estrangement is among the various aspects of urban experience which seemed to Simmel to make the stranger an iconic figure of modernity, torn from older forms of belonging and social investments and delivered only to fleeting and ephemeral compensations in a market-driven world. It is not difficult to see again how appeals to nationality or essentialist ethnicity could exert a magnetic pull for people fearful of such a condition, providing a reassuring alternative to the risk and adventure of city life associated with the stranger – that which brings excitement and freedom as well as fear and danger. They attempt to overcome the uncertainty, unpredictability and contingency that lies between opportunity and security, community and alienation, identity and difference. The dream of modernist city planning echoed these vain attempts at annulling uncertainty and contingency by trying to deny the under-determination of strangers, to reduce them safely into a background 'one need neither notice nor care about' (Bauman, 1995: 128). The puzzling under-determination always remains. The stranger manifests a difference that is and is not a difference. Strangerhood is, indeed, an indifference until its indeterminate state changes into confirmation of being properly either inside or outside, and thus once again positioned in a clear-cut category of identity or difference. As an undecidable, the stranger is 'all neither/nor', and thus militates 'against the either/or' (Bauman, 1991: 56). To understand the value of this for the question of stereotypical judgement and the sociology of censure, we need to recapitulate a little on what this form of judgement involves.

In previous chapters I have examined a range of ways in which binary oppositions, those of either/or logics of categorisation, structure perceptions and conceptions of other people or cultures around strictly defined divisions between 'them' and 'us'. The distancing achieved by these divisions, seeming to guarantee the legitimacy of various cultural norms, at the same time confirms the already existing stereotypes of 'them' in contradistinction to 'us' and validates discriminatory and exclusionary strategies directed towards those who are thus othered. The result of such moves is the construction of large blocks of unchanging sameness grouped under different category headings. These homogenised blocks are hierarchically arranged and differentially assigned as 'essence' and 'difference', with unequal consequences for the allocation and distribution of social resources (as, for example, into 'deserving' and 'undeserving' categories). We have also seen this as an integral feature of the politics of representation in which x = not y, white = 'not black', 'he' as subject = 'she' as Other. These are advanced as non-reversible equations because 'x' is the 'essence' and 'y' the unassimilable 'difference', 'x' is constitutively 'inside' and 'y' is diametrically extraterritorial. But the essentialised white – to continue with just one of these summary cases – is fundamentally dependent on the 'inessential' black for self-definition, and if 'self' can only constitute itself in this way, then its very 'essentialness' is clearly called into question.

So, when we define our friends by our enemies, the definition depends on a series of binarisms: inside and outside, positive and negative, presence and absence. These provide a symmetry whose illusion is revealed by the unequally distributed or self-arrogated right to define, to classify and assign a position for others in narrative forms. The process of defining is then an act of domination which 'dispels doubt ... assures that one goes where one should', and immunises against 'the vagaries of choice' (Bauman, 1991: 53–4). Defining may then operate as a mode of domination, but it remains insecure, since what is secured by the definition is always threatened by what has been excluded, and what is valued – intimacy and mutual responsibility among friends, for example – is established by posing the threat of their denial. Otherness as symbolic negation, then, always holds the danger of reversal, of inverting the self-same, the sameness of self, precisely because of the dichotomous binary logic on which it is based.

One of the curious features of symbolic forms and their varied careers lies in the ways they shift and move. This is never more curious than in their reversibility, when they mutate into something quite opposed to their previous value-location. The politics of symbolic forms depends on such movement, especially for challenges to existing, apparently irreversible categories and meanings, as for instance those advanced in sexist or racist stereotypes. Such challenges can then exploit the threat of their denial inherent in the discursive binarisms on which they are based. There is an important caveat to this, for there is a danger of merely inverting racism or sexism in political challenge to their binary representations. This simply offers a mirror image of these representations. It does not take us much beyond heated polemic precisely because it misunderstands the nature of prejudice. Prejudice as such is castigated on the premise that it is possible to be free of prejudice. This remote human possibility is perhaps only identifiable in the idealised figure of the saint. Since such a figure is hardly a common feature of the profane and dirty world of social encounter and interaction that we live in, creating it as the basis for anti-racism or anti-sexism is not very helpful. The problem is broader than this, however. To be free from prejudice was a central ideal of the Enlightenment, and the legacy of the Enlightenment has deeply influenced our attitude to prejudice. Yet prejudice in the more literal sense of prejudgement, involving our already established, socially and temporally located means for approaching any situation or event, is the unavoidable starting point for understanding social encounters and interactions (see Gadamer, 1996: 270–7; Pickering, 1999). The implications of this for subsequent judgement, for stereotyping and a critical understanding of the stereotype, are crucial. They should lead us to rethink the premises of enlightened reason's self-arrogated pathologisation of prejudice.

Among the various other things in which it is entailed, stereotyping contributes to the drive to order by maintaining some semblance of stability amidst the great blooming buzz of social reality. It attempts to annul ambivalence. This involves far more than the socially neutralised, ahistorical process of information reduction and synthesising elaborated in the cognitive economy model of the stereotype, for what is wrapped up in it is the struggle to assert and maintain control in a world of dislocations and ambivalences, all that Baudelaire referred to in his distillation of *modernité* as 'the ephemeral, the fugitive, the contingent' (Baudelaire, 1972: 403). It is a world characterised by what Habermas calls its 'self-renewing presentness', a temporal quality in contemporary Western culture that is the nineteenth-century European imperial ethos in reverse. It is a world in which, for Simmel, time is experienced as transitory, space as fleeting and discontinuous, and causality as fortuitous or arbitrary. When the urban fragmentation of experience is interiorised the great blooming buzz of social reality is seen as endlessly fleeting and contradictory. This again is where the dilemma of stereotyping digs in, and again where strangers keep in view what stereotyping seeks to evade. Strangers exist at the crossover point of relations between the negotiation of modern urban experience and the politics of representation in modern culture. Stereotyping takes on its specifically modern form in its efforts to deny the destabilising consequences of modernity, the contingent world of ambivalence, transitoriness, chance and the vagaries of choice it has irrevocably set in motion. The critical value of the so-often stereotyped stranger is realised exactly in relation to these efforts. As the exemplary condition of ambivalence, stranger-hood is an abiding challenge to the constantly imperilled drive to order in which stereotyping is swept up. In Bauman's words, strangers

> put paid to the ordering power of the opposition, and so to the ordering power of the narrators of the opposition. Oppositions enable knowledge and action; undecidables paralyse them. Undecidables brutally expose the arti-fice, the fragility, the sham of the most vital of separations. They bring the outside into the inside, and poison the comfort of order with suspicion of chaos. (1991: 56)

From Simmel to Bauman

As may have been suggested by the various citations from him, Bauman is pre-eminent among contemporary sociologists in his concern with the stranger. I want now to summarise some of his chief lines of thinking about strangerhood. First of all, the symbolic boundaries which stereo-types patrol lead to safe solutions to the hermeneutic problems that arise when classifications unravel and normative understandings are chal-lenged. Challenge comes from what is not yet familiar, not yet classi-fied, not yet decided, not yet put in its norm-defining place. The challenge can be countered by reclassifying, reasserting norms by resorting once more to defining identity by difference, a move which is designed to corroborate faith in 'the essential orderliness of the world' (Bauman, 1991: 58). But strangers are people out of normalised space. They are not simply unfamiliar – they are undecidable, questioning the very principle of binary oppositions and classificatory dichotomies, defying 'the easy expedient of spatial or temporal segregation' (ibid: 59). Strangers subvert the objectifying procedures of the stereotype, and refuse the symbolic distancing function of the stereotyping process, by claiming the right to subjectivity, to subject-hood, on their own ambiva-lent terms.

These terms unsettle the politics of belonging in relation to the nation and the modern nation-state. Incongruity and anomaly are constitutive of the stranger, and these qualities blur the boundary lines 'vital to the construction of a particular social order or a particular life-world'. The stranger is thus 'the bane of modernity', undermining its 'spatial ordering of the world – the fought-after co-ordination between moral and topographical closeness' by bringing into 'the inner circle of proximity the kind of difference and otherness that are anticipated and tolerated only at a distance' (Bauman, 1991: 60–1). Yet modernity in the metropolis is the symbolic time and space of strangerhood, seeming to have dissolved the comforting, knowable communities of a lost, idealised world. The modern nation-state counters this as a substitute for older modes of belonging by promoting uniformity through an 'incessant propaganda of *shared* attitudes' and '*joint* historical memories' (ibid: 64, emphases in original). It is strangers who symbolically refuse this project, however, since they are irredeemably neither 'us' nor 'them'. For modern nation-states, strangers have always 'exuded uncertainty' in the face of the attempt to impose and instil order 'as the clarity of binding divisions, classifications, allocations and boundaries'. As such there could be no room 'for those who sat astride, for the cognitively ambivalent', and this has entailed a war of attrition against strangers. Aggressive manoeuvres against strangers have involved two alternative yet complementary strategies: either assimilating them, stripping away their strangerhood till they become like 'us', and so similar and familiar; or excluding them, casting them out from 'the limits of the orderly world' in ghettoised spaces – the slum, the racially demarcated social quarter, the squatter camp, the bantustan – and so placing them, under 'the pressure of the modern order-building state', in 'a state of suspended extinction' (Bauman, 1997: 47–8).

But strangers refuse to be 'othered', to become a permanent Other, even when stigmatised, for the effort to justify exclusion by stigmatising the stranger reveals 'the limit of the transforming capacity of culture' upon which the very sense of modernity is so crucially dependent:

> Stigma is a cultural product which proclaims a limit to the potency of culture. In stigma, culture draws a boundary to the territory which it considers as its task to cultivate, and circumscribes an area which *must* and *should* lie fallow ... It is, therefore, at odds with everything modernity stands for and everything that modern society must believe in in order to reproduce its existence in the only shape it knows of and is trained to cultivate. (Bauman, 1991: 68–9, emphases in original)

Strangerhood is thus not so much the result of cultural difference as the continual doubt sitting inside identities which are the result of the production of cultural difference. It is 'an affliction caused by an attempt to efface it' (ibid: 73) and it remains as an insistent background intrusion in the normative tunings-in of social communication.

At the same time, the quality of strangerhood has its cultural attractions, as we saw in Chapter 3 with Richard Wright's observations on the emergent 'white negro' of a disaffected North America. The sense of 'black culture' as a cultural alternative to mainstream media or a parent culture, a symbolic source of something exhilarating, vibrant and unavailable in the familiar, everyday world, has in various ways been white people's experience of African-American and African-Caribbean music over a century and more, from spirituals and slave-songs to reggae and rap. The pleasures involved have been generated precisely because of the sense of estrangement in bondage suffered by black people. This is not to suggest some essentialist black identity with which white people have identified, for 'there is a radical difference between a repudiation of the idea that there is a black "essence" and recognition of the way black identity has been specifically constituted in the experience of exile and struggle' (hooks, 1993: 426). At its least reflexive, however, delight in one form or other of essentialised cultural exoticism involves 'creaming off the enticements of the Other without committing oneself to give anything in exchange'. All you have to do is sit back comfortably and enjoy the amoral vicissitudes of consumerist cycles of fashion (Bauman, 1995: 133–4). 'The most recent invention of "thematic" shopping malls with Caribbean villages, Indian reserves and Polynesian shrines closely packed together under one roof, has brought the old technique of institutional separation to the level of perfection reached in the past only by the zoo' (Bauman, 1991: 58). Not only the zoo of course, but also the imperial exhibition discussed in Chapter 4. When we enter these 'thematic' shopping malls, we are treading in the footsteps of our imperialist forebears.

The consumerist construction of the stranger is not the same as the stranger outside the gate. The stranger who provides a one-way source of temptation and fleeting pleasure is conveniently placed at a remove from the stranger constructed as threat, the enemy 'conspiring to trespass, to break in and invade' the symbolically idealised, small defensible space of 'home and hearth'. Both these physiognomies of the stranger are 'half-visible and blurred'. It is left to the interpreter 'to recast the fluid impressions into sensations of pleasure or fear' and continually recombine the contradictory and ambiguous compound of meanings and values inherent in the figure of the stranger (Bauman, 1995: 138). But if the perceived threat of strangers has been derived from the in-between spaces they inhabit, both socially and symbolically, thus obscuring the transparency of safely known categories and blurring the boundary lines in people's mental maps of the world, then for Bauman postmodern life defies any such transparency, solidity or continuity because it is defined by its condition of irreducible ontological uncertainty – 'about the future shape of the world, about the right way of living in it, and about the criteria by which to judge the rights and wrongs of one's way of living' (1997: 50). This is the condition referred to briefly in the previous chapter in which ethical doubt breeds political pragmatism. Both doubt and pragmatism are symptoms of 'the way we live now' following the breakup of the old power-bloc politics, the ascendancy of economic reason and unfettered market forces, the renewed ruthlessness of the labour market, the consumerist dissolution of 'the ties that bind', and the widespread avowal of what Bauman calls 'a palimpsest identity' dependent on the art of forgetting as much as the art of memorising – 'where memory itself is like videotape, always ready to be wiped clean in order to admit new images' (ibid: 54). Postmodernism simply wipes clean what modernist stereotyping sought artfully to forget. All we have to do is sit back comfortably and switch channels. New images appear at the click of a button.

We can still suggest a different way of living now. If we start from uncertainty rather than certainty, strangerhood becomes a quality that is central rather than peripheral to our sense of the world in which we live. The difference between the normal and abnormal, the familiar and strange, is diluted. Strangers 'are no longer authoritatively pre-selected ... as they used to be in times of the state-managed, consistent and durable programmes of order-building' (ibid). This is to pose a different and deeper sense of uncertainty whereby strangers are a necessary resource of incessant and always inconclusive identity-building. As such they are amenable neither to strategies of assimilation nor of exclusion, because their still ambivalent presence is now an integral part of the world that has emerged out of modernity. Strangers are neither abnormal nor disposable because of a newly emergent consensus that 'difference is good, precious, and in need of protection and cultivation' (ibid: 55). Even racists recognise and place value on difference, although of course in the belief that different cultures should be kept firmly apart. If we are to go beyond nationalism and ethnic essentialism, beyond individualist lifestyles and consumerist identities, then for Bauman we need to abandon the self/not-self binarisms on which strangerhood in the modern project has been built. 'The chance of human togetherness depends on the rights of the stranger, not on the question of who ... is entitled to decide who the strangers are' (ibid: 57).

To have any validity, the rights of the stranger depend on the recognition of difference in the interests of dialogue rather than the right to decide who the strangers are. That is why assessing strangers in terms of how much they conform to being like 'us' will always lead to errors of judgement. Michael Walzer (1983) has suggested that the rights of strangers depend on a commitment to belong, brought from outside but redirected at the host community, as well as permission to belong being granted by the host community. He acknowledges that we may have an obligation to give sanctuary to those who have been persecuted for religious, ethnic or political reasons in the places where they live, to those to whose flight we have contributed, as Americans did to Vietnamese refugees, and to those we have encouraged to defend certain principles we claim to embody, as was the case with the British and those forced to flee Hungary after the failed revolution in 1956. Beyond this, Walzer's criteria for the admission and exclusion of 'strangers' are little other than vague gestures to somehow being like 'us' or having historical ties with 'us', and lump together various disparate elements of what is putatively shared in collective belonging. But belonging to what? The host community for Walzer seems inevitably to be the nation, and he then falls back on the depth and significance of national belonging not only for those within this 'community', but also those strangers required to show a new and ardent commitment of belonging to it.

We have already seen how national belonging and identity encourage stereotyping in its polarised division of 'us' and 'them', its homogenisation and reification of both sides of this division, and its flattening out of social and cultural diversity. If strangers return us to a sense of historical movement and contingency, how can they be expected to belong to that which arrests history and extols an apparently unchanging form of collective identity, as in its assertions of antiquity and its inventions of tradition? How can they be expected to commit themselves to the self/not-self binarisms which their own hybrid identities contest? There seems little chance of human togetherness in expectations like these. To require a commitment to belong on 'native' terms is to negate the stranger's potential, to ignore the possibilities that may open up through cultural dialogue and translation, through being receptive to encounters in the creative contact zone between 'near' and 'far'.

We need to think about difference differently. We need to recognise that exoticised strangeness, as in 'ethnic' consumerism and tourism, is the other side of the coin of those surges of hostility when urban reserve and indifference are breached by a backyard defensiveness of 'us'/'them' divisions. This oscillation between the *frisson* of encounters with tamed difference and fear of its demonised forms has been a constant feature of modernity, the panoptical movement between them being encompassed in a single turn of the head. It has taken many forms, and it continues to do so, but it remains a constant distraction from appreciating the importance of bringing different cultural traditions and practices into a dialogue designed for the benefit of both, a creative interplay that is opposite in its significance to the symbolic containment of stereotyping.

Strangers remind us of the risk entailed in the strategy of symbolic containment. They open up the politics of representation to the poetics of transgression. This applies even to the short-term strategies adopted by ethnic or gay minorities who twist alienating stereotypes back on themselves in a playful, ironic, comic or affectionate manner, assimilating them for their own various political uses, as with the hyper-inflated semantics of 'queer' or the subversion of the stereotypical 'nigger' by *attitude*. Stereotypes can themselves be used to question and undermine the basis on which they are set up through the ways in which they are sent up, as happens when they are wryly and knowingly presented, delivered in a deadpan manner, or subverted through such techniques as role reversal and narrative exaggeration. The symbolic excesses and slippages that occur when cultural signs and codes are reshuffled in this way may serve to estrange us from our expectations and habituations, and bring us closer to facing up to the social permeation of strangerhood in late modernity.

Bringing it all Back Home

Home is a place of intense belonging. A heart needs a home, and home is where the heart is. Idealisation of the domestic hearth has been with us since the ascendancy of the Victorian middle class. Our versions of it may have changed, but we still associate the word with a benign warmth. It suggests the proper centre from which to proceed, and to which, after emigration, travel, exile and displacement, we return for restoration and resolution of all our disparate experiences while away. In modernity, this has become less and less possible, for the home we intend to return to after being away is no longer the home we left. Such a place no longer exists; much has changed in our absence. We ourselves are no longer the same. We look at our old home differently, see previously familiar things as if they are strange. We have become, in how we see and think, something of a stranger. Strangers remind us of the arbitrary and fleeting character of these associations gathered around the idea of home, for by their presence they define an in-between, transitional stage between a home lost and another home not yet found. The stranger brings the periphery into the centre, difference into the same, unfamiliarity into familiarity, in ways which unravel the certitude and resolution in the idealisation of home.

Strangers can come from anywhere and so relate to a far broader category than that of the immigrant or refugee, although these can of course be included. Strangers in themselves do not 'flood in', 'swamp' or 'invade'; they are already here, we are among them, 'we' *are* 'them' depending on where we go, where we stand, who we're among. In talking about the figure of the stranger we're not dealing with the great fear of modernity in its binary constructions of difference, of the Other being found not where it should belong, out there at the designated periphery, but here, as in the worst nightmare, within the home, within the heart. We are dealing instead with the perturbation of the 'inside' of attachment being faced from the 'outside' through a certain difference that is never clearly defined. Such difference is rarely particularised, rarely given a clearly identifying name. The stranger fills a category which only designates in general terms a different set of life experiences, a different biographical trajectory, a different relation to history to those who look out from the settled place of home. This is why the stranger brings an element of coolness and a feeling of contingency into social relations, even where these also involve the realisation of certain shared elements of experience. What connects people through these shared experiences has lost its specific and centripetal character (Wolff, 1964: 406). The figure of the stranger is characteristic of modern urban society because it is in such a society that a new dimension of experience opens up for kinds of social relationships built on coolness and contingency. This new dimension calls certainty, resolution and attachment into doubt, placing equivocality, irresolution and detachment in a promiscuous relation to them. Strangers are figures of modernity because they show there is no longer any safe, settled home to return to, no centre at the heart of the world, no fixed, unchanging homeland to which they should commit themselves to belonging. Everything is transitional and contingent, and every safe arrival is another point of relentless departure.

It is in such modern conditions that stereotyping has exerted its immense pressures on social relationships. Such conditions condemn stereotyping to its incessant work of reiteration at the same time as generating its energies to operate towards an end that can never be reached – the centring of identity through the fixity of the Other. The virtue of the stranger is to show the paradoxical quality of stereotyping, the traces left within it by its efforts to annul the dilemma between open and closed thinking. By representing transience and ambivalence, the stranger suggests an alternative to hidebound convention and hard-and-fast boundaries, encourages more flexible ways of seeing, and reawakens the dilemma which stereotyping strives to forget. Stereotyping, when effective, is taken as common sense, and when it is successful in this way it shuts down awareness of the contrary themes in common-sense thinking. Strangers open them up again, which is why they are discomfiting. They disturb because they do not quite fit. Stereotyping is a search for the comfort of precision, but strangers disrupt this search by representing the discomfort of imprecision. In doing so they may show people how they are incarcerated in the conventions they live by.

In this way strangers appeal to the imagination rather than to fantasy, to imagining differently rather than utilising entertaining images, for the sake of similitude, as a one-way source of temptation and pleasure. Strangers may suggest something inside ourselves whose potential has not yet been realised, something we may feel but not yet know, something intimated but not yet intimate. But such possibilities are not simply to do with ourselves. They are concerned just as much with the ethical structure of social relations, with the grounds of intersubjectivity and association in our shared lives. Strangers return us to the possibilities which stereotyping forecloses. They presuppose a different kind of judgement to that which stigmatises the social deviant, one which is comparative in its assessments, refusing the setting up and perpetuation of polar oppositions between normality and deviancy, inside and outside, belonging and unbelonging. Such a form of social judgement is based on an acceptance that we all in some way share the condition of strangerhood, that there are no absolute certainties or fixed boundaries, and that judgement without imagination is a failure of judgement. It is only the exercise of dogmatic reason.

There is a danger in all this of idealising the stranger as a counter to the idealisation of the home. While the counter is important because it is the false certitudes of home that stereotyping relies on, we must remember that encounters with strangers are far more pervasive and multiple than in Simmel's time. This is partly a consequence of media expansion and the centrality of the media to contemporary social and cultural relations, but it is also a result of decolonisation and the importation of cheap migrant labour into Western societies. As well as economic exploitation, for the incomer this can entail huge losses, severe disruptions and intense displacement both from home and within a foreign city. To be a migrant worker is to be adrift in space, in time and in identity (see for example, Berger and Mohr, 1975; O'Grady and Pyke, 1998; White, 1998). But the strangers of modernity are multiple, cutting across social categories, and because of this they work off each other. The melancholy of the migrant worker in the alien city is shadowed by the sorrow of unfulfilled promises in the realities of urban experience. It is echoed in the empty dreams of modern consumerism as compensation for the endless disruptions of social relations in the city. These are not disparate experiences, for they come together in the same dislocation from the past, the same disappointment with where history seems to have led us.

It is no longer possible to long for a world we have lost when what we have lost is no longer known. For already established people in Western societies, this means that strangeness has intensified. The sharpness of division between centre and periphery in the days of empire has dissolved; difference resides within the heartlands of similitude. This may increase anxiety and fear in relations with others, for strangeness within similitude cannot be so easily distanced, through stereotyping or some other norm-defending process, as can strangeness associated with starkly delineated difference. But this is the new challenge. The fences are down, the boundaries blurred, norms become opaque. What is strange is now more diffusely experienced, what is alien does not of itself seem to threaten what is indigenous, at least in so far as the distinctions between them have eroded, and we face a potentially far richer mutuality of interchange, across the diversity of the world's cultures and subcultures. At the very least, difference is less different, less stark and dramatic, less unassimilated than in the days of state-constructed orderliness and normality, the lines of which cannot now be readily assumed or left unquestioned.

What we encounter today is a far greater degree of cultural exchange, crossover, symbolic intermapping, métissage and hybridity than in the new urban environments first anatomised by Baudelaire, Simmel, Benjamin and the Chicago sociologists. There can be no ethical neutrality in these encounters, and no romanticisation of multicultural difference in a world still reeling with virulent nationalisms, racisms, ethnic cleansings and the widespread oppression of social minorities. These remain the real pathologies of which stereotypical Otherness is but one symptom. But the new situation is a global situation in which alterity can no longer be defined, assessed and placed by some absolute yardstick. We have to learn anew all the old identities, all the old 'we' and 'us' affiliations, all the old 'they' and 'them' dissociations, involved in the pursuit of collective cultural goods and values. If Simmel's sociology has enduring value, one aspect of this lies in his emphasis on the ways in which encounters with strangers, and the problems, displacements and conflicts they generate, are necessary components of sociality.

The senses of belonging and order depend upon an illusion of solidity, of people and things being in their place, of present arrangements seeming fixed. If we see this as an illusion, as in greater or lesser degree the stranger does, we need to come to terms with ambivalence instead of attempting to expurgate it in the interests of absolute boundaries, fixed arrangements. Ambivalence is necessary for open and tolerant forms of social encounter and interaction, for ambivalence unravels fixity, the solidity of hard-and-fast boundaries between little worlds, the fetishistic certainty of stereotypical attributions. Ambivalence is a liminal condition, and liminality hinges upon being in-between, receptive to contingency, open to the open-endedness of historical process.

The centrality of strangerhood disperses the terms of exception, deviance and difference against which regulation, normality and similitude used to be measured, showing them as all standing under the same uncertain, changeable sky. It is perhaps when we at last see things in this way that we can truly learn from the stranger, for there is something in the way of seeing of the stranger that perpetually disconcerts. This is akin to the relative detachment anyone may feel on returning to familiar places, to a routinely known area of the world, after months or years living abroad. We begin then to look at our formerly taken-for-granted part of the world through the eyes of the stranger, and find strange its naturalised everyday configuration. This rarely lasts long. We soon regain our earlier, habituated way of looking at and tacitly accepting the way this familiar world appears to fit together. But the eyes of the stranger remind us of the ways in which it can be unsettled, the glimpse we had of its insecure and uncertain foundations, for home truths are for the stranger never absolute truths, and as such they cannot be assimilated without being changed.

This may remind us of the feeling we had, on returning home, that the configuration of the world from our earlier habituated perspective need not necessarily be that way. The stranger may remind us of the historical contingency of the social configuration, its constructedness in time and its changeability over time. The stranger may help us move from what appears to be stereotypically fixed in its evaluative co-ordinates to a critical position of ambivalence between committed involvement and sceptical detachment. We are, when at home, both suspicious and envious of strangers because of their freedom to see differently, to pick and choose, support and reject, come and go, and never be really and truly 'at home' in such a way that 'home truths' remain true. If we move beyond both these attitudes, we may realise that it is possible to live without certainty, to entrust our lives to contingency, and to distrust the dogmas of belonging. This is a difficult move, but it is the only move we can begin to make once we realise that we are now all in the generalised position of strangers, coming today and staying tomorrow, with no natural belonging or unbelonging, forever in the ambivalence of being in-between our variously constructed and mediated worlds, forever in transit between our different lives. This is where we have been all along, but we are only just learning to live as the vagabonds of history.

Bibliography

Achebe, C. (1989) *Hopes and Impediments,* New York: Doubleday.

Adorno, T.W. and Horkheimer, M. (1979) *Dialectic of Enlightenment,* London: Verso (orig. pub. 1947).

Adorno, T.W., Frenleel-Brunswick, E., Levinson, D.J. and Sanford, R.N. (1995) *The Authoritarian Personality,* New York: Harper (orig. pub. 1950).

Ageron, C.R. (1968) *Les Algériens Muselmans et la France (1871–1919),* Vol. 1, Paris: Presses Universitaires de France.

Allport, G.W. (1954) *The Nature of Prejudice,* Cambridge, MA: Addison Wesley.

Altick, R. (1978) *The Shows of London,* Cambridge, MA: Harvard University Press.

Anderson, B. (1986) *Imagined Communities,* London: Verso.

Anonymous (1861) 'National Character', *Cornhill Magazine,* Vol. 4, July–December, 584–98.

Arberry, A.J. (1960) *Oriental Essays,* London: George Allen & Unwin.

Arnold, G. (1980) *Held Fast for England: G.A. Henty, Imperialist Boys' Writer,* London: Hamish Hamilton.

Arnold, T. (1841) *An Inaugural Lecture on the Study of Modern History,* Oxford: Parker.

Asad, T. (ed.) (1973) *Anthropology and the Colonial Encounter,* New York: Humanities Press.

Ashmore, R.D. and Del Boca, F.K. (1979) 'Sex Stereotypes and Implicit Personality Theory', *Sex Roles,* 5: 219–48.

Ashmore, R.D. and Del Boca, F.K. (1981) 'Conceptual Approaches to Stereotypes and Stereotyping' in Hamilton, D. (ed.) *Cognitive Processes in Stereotyping and Intergroup Behaviour.* Hillsdale, NJ: Erlbaum.

Awatere, D. (1984) *Maori Sovereignty,* Auckland: Broadsheet Publications.

Babcock, B. (1978) *The Reversible World: Symbolic Inversion in Art and Society,* Ithaca, NY: Cornell University Press.

Ballantyne, R. (1880) *Six Months at the Cape; or, Letters to Periwinkle from South Africa,* London: James Nisbet & Co.

Ballantyne, R. (1888) *Blue Lights; or, Hot Work in the Soudan,* London: James Nisbet & Co.

Barker, M. (1984) *A Haunt of Fears,* London: Pluto.

Barker, M. (1989) *Comics: Ideology, Power & Politics,* Manchester: Manchester University Press.

Barnett, A. (1982) *Iron Britannia,* London: Allison & Busby.

Barr, P. (1970) *The Coming of the Barbarians*, London: Macmillan – now Palgrave.

Barrell, J. (1991) *The Infection of Thomas de Quincey: A Psychopathology of Imperialism*, New Haven, CT: Yale University Press.

Barthes, R. (1973) *Mythologies*, St Albans: Paladin (orig. pub. 1957).

Barzun, J. (1937) *Race: A Study in Superstition*, New York: Harcourt Brace.

Baudelaire, C. (1972) *Selected Writings on Art and Artists*, Harmondsworth: Penguin.

Bauman, Z. (1990) *Thinking Sociologically*, Oxford: Blackwell.

Bauman, Z. (1991) *Modernity and Ambivalence*, Cambridge: Polity.

Bauman, Z. (1995) *Life in Fragments*, Oxford: Blackwell.

Bauman, Z. (1997) 'The Making and Unmaking of Strangers' in Werbner, P. and Modood, T. (eds) *Debating Cultural Hybridity: Multi-Cultural Identities and the Politics of Anti-Racism*, London: Zed Books.

Beauvoir, S. de (1968) *Force of Circumstance*, Harmondsworth: Penguin.

Beauvoir, S. de (1984) *The Second Sex*, Harmondsworth: Penguin.

Beauvoir, S. de (1999) *America Day by Day*, Berkeley, CA: University of California Press (orig. pub. 1954).

Becker, H. (1966) *Outsiders*, New York: Free Press (orig. pub. 1963).

Beckingham, C.F. (1979) 'Edward W. Said: Orientalism', *Bulletin of the School of Oriental and African Studies*, 42(3): 562–4.

Bennett, G. (1953) *The Concept of Empire*, London: Black.

Berger, J. and Mohr, J. (1975) *A Seventh Man*, Harmondsworth: Penguin.

Berridge, V. (1978) 'East End Opium Dens and Narcotic Use in Britain', *London Journal*, 4(1): 3–28.

Betts, R.F. (1961) *Assimilation and Association in French Colonial Theory 1890–1914*, New York: Columbia University Press.

Bhabha, H.K. (1996) 'Culture's In-Between' in Hall, S. and du Gay, P. (eds) *Questions of Cultural Identity*, London: Sage.

Bhabha, H.K. (1997) *The Location of Culture*, London: Routledge (orig. pub. 1994).

Biddis, M.D. (1976) 'The Politics of Anatomy: Dr Robert Knox and Victorian Racism', *Proceedings of the Royal Society of Medicine*, LXIX: 245–50.

Biddis, M.D. (ed.) (1979) *Images of Race*, Leicester: Leicester University Press.

Billig, M. (1978) *Fascists: A Social Psychological Study*, New York: Harcourt.

Billig, M. (1985) 'Prejudice, Categorisation and Particularisation: From a Perceptual to a Rhetorical Approach', *European Journal of Social Psychology*, 15: 79–103.

Billig, M. (1991) *Ideology and Opinions*, London: Sage.

Billig, M. (1994) 'Repopulating the Depopulated Pages of Social Psychology', *Theory and Psychology*, 4: 307–35.

Billig, M. (1995a) 'Prejudice' in Kuper, A. and Kuper, J. (eds) *The Social Science Encyclopedia*, 2nd edn, London: Routledge.

Billig, M. (1995b) *Banal Nationalism*, London: Sage.

Billig, M. (1996a) 'Remembering the Particular Background of Social Identity Theory' in Robinson, W. (ed.) *Social Groups and Identities: Developing the Legacy of Henri Tajfel*, Oxford: Butterworth Heinemann.

Billig, M. (1996b) *Arguing and Thinking*, Cambridge: Cambridge University Press (orig. pub. 1987).

Blake, A. (1996) 'Foreign Devils and Moral Panics: Britain, Asia and the Opium Trade' in Schwarz, B. (ed.) *The Expansion of England*, London: Routledge.

Bolt, C. (1984) 'Race and the Victorians' in Eldridge, C.C. (ed.) *British Imperialism in the Nineteenth Century*, London: Macmillan – now Palgrave.

Bolton, R. (1989) 'In the American East: Richard Avedon Incorporated' in Bolton, R. (ed.) *The Contest of Meaning: Critical Histories of Photography*, Cambridge, MA: The MIT Press.

Booth, M. (1990) *The Triads*, London: Grafton Books.

Bourke, J. (1994) *Working-Class Cultures in Britain 1890–1960*, London: Routledge.

Box, S. (1983) *Power, Crime and Mystification*, London: Tavistock.

Brantlinger, P. (1985) 'Victorians and Africans: The Genealogy of the Myth of the Dark Continent', *Critical Inquiry*, **12**(1): 166–203.

Broca, P. (1864) (ed. and trans. C. Carter Blake) *On the Phenomena of Hybridity in the Genus Homo*, London: Anthropological Society.

Bronfen, E. (1992) *Over Her Dead Body: Death, Femininity and the Aesthetic*, Manchester: Manchester University Press.

Buchan, J. (1910) *Prester John*, London: Thomas Nelson.

Buck-Morss, S. (1989) *The Dialectics of Seeing: Walter Benjamin and the Arcades Project*, London: MIT Press.

Burton, R. (1860) *The Lake Regions of Central Africa*, London: Longman.

Calhoun, C. (1995) *Critical Social Theory*, Oxford: Blackwell.

Calhoun, C. (1997) *Nationalism*, Buckingham: Open University Press.

Canguilhem, G. (1989) *The Normal and the Pathological*, New York: Zone Books (orig. pub. 1966).

Cannadine, D. (1984) 'The Context, Performance and Meaning of Ritual: The British Monarchy and the "Invention of Tradition"', in Hobsbawm, E. and Ranger, T. (eds) *The Invention of Tradition*, Cambridge: Cambridge University Press.

Carey, J. (1989) *Communication as Culture*, Boston: Unwin Hyman.

Carline, R. (1971) *Pictures in the Post: The Story of the Picture Postcard*, London: Gordon Fraser.

Carlyle, T. (1897) 'Occasional Discourse on the Nigger Question' in his *Latter-Day Pamphlets*, London: Chapman & Hall (orig. pub. 1849 in *Fraser's Magazine*).

Chaney, D. (1994) *The Cultural Turn*, London: Routledge.

Chen, C.H. (1996) 'Feminization of Asian (American) Men in the U.S. Mass Media: An Analysis of "The Ballad of Little Jo"', *Journal of Communication Inquiry*, **20**(2): 57–71.

Childs, P. and Williams, P. (1997) *An Introduction to Post-Colonial Theory*, London: Prentice Hall/Harvester Wheatsheaf.

Clark, L. (1984) *Social Darwinism in France*, Alabama: University of Alabama Press.

Clegg, J. (1994) *Fu Manchu and the 'Yellow Peril'*, Stoke-on-Trent: Trentham Books.

Clifford, J. (1988) *The Predicament of Culture: Twentieth-Century Ethnography, Literature and Art*, Cambridge, MA: Harvard University Press.

Cockburn, A. (1987) *Corruptions of Empire*, London: Verso.

Cohen, A. (1982) *Belonging: Identity and Social Organisation in British Rural Cultures*, Manchester: Manchester University Press.

Cohen, A. (1985) *The Symbolic Construction of Community*, London: Tavistock.

Cohen, A. (ed.) (1986) *Symbolising Boundaries: Identity and Diversity in British Cultures*, Manchester: Manchester University Press.

Cohen, P. (1997) *Rethinking the Youth Question: Education, Labour and Cultural Studies*, Basingstoke: Macmillan – now Palgrave.

Cohen, S. (ed.) (1971) *Images of Deviance*, Harmondsworth: Penguin.

Cohen, S. (1973) *Folk Devils and Moral Panics*, St Albans: Paladin (orig. pub. 1972).

Cohen, S. and Young, J. (eds) (1973) *The Manufacture of News: Deviance, Social Problems and the Mass Media*, Oxford: Basil Blackwell.

Cohen, W.B. (1980) *The French Encounter with Africans*, Bloomington: Indiana University Press.

Colley, L. (1994) *Britons: Forging the Nation, 1707–1837*, London: Pimlico.

Condor, S. (1988) '"Race" Stereotypes and Racist Discourse', *Text*, **8**: 1–2, 69–90.

Conrad, J. (1976) *Heart of Darkness*, London: Pan (orig. pub. 1902).

Coombes, A. (1985) '"For Good and for England": Contributions to an Image of Africa in the First Decade of the Twentieth Century', *Art History*, **8**(4): 453–66.

Corbey, R. (1995) 'Ethnographic Showcases, 1870–1930' in Pieterse, J.N. and Parekh, B. (eds) *The Decolonisation of Imagination*, London: Zed Books.

Corrigan, P. and Sayer, D. (1985) *The Great Arch: English State Formation as Cultural Revolution*, Oxford: Blackwell.

Cottrell, R. (1976) *Simone de Beauvoir*, New York: Frederick Ungar.

Cresswell, T. (1996) *In Place/Out of Place: Geography, Ideology, and Transgression*, Minneapolis: University of Minnesota Press.

Curtin, P. (1960–63) '"Scientific" Racism and the British Theory of Empire', *Journal of the Historical Society of Nigeria*, **2**: 40–51.

Curtin, P. (1965) *The Image of Africa: British Ideas and Action, 1780–1850*, London: Macmillan – now Palgrave.

Curtin, P. (ed.) (1971) *Imperialism*, New York: Harper & Row.

Curtis, L.P. (1971) *Apes and Angels: The Irishman in Victorian Caricature*, Washington: Smithsonian Institution Press.

Darwin, C. (1913) *The Descent of Man*, London: John Murray (orig. pub. 1871).

Davidson, B. (1974) *Africa in History: Themes and Outlines*, London: Collier.

Davies, A. (1998) 'Youth Gangs, Masculinity and Violence in Late Victorian Manchester and Salford', *Journal of Social History*, 32(2): 349–69.

Davin, A. (1996) *Growing Up Poor: Home, School and Street 1870–1914*, London: Rivers Oram Press.

Davis, D.B. (1970) *The Problem of Slavery in Western Culture*, Harmondsworth: Penguin.

Dawson, G. (1994) *Soldier Heroes: British Adventure, Empire and the Imagining of Masculinities*, London: Routledge.

Deshpande, S. (1993) 'Them and Us' in Chew, S. and Rutherford, A. (eds) *Unbecoming Daughters of the Empire*, Sydney: Dangeroo Press.

Deutsch, K.W. (1969) *Nationalism and its Alternatives*, New York: Knopf.

Devereux, G. (1975) 'Ethnic Identity: Its Logical Foundations and Dysfunctions' in de Vos, G. and Romanucci-Ross, L. (eds) *Ethnic Identity*, Chicago: University of Chicago Press.

Devine, P.G. (1989) 'Stereotypes and Prejudice: their Automatic and Controlled Components', *Journal of Personality and Social Psychology*, 56: 5–18.

Dickens, C. (1961) *The Mystery of Edwin Drood*, New York: Signet (orig. pub. 1870).

Disraeli, B. (1927) *Tancred*, London: Peter Davies.

Dixon, B. (1977) *Catching Them Young 2: Political Ideas in Children's Fiction*, London: Pluto.

Doré, G. and Jerrold, B. (1872) *London: A Pilgrimage*, London: Grant.

Dore, R. (1978) *Shinohata: A Portrait of a Japanese Village*, London: Allen Lane.

Drotner, K. (1992) 'Modernity and Media Panics' in Skovmand, M. and Schrøder, K. (eds) *Media Cultures: Reappraising Transnational Media*, London: Routledge.

Du Bois, W.E.B. (1996) *The Souls of Black Folk*, London: Penguin (orig. pub. 1903).

Dunae, P. (1977) 'Boys' Literature and the Idea of Race: 1870–1900', *Wascana Review*, Spring, pp. 84–107.

Dunae, P. (1980) 'Boys' Literature and the Idea of Empire, 1870–1914, *Victorian Studies*, 24: 105–21.

Dunae, P. (1989) 'New Grub Street for Boys' in Richards, J. (ed.) *Imperialism and Juvenile Literature*, Manchester: Manchester University Press.

Durkheim, E. (1984) *The Division of Labour in Society*, Basingstoke: Macmillan – now Palgrave.

Dyer, R. (1979) 'The Role of Stereotypes' in Cook, J. and Levington, M. (eds) *Images of Alcoholism*, London: BFI; reprinted in Dyer, R. (1993) *The Matter of Images*, London: Routledge.

Ehrenberg, I. (1976) *The Life of the Automobile*, New York: Urizen Books (orig. pub. 1929).

Emerson, R.W. (1966) *English Traits*, London: Oxford University Press (orig. pub. 1856).

Enloe, C. (1989) *Bananas, Beaches and Bases: Making Feminist Sense of International Politics*, Berkeley, CA: University of California Press.

Ericson, R.V., Baranek, P.M. and Chan, J.B.L. (1987) *Visualising Deviance*, Milton Keynes: Open University Press.

Erikson, K.T. (1966) *Wayward Puritans: A Study in the Sociology of Deviance*, New York: Wiley.

Evans, R. (1997) *In Defence of History*, London: Granta.

Evans, R. (1998) *Tales from the German Underworld: Crime and Punishment in the Nineteenth Century*, New Haven, CT: Yale University Press.

Fabian, J. (1983) *Time and the Other: How Anthropology Makes its Object*, New York: Columbia University Press.

Fanon, F. (1970) *The Wretched of the Earth*, Harmondsworth: Penguin.

Fanon, F. (1972) *Black Skin, White Masks*, London: Paladin.

Farmer, P. (1994) *The Uses of Haiti*, Monroe, ME: Common Courage Press.

Fenn, G.M. (1907) *George Alfred Henty*, London: Blackie & Son.

Fletcher, C.R.L. and Kipling, R. (1911) *A School History of England*, Oxford: Clarendon Press.

Forster, I. (1989) 'Nature's Outcast Child: Black People in Children's Books', *Race and Class*, 31(1): 59–77.

Foucault, M. (1977a) *Discipline and Punish*, London: Allen Lane.

Foucault, M. (1977b) *Language, Counter-Memory, Practice*, Ithaca, NY: Cornell University Press.

Foucault, M. (1989) *Madness and Civilisation: A History of Insanity in the Age of Reason*, London: Routledge.

Fried, M.H. (1975) 'A 4 Lettter Word that Hurts' in Bernard, H.R. (ed.) *The Human Way: Readings in Anthropology*, New York: Macmillan – now Palgrave.

Friedman, L.J. (1977) *Sex Role Stereotyping in the Mass Media*, New York: Garland Publishing.

Friedman, J. (1983) 'Civilisational Cycles and the History of Primitivism', *Social Analysis*, 14: 31–52.

Frisby, D. (1984) *Georg Simmel*, London: Tavistock.

Frith, S. (1999) 'Advancing Cultural Studies (Or Keeping the Fly in the Ointment)' in Fornäs, J. (ed.) *Advancing Cultural Studies*, Stockholm: Stockholm University.

Fryer, P. (1984) *Staying Power: The History of Black People in Britain*, London: Pluto Press.

Fullbrook, A. and Fullbrook, K. (1998) *Simone de Beauvoir: A Critical Introduction*, Cambridge: Polity.

Fuss, D. (1994) 'Interior Colonies: Frantz Fanon and the Politics of Identification', *Diacritics*, 24(2–3): 20–42.

Fyfe, C. (1992) 'Race, Empire and the Historians', *Race and Class*, **33**(4): 15–30.

Gadamer, H.G. (1975) *Truth and Method*. London: Sheed & Ward; note also the 1996 edition.

Gauguin, P. (1890) *Noa, Noa*, Oxford: Cassirer, 1961.

Gayford, M. (1992) 'The Good, The Bad, and the Interesting', *Modern Painters*, **6**: 1.

Geist, J.F. (1983) *Arcades*, Cambridge, MA: MIT Press.

Gellhorn, M. (1989) *The View from the Ground*, London: Granta.

Gellner, E. (1964) *Thought and Change*, London: Weidenfeld & Nicolson.

Gellner, E. (1997) *Nations and Nationalism*, Oxford: Blackwell (orig. pub. 1983).

Gibson, N. (1999) 'Fanon and the Pitfalls of Cultural Studies' in Alessandrini, A. (ed.) *Frantz Fanon: Critical Perspectives*, London: Routledge.

Giddens, A. (1983) *A Contemporary Critique of Historical Materialism*, London: Macmillan – now Palgrave.

Gillespie, M. (1999) 'Breaking Boundaries? New British TV Comedy and Anti-racism' in *European Media Conference: Cultural Diversity: Against Racism*, Cologne/Vienna: Westdeutscher Rundfunk Köln.

Gilman, S.L. (1976) *Introducing Psychoanalytic Theory*, New York: Brunner/Mazel.

Gilman, S.L. (1985) *Difference and Pathology*, Ithaca, NY: Cornell University Press.

Gilman, S.L. (1991) *Inscribing the Other*, Lincoln, NE: University of Nebraska Press.

Gilroy, P. (1987) *There Ain't No Black in the Union Jack*, London: Hutchinson.

Gilroy, P. (1999) 'Hatred of the Partially Familiar', *Times Higher Education Supplement*, 25 June.

Glassner, B. (1980) *Essential Interactionism: On the Intelligibility of Prejudice*, London: Routledge & Kegan Paul.

Glendenning, F.A. (1973) 'School History Textbooks and Racial Attitudes, 1804–1911', *Journal of Educational Administration and History*, **5**: 33–44.

Glynn, C.J., Herbst, S., O'Keefe, G.J. and Shapiro, R.Y. (1999) *Public Opinion*, Boulder, CO: Westview Press.

Goffman, E. (1972) *Encounters*, Harmondsworth: Penguin.

Goldberg, D. (1993) *Racist Culture*, Oxford: Blackwell.

Golding, P. and Middleton, S. (1982) *Images of Welfare: Press and Public Attitudes to Poverty*, Oxford: Martin Robertson.

Guha, R. and Spivak, G.C. (eds) (1988) *Selected Subaltern Studies*, Oxford: Oxford University Press.

Gunter, B. (1986) *Television and Sex Role Stereotyping*, London: John Libbey.

Haas, E.B. (1964) *Beyond the Nation State*, Stanford: Stanford University Press.

Hacking, I. (1990) *The Taming of Chance*, Cambridge: Cambridge University Press.

Haggis, J. (1990) 'Gendering Colonialism or Colonising Gender?' *Women's Studies International Forum*, **12**: 105–12.

Haggis, J. (1998) 'White Women and Colonialism' in Midgley, C. (ed.) *Gender and Imperialism*, Manchester: Manchester University Press.

Hall, S. (1993a) 'Culture, Community, Nation', *Cultural Studies*, 7(1): 349–63.

Hall, S. (1993b) 'Metaphors of Transformation', introduction to White, A. *Carnival, Hysteria, and Writing*, Oxford: Clarendon Press.

Hall, S. (1996) 'When Was "The Post-Colonial"? Thinking at the Limit' in Chambers, I. and Curti, L. (eds) *The Post-Colonial Question*, London: Routledge.

Hall, S. and Jefferson, T. (eds) (1975) *Resistance through Rituals: Youth Subcultures in Postwar Britain*, London: Hutchinson.

Hall, S., Critcher, C., Jefferson, T., Clarke, J. and Roberts, B. (1978) *Policing the Crisis: Mugging, The State and Law and Order*, London: Macmillan – now Palgrave.

Halloran, J., Elliott, P. and Murdock, G. (1970) *Demonstrations and Communication*, Harmondsworth: Penguin.

Hamburg, C. (1956) *Symbol and Reality: Studies in the Philosophy of Ernst Cassirer*, The Hague: Martinus Nijhoff.

Hamilton, D.L. (ed.) (1981) *Cognitive Processess in Stereotyping and Intergroup Behaviour*. Hillsdale, NJ: Erlbaum.

Harding, J. (1968) 'Stereotypes', *International Encyclopaedia of Social Sciences*, pp. 259–62, New York; Collier Macmillan.

Harré, R. (1981) 'Rituals, Rhetoric and Social Cognition' in Forgas, J.P. (ed.) *Social Cognition*, London: Academic Press.

Harris, J. (1993) *Private Lives, Public Spirit: A Social History of Britain, 1870–1914*, Oxford: Oxford University Press.

Harvey, D. (1991) *The Condition of Postmodernity*, Cambridge, MA: Blackwell.

Hawthorn, J. (1992) *Joseph Conrad: Narrative Technique and Ideological Commitment*, London: Edward Arnold.

Hechter, M. (1975) *Internal Colonialism: The Celtic Fringe in British National Development*, Berkeley, CA: University of California Press.

Hegel, G.W.F. (1967) *The Phenomenology of Mind*, New York: Harper & Row (orig. pub. 1807).

Henty, G.A. (1883) *By Sheer Pluck: A Tale of the Ashanti War*, London: Blackie & Son.

Henty, G.A. (1894) *Through the Sikh War*, London: Blackie & Son.

Henty, G.A. (1902) *With Roberts to Pretoria*, London, Blackie & Son.

Hobsbawm, E. (1997) *Nations and Nationalism since 1780*, Cambridge: Cambridge University Press.

Hobsbawm, E. and Ranger, T. (eds) (1984) *The Invention of Tradition*, Cambridge: Cambridge University Press.

Hobson, J. (1895/96) 'Mr Kidd's Social Evolution', *American Journal of Sociology*, 1: 299–312.

Hochschild, A. (1999) *King Leopold's Ghost: A Story of Greed, Terror and Heroism in Colonial Africa*, Basingstoke: Macmillan – now Palgrave.

Hogg, M.A. and Abrams, D. (1988) *Social Identification: A Social Psychology of Intergroup Relations and Group Processes*, London: Routledge.

Holquist, M. (1989) 'The Inevitability of Stereotype: Colonialism in The Great Gatsby' in Hernadi, P. (ed.) *The Rhetoric of Interpretation and the Interpretation of Rhetoric*, Durham: Duke University Press.

Honour, H. (1989) *The Image of the Black in Western Art*, 4 vols, Cambridge, MA: Harvard University Press.

hooks, b. (1993) 'Postmodern Blackness' in Williams, P. and Chrisman, L. (eds) *Colonial Discourse and Post-Colonial Theory*, Hemel Hempstead: Harvester Wheatsheaf.

Hoppenstand, G. (1983) 'Yellow Devil Doctors and Opium Dens: A Survey of the Yellow Peril Stereotypes in the Media' in Geist, C.D. and Nachbar, J. (eds) *Popular Culture Reader*, Ohio: Bowling Green University Popular Press.

Howitt, D. and Owusu-Bempah, J. (1994) *The Racism of Psychology*, New York: Harvester Wheatsheaf.

Hume, D. (1974) *Essays – Moral, Political and Literary*, Oxford: Oxford University Press (orig. pub. 1741/42).

Hunt, J. (1863–64) 'On the Negro's Place in Nature', *Memoirs Read before the Anthropological Society of London*, **1**: 1–64.

Huttenback, R.A. (1965–66) 'G.A. Henty and the Imperial Stereotype', *Huntington Library Quarterly*, **29**: 63–75.

Hwang, D.H. (1989) 'People Like Us', *Guardian*, 21 April.

Hyman, H.H. and Sheatsley, P.B. (1954) 'The Authoritarian Personality – A Methodological Critique' in Christie, K. and Jahoda, M. (eds) *Studies in the Scope and Method of The Authoritarian Personality*, Glencoe: Free Press.

James, B. and Saville-Smith, K. (1990) *Gender, Culture and Power: Challenging New Zealand's Gendered Culture*, Oxford: Oxford University Press.

James, C.L.R. (1994) *The Black Jacobins*, London: Allison & Busby (orig. pub. 1938).

James, L. (1973) 'Tom Brown's Imperialist Sons', *Victorian Studies*, **17**: 89–99.

Jenkins, P. (1992) *Intimate Enemies: Moral Panics in Contemporary Great Britain*, New York: Aldine de Gruyter.

Jesson, B. (1983) 'Reviewing the "Maori Sovereignty" Debate', *The Republican*, **48**(3–4): 19–20.

Jones, G. (1980) *Social Darwinism in English Thought: The Interaction Between Biological and Social Theory*, Brighton: Harvester Press.

Jordanova, L. (1989) *Sexual Visions: Images of Gender in Science and Medicine between the Eighteenth and Twentieth Centuries*, Brighton: Harvester Wheatsheaf.

Joyce, T.A. (1910–11) 'Negro', *Encyclopedia Britannica*, 11th edn.

Katz, D. and Braly, K. (1933) 'Racial Stereotypes of One Hundred College Students', *Journal of Abnormal and Social Psychology*, **28**: 280–90.

Katz, D. and Braly, K. (1935) 'Racial Prejudice and Racial Stereotype', *Journal of Abnormal and Social Psychology*, **30**: 175–93.

Keefe, T. (1983) *Simone de Beauvoir: A Study of her Writings*, Totoawa, NJ: Barnes & Noble.

Kiernan, V.G. (1972) *The Lords of Human Kind*, Harmondsworth: Penguin.

Kim, E.H. (1982) *Asian American Literature*, Philadelphia: Temple University Press.

Kingsley, F.E. (ed.) (1977) *Charles Kingsley: His Letters and Memories of His Life*, London: Henry S. King.

Klineberg, O. (1950) *Tensions Affecting International Understanding: A Survey of Research*, New York: Social Science Research Council.

Knox, R. (1862) *The Races of Man*, London: Renshaw (orig. pub. 1850)

Kolakowski, L. (1999) *Freedom, Fame, Lying and Betrayal: Essays on Everyday Life*, London: Penguin.

Koselleck, R. (1985) *Futures Past: On the Semantics of Historical Time*, Cambridge, MA: The MIT Press.

Kristeva, J. (1982) *Powers of Horror: An Essay on Abjection*, New York: Columbia University Press.

Kuper, A. (1988) *The Invention of Primitive Society*, London: Routledge.

La Rochefoucauld (1931) *Maxims*, London: Haworth Press.

Lake, M. (1998) 'Australian Frontier Feminism and the Marauding White Man' in Midgley, C. (ed.) *Gender and Imperialism*, Manchester: Manchester University Press.

Lane, J. (2000) *Pierre Bourdieu: A Critical Introduction*, London: Pluto Press.

Layton-Henry, Z. (1984) *The Politics of Race in Britain*, London: George Allen & Unwin.

Lebow, R.N. (1976) *White Britain and Black Ireland: The Influence of Stereotypes on Colonial Policy*, Philadelphia: Institute for Study of Human Issues.

Lessing, D. (1987) *The Wind Blows Away Our Words*, London: Picador.

Leyens, J.P., Yzerbyt, V. and Schadrom, G. (1994) *Stereotypes and Social Cognition*, London: Sage.

Lindop, G. (1981) *The Opium Eater: A Life of Thomas de Quincey*, London: J.M. Dent & Sons.

Lippmann, W. (1915) *The Stakes of Diplomacy*, New York: Henry Holt.

Lippmann, W. (1925) *The Phantom Public*. New York: Harcourt Brace.

Lippmann, W. (1961) *Drift and Mastery*, Englewood Cliffs, NJ: Prentice Hall (orig. pub. 1914).

Lippmann, W. (1962) *A Preface to Politics*, Michigan: University of Michigan Press (orig. pub. 1914).

Lippmann, W. (1965) *Public Opinion*, London: The Free Press/Collier Macmillan (orig. pub. 1922).

Livingstone, D. (1857) *Missionary Travels and Researches*, London: John Murray.

Llobera, J. (1998) 'Nationalism/Internationalism' in Jenks, C. (ed.) *Core Sociological Dichotomies*, London: Sage.

Lorcin, P. (1995) *Imperial Identities: Stereotyping, Prejudice and Race in Colonial Algeria*, London: I.B. Tauris.

Lorimer, D. (1978) *Colour, Class and the Victorians*, Leicester: Leicester University Press.

Lorimer, D. (1996) 'Race, Science and Culture: Historical Continuities and Discontinuities, 1850–1914' in West, S. (ed.) *The Victorians and Race*, Aldershot: Scolar Press.

Lowe, L. (1991) *Critical Terrains: French and British Orientalisms*, Ithaca, NY: Cornell University Press.

Lugard, F.D. (1926) *The Dual Mandate in British Tropical Africa*, Edinburgh: William Blackwood & Sons.

McClintock, A. (1995) *Imperial Leather: Race, Gender and Sexuality in the Colonial Contest*, New York: Routledge.

McDonald, M. (1993) 'The Construction of Difference: An Anthropological Approach to Stereotypes' in MacDonald, S. (ed.) *Inside European Identities*, Providence: Berg.

McGrane, B. (1989) *Beyond Anthropology: Society and the Other*, New York: Columbia University Press.

MacKenzie, J. (1983) 'Ephemera – Reflection or Instrument?', *The Ephemerist*, **2**: 4–7.

MacKenzie, J. (1985) *Propaganda and Empire: The Manipulation of British Public Opinion 1880–1960*, Manchester: Manchester University Press.

MacKenzie, J. (1995) *Orientalism: History, Theory and the Arts*, Manchester: Manchester University Press.

MacLaughlin, J. (1999) '"Pestilence on their Backs, Famine in their Stomachs": the Racial Construction of Irishness and the Irish in Victorian Britain' in Graham, C. and Kirkland, R. (eds) *Ireland and Cultural Theory*, Basingstoke: Macmillan – now Palgrave.

McLynn, F. (1993) *Hearts of Darkness: The European Exploration of Africa*, London: Pimlico.

McQuire, S. (1998) *Visions of Modernity: Representation, Memory, Time and Space in the Age of the Camera*, London: Sage.

McRobbie, A. (1994) *Postmodernism and Popular Culture*, London: Routledge.

McRobbie, A. and Thornton, S. (1995) 'Rethinking "Moral Panic" for Multi-Mediated Social Worlds', *British Journal of Sociology*, **46**(4): 559–74.

Mangan, J.A. (1981) *Athleticism in the Victorian and Edwardian Public School*, Cambridge: Cambridge University Press.

Marchetti, G. (1993) *Romance and the Yellow Peril: Race, Sex and Discursive Hollywood Strategies in Hollywood Fiction*, Berkeley, CA: University of California Press.

Marx, K. (1988) *Collected Works*, Vol. 30, London: Lawrence & Wishart.

Mause, L. de (1986) 'The Secret Psyche of Ronald Reagan', *Guardian*, 29 December.

Melville, H. (1972) *Typee*, Harmondsworth: Penguin.

Miller, C.L. (1985) *Blank Darkness: Africanist Discourse in French*, Chicago: University of Chicago Press.

Milligan, B. (1995) *Pleasures and Pains: Opium and the Orient in Nineteenth-Century British Culture*, Charlottesville, VA: University Press of Virginia.

Mills, C. Wright (1963) *Power, Politics and People*, New York: Ballantine (orig. pub. 1943).

Mills, S. (1997) *Discourse*, London: Routledge.

Mitchell, D. (ed.) (1977) *A Dictionary of Sociology*, London: Routledge & Kegan Paul.

Moi, T. (1998) '"Independent Women" and "Narratives of Liberation"' in Fallaize, E. (ed.) *Simone de Beauvoir: A Critical Reader*, London: Routledge.

Mommsen, W.J. (1974) 'Power, Politics, Imperialism and National Emancipation' in Moody, T.W. (ed.) *Nationality and the Pursuit of National Independence*, Belfast: Appletree.

Moore-Gilbert, B. (1997) *Postcolonial Theory: Contexts, Practices, Politics*, London: Verso.

Morrison, T. (1993) *Playing in the Dark: Whiteness and the Literary Imagination*, London: Picador.

Mosse, G. (1976) 'Mass Politics and the Political Liturgy of Nationalism' in Kamenka, E. (ed.) *Nationalism: The Nature and Evolution of an Idea*, London: Edward Arnold.

Mosse, G. (1985) *Nationalism and Sexuality: Middle-Class Morality and Sexual Norms in Modern Europe*, Madison, WI: University of Wisconsin Press.

Mudimbe, V.Y. (1988) *The Invention of Africa: Gnosis, Philosophy and the Order of Knowledge*, Bloomington, IN: Indiana University Press.

Murphy, S. and Rosenbaum, M. (1999) *Pregnant Women on Drugs: Combating Stereotypes and Stigma*, New Brunswick, NJ: Rutgers University Press.

Myrdal, G. (1944) *An American Dilemma*, New York: Harper.

Nava, M. (1988) 'Cleveland and the Press: Outrage and Anxiety in the Reporting of Child Sexual Abuse', *Feminist Review*, 28: 103–22.

Nedelman, B. (1990) 'On the Concept of "Erlaben" in Georg Simmel's Sociology' in Kaern, M., Phillips, B.S. and Cohen, R.S. (eds) *Georg Simmel and Contemporary Sociology*, Dordrecht: Kluwer Academic.

Newman, G. (1997) *The Rise of English Nationalism*, Basingstoke: Macmillan – now Palgrave.

O'Barr, W. (1994) *Culture and the Ad: Exploring Otherness in the World of Advertising*, Boulder, CO: Westview Press.

O'Grady, T. and Pyke, S. (1998) *I Could Read the Sky*, London: Harvill Press.

Oakes, P.J., Haslam, S.A. and Turner, J.C. (1994) *Stereotyping and Social Reality*, Oxford: Blackwell.

Oehling, R.A. (1980) 'The Yellow Menace: Asian Images in American Film' in Miller, R. (ed.) *The Kaleidscopic Lens: How Hollywood Views Ethnic Groups*, Englewood, NJ: Jerome S. Ozer.

Orwell, G. (1984) 'Notes on Nationalism', *The Collected Essays, Journalism and Letters*, 4 vols, 3:1943–45 Harmondsworth: Penguin.

Ostendorf, B. (1982) *Black Literature in White America*, Brighton: Harvester.

Park, R. (1915) 'The City: Suggestions for the Investigation of Human Behavior in the City Environment', *American Journal of Sociology*, **20**(5): 577–612.

Parker, A. et al. (eds) (1992) *Nationalisms and Sexualities*, New York: Routledge.

Parry, B. (1987) 'Problems in Current Theories of Colonial Discourse', *Oxford Literary Review*, **9**(1–2): 27–58.

Parry, B. (1992) 'Overlapping Territories and Intertwined Histories: Edward Said's Postcolonial Cosmopolitanism' in Sprinker, M. (ed.) *Edward Said: A Critical Reader*, Oxford: Blackwell.

Parry, B. (1994) 'Signs of the Times', *Third Text*, **28/29**: 5–24.

Pearson, G. (1983) *Hooligan*, London: Macmillan – now Palgrave.

Pennycook, A. (1998) *English and the Discourses of Colonialism*, London: Routledge.

Perkins, T.E. (1979) 'Rethinking Stereotypes' in Barrett, M., Corrigan, P., Kohn, A. and Wolff, J. (eds) *Ideology and Cultural Production*, London: Croom Helm.

Phillips, J. (1987) *A Man's Country? The Image of the Pakeha Male*, Auckland: Penguin.

Philo, G. and Beattie, L. (1999) 'Race, Migration and Media' in Philo, G. (ed.) *Message Received*, Harlow: Longman.

Pickering, M. (1997a) *History, Experience and Cultural Studies*, Basingstoke: Macmillan – now Palgrave.

Pickering, M. (1997b) 'John Bull in Blackface', *Popular Music*, **16**(2): 181–201.

Pickering, M. (1999) 'History as Horizon: Gadamer, Tradition and Critique', *Rethinking History*, **3**(2): 177–95.

Pieterse, J.N. (1992) *White on Black: Images of Africa and Blacks in Western Popular Culture*, New Haven, CT: Yale University Press.

Pilardi, J.-A. (1999) *Simone de Beauvoir: Writing the Self*, Westport, CO: Praeger.

Porter, D. (1983) 'Orientalism and its Problems' in Barker, F., Hulme, P., Iversen, M. and Loxley, D. (eds) *The Politics of Theory*, Colchester: University of Essex.

Potter, W.J. (1998) *Media Literacy*, London: Sage.

Pratt, M.L. (1992) *Imperial Eyes: Travel Writing and Transculturation*, London: Routledge.

Reade, W. (1872) *The Martyrdom of Man*, London: Thinker's Library.

Reid, T. (n.d.) *The Giraffe Hunters*, London: Routledge & Sons.

Reinarman, C. (1994) 'The Social Construction of Drug Scares' in Adler, P. and Adler, P. (eds) *Constructions of Deviance*, Belmont, CA: Wadsworth.

Rigby, P. (1996) *African Images: Racism and the End of Anthropology*, Oxford: Berg.

Robins, K., Webster, F. and Pickering, M. (1987) 'Propaganda, Information and Social Control' in Hawthorn, J. (ed.) *Propaganda, Persuasion and Polemic*, London: Edward Arnold.

Rodney, W. (1982) *How Europe Underdeveloped Africa*. Washington, DC: Howard University Press.

Rosebery, Lord (1900) *Questions of Empire*, London: Arthur L. Humphreys.

Russell, B. (1939) 'The Intellectual in the Modern World', *American Journal of Sociology*, 44(4): 491–8.

Russell, C. and Lewis, H. (1900) *The Jew in London*, London: Fisher Unwin.

Rutherford, J. (1997) *Forever England: Reflections on Race, Masculinity and Empire*, London: Lawrence & Wishart.

Rydell, R. (1984) *All the World's a Fair: Visions of Empire at American International Expositions, 1876–1916*, Chicago: University of Chicago Press.

Said, E. (1979) *The Question of Palestine*, London: Routledge & Kegan Paul.

Said, E. (1981) *Covering Islam*, London: Routledge & Kegan Paul.

Said, E. (1984) *The World, the Text and the Critic*, London: Faber and Faber.

Said, E. (1985a) *Orientalism*, Harmondsworth: Penguin (orig. pub. 1978).

Said, E. (1985b) 'Orientalism Reconsidered' in Barker, F., Hulme, P., Iversen, M. and Loxley, D. (eds) *Europe and its Others*, Vol. 1, Colchester: University of Essex.

Said, E. (1988) 'Identity, Negation and Violence', *New Left Review*, 171: 46–60.

Said, E. (1994) *Culture and Imperialism*, London: Vintage.

Salt, J. (1998) 'Europe and the "Islamic Threat": Putting the Spectre into Perspective' in Murray, P. and Holmes, L. (eds) *Europe: Rethinking the Boundaries*, Aldershot: Ashgate.

Samelson, F. (1978) 'From "Race Psychology" to "Studies in Prejudice": Some Observations on the Thematic Reversal in Social Psychology', *Journal of the History of the Behavioural Sciences*, 14: 265–78.

Sampson, E.E. (1993) *Celebrating the Other*, Boulder, CO: Westview Press.

Samuel, R. (ed.) (1989) *Patriotism: The Making and Unmaking of British National Identity*, 3 vols., London: Routledge.

Sapir, E. (1970) *Culture, Language and Personality*, Berkeley, CA: University of California Press.

Sapper (Cyril McNeile) (1919) *Mufti*, London: Hodder & Stoughton.

Sartre, J.-P. (1962) *Anti-Semite and Jew*, New York: Grove Press (orig. pub. 1946).

Sartre, J.-P. (1969) *Being and Nothingness*, London: Methuen (orig. pub. 1943).

Sartre, J.-P. (1982) *Critique of Dialectical Reason*, London: Verso.

Scannell, P. and Cardiff, D. (1991) *A Social History of British Broadcasting, Volume 1: Serving the Nation*, Oxford: Oxford University Press.

Schapera, I. (ed.) (1960) *Livingstone's Private Journals, 1851–1853*, London: Chatto & Windus.

Schlesinger, P. (1991) *Media, State and Nation*, London: Sage.

Schweitzer, A. (1922) *On the Edge of the Primeval Forest*, London: Black.

Seiter, E. (1986) 'Stereotypes and the Media: A Re-evaluation', *Journal of Communication*, 36(2): 14–26.

Sennett, R. (1986) *The Fall of Public Man*, London: Faber and Faber.

Sennett, R. (1996) 'The Foreigner' in Heelas, P., Lash, S. and Morris, P. (eds) *Detraditionalization: Critical Reflections on Authority and Identity*, Oxford: Blackwell.

Sherif, M. (1967) *Group Conflict and Cooperation*. London: Routledge & Kegan Paul.

Shi-xu (1997) *Cultural Representations*, Frankfurt am Main: Peter Lang.

Shoberl, F. (1838) *Forget Me Not: A Christmas, New Year and Birthday Present*, London: Ackermann.

Shohat, E. and Stam, R. (1994) *Unthinking Eurocentrism: Multiculturalism and the Media*, London: Routledge.

Signorielli, N. (ed.) (1985) *Role Portrayal and Stereotyping on Television*, Westport, CO: Greenwood Press.

Simmel, G. (1978) *The Philosophy of Money*, London: Routledge.

Simons, M.A. and Benjamin, J. (1979) 'Simone de Beauvoir: An Interview', *Feminist Studies*, **5**: Summer.

Sindall, R. (1990) *Street Violence in the Nineteenth Century: Media Panic or Real Danger?* Leicester: Leicester University Press.

Sinha, M. (1995) *Colonial Masculinity*, Manchester: Manchester University Press.

Smiles, S. (1911) *Self-Help*, London: S.W. Partridge.

Smith, A. (1986) *The Ethnic Origins of Nations*, Oxford: Blackwell.

Smith, A. (1991) *National Identity*, London: Penguin.

Speke, J.H. (1863) *Journal of the Discovery of the Nile*, London: Blackwood.

Spencer, H. (1874) *Descriptive Sociology*, London: Williams & Norgate.

Spender, D. (1982) *Women of Ideas and What Men Have Done to Them*, London: Pandora.

Spivak, G.C. (1984) 'The Rani of Sirmur' in Barker, F., Hulme, P., Iversen, M. and Loxley, D. (eds) *Europe and its Others*, Vol. 1, Colchester: University of Essex.

Spivak, G.C. (1985) 'Three Women's Texts and a Critique of Imperialism', *Critical Inquiry*, **12**(1): 243–61.

Spivak, G.C. (1987) *In Other Worlds*, London: Routledge.

Spivak, G.C. (1988) 'Can the Subaltern Speak?' in Nelson, C. and Grossberg, L. (eds) *Marxism and the Interpretation of Culture*, Basingstoke: Macmillan – now Palgrave.

Spivak, G.C. (1993) *Outside in the Teaching Machine*, London: Routledge.

Springhall, J. (1998) *Youth, Popular Culture and Moral Panics*, Basingstoke: Macmillan – now Palgrave.

Stafford, P. (1984) 'How Strength is Drawn from Myth and Stereotype', *Times Higher Education Supplement*, 10 February.

Stallybrass, P. and White, A. (1986) *The Politics and Poetics of Transgression*, London: Methuen.

Stanley, L. (ed.) *The Diaries of Hannah Cullwick*, London: Virago.

Steel, R. (1980) *Walter Lippmann and the American Century*, London: Bodley Head.

Stepan, N. (1982) *The Idea of Race in Science: Great Britain, 1800–1960*, London: Macmillan – now Palgrave.

Stephan, W.G. and Rosenfield, D. (1982) 'Racial and Ethnic Stereotypes' in Miller, A.G. (ed.) *In the Eye of the Beholder: Contemporary Issues in Stereotyping*, New York: Praeger.

Stocking, G.W. (1987) *Victorian Anthropology*, New York: Free Press.

Suleri, S. (1992) *The Rhetoric of English India*, Chicago: Chicago University Press.

Sumner, C. (ed.) (1990) *Censure, Politics and Criminal Justice*, Milton Keynes: Open University Press.

Sumner, C. (1994) *The Sociology of Deviance: An Obituary*, Buckingham: Open University Press.

Swingewood, A. (1984) *A Short History of Sociological Thought*, London: Macmillan – now Palgrave.

Szwed, J. (1975) 'Race and the Embodiment of Culture', *Ethnicity*, 2: 19–33.

Tajfel, H. (1963) 'Stereotypes', *Race*, 5(2): 3–14.

Tajfel, H. (1981) *Human Groups and Social Categories*, Cambridge: Cambridge University Press.

Tajfel, H. and Fraser, C. (1978) *Introducing Social Psychology*, Harmondsworth: Penguin.

Taylor, I. (1999) *Crime in Context: A Critical Criminology of Market Societies*, Cambridge: Polity.

Taylor, S.E. (1981) 'A Categorisation Approach to Stereotyping' in Hamilton, D.L. (ed.) *Cognitive Processes in Stereotyping and Intergroup Behaviour*, Hillsdale, NJ: Erlbaum.

Thomas, W.I. (1908) 'The Psychology of the Yellow Journal', *American Magazine*, March, pp. 491–6.

Thompson, K. (1998) *Moral Panics*, London: Routledge.

Thompson, L. (1985) *The Political Mythology of Apartheid*, New Haven, CT: Yale University Press.

Thornton, S. (1994) 'Moral Panic, The Media and British Rave Culture' in Ross, A. and Rose, T. (eds) *Microphone Fiends*, London: Routledge.

Thornton, S. (1995) *Club Cultures: Music, Media and Subcultural Capital*, Oxford: Polity.

Tönnies, F. (1963) *Community and Association*, London: Routledge & Kegan Paul.

Trevarthen, J. (1901) 'Hooliganism', *The Nineteenth Century*, 49: 84–9.

Turner, B.S. (1974) *Weber and Islam*, London: Routledge & Kegan Paul.

Turner, B.S. (1978) *Marx and the End of Orientalism*, London: Allen & Unwin.

Turner, B.S. (1989) 'From Orientalism to Global Sociology', *Sociology*, 23(4): 629–38.

Tylor, E.B. (1913) *Anthropology: An Introduction to the Study of Man and Civilisation*, London: Watts (orig. pub. 1881).

van Zoonen, L. (1994) *Feminist Media Studies*, London: Sage.

Varadharajan, A. (1995) *Exotic Parodies: Subjectivity in Adorno, Said, and Spivak*, Minneapolis: University of Minnesota Press.

Walzer, M. (1983) *Spheres of Justice*, Oxford: Basil Blackwell.

Ward, H. (1910) *A Voice from the Congo*, London: William Heinemann.

Ward, R. (1966) *The Australian Legend*, Melbourne: Oxford University Press.

Watney, S. (1987) *Policing Desire: Pornography, AIDS and the Media*, London: Methuen.

Weber, E. (1976) *Peasants into Frenchmen*, Stanford: Stanford University Press.

Weeks, J. (1985) *Sexuality and its Discontents*, London: Routledge.

Wetherell, M. and Potter, J. (1992) *Mapping the Language of Racism*. New York: Harvester Wheatsheaf.

White, R. (1990) *White Mythologies*, London: Routledge.

White, R. (1998) *Remembering Ahanagran*, Cork: Cork University Press.

Wilkinson, R. (1964) *The Prefects: British Leadership and the Public School Tradition*, London: Oxford University Press.

Williams, G. (1991) *The Welsh in Patagonia*, Cardiff: University of Wales Press.

Williams, J.A. (1984) 'Gender and Inter-group Behaviour: Towards an Integration', *British Journal of Social Psychology*, **23**: 311–16.

Williams, R.H. (1991) *Dream Worlds: Mass Consumption in Late Nineteenth Century France*, Oxford: University of California Press (orig. pub. 1982).

Willmott, B. (1989) 'Introduction: Culture and National Identity' in Novitz, D. and Willmott, B. (eds) *Culture and Identity in New Zealand*, Wellington: GP Books.

Wolff, K.H. (ed.) (1964) *The Sociology of Georg Simmel*, New York: Free Press (orig. pub. 1950).

Wright, P. (1985) *On Living in an Old Country*, London: Verso.

Wright, R. (1988) *Black Boy*, London: Picador (orig. pub. 1945).

Wyatt, H.F. (1897) 'The Ethics of Empire', *The Nineteenth Century*, **XLI**: 516–30.

Xing, J. (1998) *Asian America Through the Lens*, London: Altamira Press.

Young, J. (1971) *The Drugtakers*, London: Paladin.

Young, R. (1995) *White Mythologies*, London: Routledge (orig. pub. 1990).

Younghusband, F. (1896) *The Heart of a Continent*, London: John Murray.

Zickmund, S. (1997) 'Approaching the Radical Other: The Discursive Culture of Cyberhate' in Jones, S.G. (ed.) *Virtual Culture: Identity and Communication in Cybersociety*, London: Sage.

Author Index

Subject Index